1986

Ah, Men!

AH, MEN!

What Do Men Want?
A Panorama of the Male in Crisis—
His Past Problems,
Present Uncertainties, Future Goals

Burt Avedon

A&W Publishers, Inc.
New York

Published by
A & W Publishers, Inc.
95 Madison Avenue
New York, New York 10016

Designed by Helen Roberts

Library of Congress Cataloging in Publication Data

Avedon, Burt.
Ah, men!

1. Men—United States. 2. Men—United States—Attitudes. 3. Sex role. I. Title.
HQ1090.A93 301.41'1'0973 78-74675
ISBN 0-89479-048-X

Printed in the United States of America

To the wonderful woman in my life—a lady of all things, big and small, who inspired me to love in all its measure. To the daughters, hers and mine, all through blood or emotion, who taught me the weight of responsibility, the disappointment of unrealized dreams, and the joy of loving Dana, Renee, Tracy. To their Bionic Grandma, my mother. And to Loren, a most understanding guy.

Contents

Acknowledgments

This book, like most, is the product of collective energies and intellects. Almost every word and thought expressed in the work carries the coloring of two bright young writers who will soon have books out under their own names: Martin Targoff, former editor, now author, whose agile mind brought so much to the research and interview phase of this book, and Scott Jackson, historian and author, who ably assisted me with the organization and writing.

To my editor, Angela Miller, for her effort and patience. To my agent, Peri Winkler, who believed in the book and encouraged the author. *Ah, Men!*

Introduction

MEN KNOW what it's like. Thirty . . . forty . . . fifty. Hair thinning but still there. Some paunch but not unattractive. Rising in our career, though not as fast or as high as we once dreamed. Marriage on the rocks, dead, or deep in the throes of acrimonious divorce. Doubts about ourselves and where we are heading.

Then it happens. We can't get it up anymore. Just a temporary condition, we tell ourselves. No reason to get upset. These things happen to men our age. It must be our wives. "Just haven't been able to get excited about her for a while now."

If it persists too long, our reaction is mute terror. We turn everything inward once again, pouring it all through the deadening filter of our intellect, never seeking help. We analyze, dissect, rationalize, philosophize, but we can't distance ourselves from our fear. All at once we feel our very identity dissipating.

That's the way it happened with my friend Larry, the all-American boy, college football player, golfer who shot in the high eighties, wonder of the insurance business when he first started, a man who once prided himself on his sense of humor and his sexual potency.

For Larry, feelings were always nothing more than inconvenient distractions. They sidetracked him from the task at hand, but could be mimicked and used, denied and defied at will. Somehow, he always expected his wife to know what was really going on inside of him, especially when his problem began. But when it became apparent that she was as ignorant of the real Larry Cranston as a total stranger might be, he began to resent her.

Had Julie ever really cared about him? He wondered and at times doubted she ever had. Still, it had seemed good at the beginning. Julie was a very attractive girl who he thought would be supportive of his career, a good homemaker, a mother for his children, a good lover. But somewhere along the line it had soured.

Maybe it was Julie's affair seven years ago. It came so unexpectedly. But Larry had borne it well. They patched things up, and whatever Larry felt he kept inside. He did start drinking more . . . and putting on more weight. He also began to feel less and less the master of his destiny.

Then his impotence. Occasional at first. More regularly later. His marriage was little more than a hollow shell. The last five years had been hell.

His problems spread beyond his home. As he became more prone to the extreme highs and lows of his often manic-depressive state, his subordinates at the office began trying to pick up the warning signals of imminent disaster. They began using euphemisms for his behavior—"Larry's just unpredictable," they would say.

Of course, Larry was no dummy. He knew what was going on. His life was coming apart.

Then Julie had the gall to confront him with her second affair, telling him that her new lover made her feel more like a woman than he ever had. She wanted freedom, and she made it clear she knew how to use it.

Larry blew it all then. He reacted instinctively, knocked her across their paneled den with a right cross to the temple. Julie wound up with a black eye, four stitches, and custody of their two daughters during the separation. Larry's lawyers kept his spirits up, but it looked bad no matter what they said. The child support and alimony would cripple him.

Poor Larry. He had no choice but to withdraw, roll up his sleeves, and get back to work. No respite. No time for reflection or self-pity.

Suddenly the office seemed full of hard-working, talented young bucks, jockeying for position. *Watch your ass,* Larry told himself. As if he didn't have enough to worry about from the men, women were now moving up the corporate ladder as well. Some seemed right at his heels. Larry resented these women most of all, especially the attractive ones who strutted their stuff around the office, taking advantage of their femininity one minute and behaving like men the next.

Women . . . they always seem to be the cause of it all. Always baffling, always manipulating. All of a sudden they want everything their way. Do they even know what the hell it is they want? Don't they know what they're doing to me . . . to us?

The phone rings, interrupting Larry's inner dialogue. He looks at his watch.

Six-fifteen, right on the nose as planned. The office is empty except for the cleaning ladies. Larry pauses momentarily, lets the phone ring two more times, then picks up the receiver with studied composure.

God, he tells himself, *don't breathe so hard or you'll sound like an out-of-breath old man.*

"Hello. Cranston."

"Listen, Larry," she says, getting right to the point. "I've thought this whole thing over, and I've decided it might be fun."

Larry thinks of Jana sashaying about the office. His heart races on.

"There's one catch, Larry. I've never been with a man your age, and I realize you corporate honchos are used to having things your way. But it can't be that way with me. I've finally reached a point in my life where I can get things on my own terms."

Larry listens, excited and bemused. He has set this scene in his mind a hundred times during the last few months. He runs his hand down his slacks and turns to look out at the Manhattan skyline. The sun is going down over Jersey.

"Whatever you say, Jana, only let's get together tonight."

Though the words come out smooth and controlled, Larry feels as if he is stammering.

Silence. Then she speaks.

"Well, come on over in about an hour. . . . Look, pick up a bottle of red wine on the way. I'll cook something for dinner. We can talk."

Ah. Everything will go as planned. Dinner . . . seduction . . . glorious rejuvenation!

"Larry," there is some hesitancy in her voice, "if things reach a point when it all gets honest and simple and sexual, you must be prepared to leave things to me, to let me run things a little. If it works out O.K., we'll take it from there."

A few minutes later Larry hurries out of the elevator and onto Madison Avenue, lost in uncertainty.

"It's always something," he mutters, but at least Jana seems worth it. She's a sultry and self-confident twenty-seven, long-legged, a woman whose presence makes his being leap up and shout.

He buries his face in his scarf as he turns down East Fifty-fifth Street. At Fifth Avenue he hails a downtown cab, but it stops for two women in gray suits, armed with briefcases. Larry hails another and heads for Jana's.

The cab stops for a red light at Eighth Street. The meter ticks off another dime.

Two young people, probably college students, cross the street arm in arm in front of the cab. *Shit, I envy those kids. . . . They have it all over us. At their age they've probably done it all. Lived together, had relationships and every kind of sex imaginable. Different upbringing, I guess. They even dress and look alike.*

Larry chuckles to himself after passing a group of gay men on the corner of Christopher Street. Is that one of the alternatives? One can become gay, or withdraw, or learn to play the game all over again.

Larry wonders if he could change his own ground rules at this late date in life, but it seems almost as absurd to him as the gay alternative. It would be a drastic turnabout, though. But, as the old cliché goes, you can't teach an old dog new tricks.

The cab pulls up in front of Jana's apartment on the corner of West Fourth and Bank. Larry feels pangs of apprehension in the pit of his stomach as he steps out of the cab. His mouth is dry. *This is it,* he thinks, the culmination of months of fussing with his appearance in the morning to look younger. Jana is everything Julie wasn't. She is what Larry looks forward to when he gets up for work in the morning—to her smile, her fragrance, to the easy way she moves, to their conversations in Larry's office. She is sensitive and intelligent, and Larry went out of his way to make her feel comfortable and valuable by asking her opinions about her colleagues and the workings of the company. Her commentaries would range from the glowing and enthusiastic to the irreverent and outright hostile. Whatever they were, they were always refreshingly honest.

Of course, Larry would use these occasions to drop some loaded but awkward innuendo about sex, and Jana's subsequent pouts would indicate that she always found them tiresome and unnecessary before saying something frank that would invariably embarrass him. Jana was quite a woman, unlike anyone Larry had ever known. If anyone could teach Larry the new ropes, it would be a woman like Jana. And if anyone could restore his potency, it would be her.

With this running through his mind, Larry enters the front door and bounds up the two flights of steps to her apartment. She opens the door smiling, happy to see him. In moments they are seated at her table, drinking wine. Jana's face is highlighted by a single lamp. Her hair, pinned to her head, is raven and thick, her eyes are large and hazel. Larry thinks she looks like a beautiful South American peasant woman. But then again, he always had a tendency to romanticize these things.

Larry sits guardedly at first, his conversation innocuous but occasionally funny. Before long, Jana has him talking about his wife, his daughters, how he really feels about his job, what he likes to do for fun. She feeds him a wonderful dinner and the hours pass quickly.

Larry suddenly thinks he is in love and feels vulnerable and uncomfortable. *What would their sex life be together?* he wonders. God, what a pathetic spectacle that would be—a confused, soon-to-be divorced, middle-aged man who can't even count on getting it up with this young, vivacious woman.

"Larry, you're invited to spend the night if you like."

It lands like a bomb. Larry nods his head and dumbly stares at her, transfixed.

"We can sleep together tonight, and I want you to accept it for what it is and nothing more—just good sex between two people who like each other."

Larry feels chills.

"I really don't want one of those ludicrous office romances," she continues. "We just tell each other what we like and make love. Can you accept that?"

Jana is gently stroking Larry's trembling arm. Minutes later they are on her bed, naked. Larry is stupefied by her beauty, but suddenly his brain is awash with images of technique: He sees the whole thing as a movie of how he would like to make love to her. He will screw her masterfully. She will gasp with the pleasure of his erection.

But nothing is really happening, dammit!

Come on, Larry. There it is. She wants you, buddy, so come on and get in there every which way. Please, just this one time, he prays to some god. *Come on, man! What's your problem anyway? . . . O.K., let's just take it easy for a few seconds and not panic. Regroup here. Need to relax and have a little confi-*

dence or this thing's never gonna work. He pauses to muster every bit of energy. *Now let's go . . . just lie back and feel. I, Larry Cranston, am a mature, intelligent, worthwhile, and, yes, desirable man. Otherwise, why would she be here with me? I command thee, rise! Rise, you bastard! Obey your master!*

Nothing works. His penis merely dangles there before this beautiful woman, an ineffectual sliver of manhood if there ever was one, in brazen disobedience to the shrill commands of Larry's brain.

Later, Jana lies sleeping beside Larry, her breathing even, her hair cascading down her shoulder. Larry is wide-eyed staring into the darkness. "You men put yourselves through hell," she had said after they discussed his problem. "You should have gone to see a therapist a long time ago."

Then, slowly and gently, she had fondled him erect. He came only seconds after entering her, then went limp as a wet dishrag.

Sex is like everything else in my world, he thinks. *Leaving nothing, when all is said and done, but myself.*

Doesn't Rabbi Hillel say, "If I am not for myself, then who will be for me?" Seeking help would have constituted an admission of being less than a complete man, but temporary impotence is like a lapse of consciousness, a denial, or a repudiation somehow, the manifestation of disgust with living in a world that vaunts achievement, strength, beauty, money, social status, technology, and instant gratification, but denies humanity. A world of too much loneliness and too many voids that people are afraid to think about. Too many unfulfilled dreams and too many roles to play. Too much pace and not enough substance. Too many illusions.

Should I have apologized for ejaculating prematurely? he wonders.

It's going to be a long way back, Larry.

Ah, Larry! Ah, men! Once so proud, bold and secure. Now we seem like the great herds of buffalo that roamed the plains —an endangered species. Women have been telling us that we occupy a favored position in American society. We've been reproached and chastised for having more room to move, more life options, and more power than women. But is this truth or cultural mythology?

We have to ask what it means to be a man in today's world.

Are men really an endangered species? What's happening to masculinity? Are we merely a group of confused, emotionally sterile souls who fear intimacy with each other and with women? What do we really expect of women anyway? Are we still searching for the prostitute/madonna?

Many men seem to be asking these and numerous other questions about themselves today, only to discover that the more things change, the more unanswerable the questions become. One thing is certain: Profound and rapid changes in women have left many men lagging far behind, reeling in quiet confusion as to what their roles should be.

In the past, men defined themselves by neatly prescribed social roles and clear-cut codes of masculine behavior. But because the roles of the two sexes function interdependently, it is axiomatic that changes in one will cause changes in the other. At work, at home, and in bed, fundamental alterations in the relationship between men and women have been exerting hitherto unknown pressures on men.

Suddenly, the old familiar male pattern seems to be changing before our eyes. We find ourselves in a different arena, where the very meaning of words like *masculine* and *feminine* are rapidly changing. It's new and exciting—and frightening.

Of course, some men are much more fortunate than others in their ability to adjust. Their fluidity, sensitivity, and sense of themselves are strong; but they also speak of a nagging feeling that many of their new attitudes are hedged with contradictions. These men tend to be younger, in their twenties and thirties, and have grown up in a countercultural environment. They generally have been more receptive to the feminist influence than any other segment of the male population. They are quick to respond to new currents in our culture, recognizing the positive, potentially liberating possibilities of new male values. Nevertheless, they still have difficulty integrating their new values with the realities of their living.

Others resist the winds of change with steadfast determination. And, in the long run, they will be unsuccessful at stemming the tide of history.

This book is for the majority of men, like me, some of the Larry Cranstons of the world and others who found themselves caught between the vanguard of change and the reactionaries who oppose it. Like most men, I came of age with traditional assumptions derived from our notion of male supremacy. I too felt considerable anxiety at the disappearance of traditional landmarks of masculinity and bastions of male privilege. I too was trapped between the old and the new, feeling much like an old, sturdy piece of furniture, which could be sanded and refinished with new values and outlooks but whose grain would remain unchanged underneath.

I conceived this exploration when I realized that I and many other "middle" men were experiencing the chaos of transition. Although I sensed the impracticality of much that was associated with traditional masculine behavior, I still found myself inhibited by it. As I came into contact with growing numbers of working women, I was forced to rethink sexual stereotypes. I continued to open the car door for women, but I found more and more of them stepping on my foot. As I began to take a serious look at woman's role and the quality of her life, I also began to take a serious look at the quality of my own life and the lives of men in general—*for the first time!*

Some of what I found was encouraging. I found that some men are beginning to experience and express feelings and emotions once anathematized as "feminine," learning how to confess fears, to admit vulnerability, to touch other men without worrying about possible homosexual connotations, and to experience the joys of fatherhood in completely new ways. This is encouraging.

Nevertheless, other men are having a more difficult time. Swept away by fear, or wallowing in self-pity, they have sounded the bugles of emotional and sexual retreat. Everywhere one looks, the growing numbers of withdrawn, ambivalent men are testimony to the ravages of change.

No one said it was going to be easy. After all, we have never seen a society in which men did not dominate, nor one in which traditional masculine values were not lauded from schoolboy playing fields to executive suites. However, once men show signs of adjusting and embrace new options, their questions and ideas will probably define the paths along which future generations will be able to advance. Out of their ranks will come men who are willing and able to deal with the real questions of human liberation. If nothing else, it has become clear during this exciting and sometimes painful period of transition, uncertainty, and experimentation that all of us—macho and milquetoast; gay, straight, and bi—can rid ourselves of the confines of sex roles, alter our sexual consciousness, yet still be enslaved by anxieties and expectations.

It's going to take more than a while before we can get beyond the present dilemma, but, for the male caught in the cultural maze of today, the time to begin is now. He can only begin to try to understand the nature of the forces at work on him by stepping back and taking a hard look. With a willingness to learn and change, there is no reason why men cannot take a new, more comfortable position in a freer world.

This book is not a collection of arid statistical data but primarily a mosaic of ideas, attitudes, and useful information—a panorama that highlights changes in the roles of men and raises, and frequently answers, questions about how men can and should change.

A wide range of interesting people have been generous enough to contribute to this work. They were selected because of their work and/or because something that they have done or said falls neatly into the mosaic. Others are included because they represent a particular point of view. Several occupy positions from which they can mold popular thought on this subject.

If one theme must emerge, it will be that the problems of men are virtually inextricable from discussions about success, power, our economic way of life; the historical development of sex roles, feminism, and the sociology of the seventies; how men are brought up and how they bring up their children; the nature of male sexuality, changing sexual attitudes, and the relationship between the sexes; violence, aggression, and our anthropological heritage.

The contributors are writers, poets, editors, feminists, social theorists, doctors, sex therapists, psychologists, an anthropologist, actors, and one of the greatest athletes in the world. Each personality is singularly fascinating, but together they form a potent brew. Woven into the structure of this book, their perceptions and perspectives are invaluable. Sincere thanks to Helen Gurley Brown, Art Buchwald, James Dickey, Dr. Albert Ellis, Warren Farrell, Dan Greenburg, Gael Greene, Bob Guccione, Sterling Hayden, Joseph Heller, Elizabeth Janeway, Bruce Jenner, Michael Korda, Ashley Montagu, Anthony Pietropinto, George Plimpton, Tony Randall, Alvin Toffler, Tom Tryon, Gore Vidal, and James Whitmore. They all care.

Finally, it must be said in passing that, while this book is not an apologia for male chauvinism and does not intend to lament the passing of masculine privilege or to evoke nostalgic sentiment for the good old days when "real men" roamed the earth, it does recognize from the outset that men are very special creatures indeed. "Special," however, does not for a moment mean "better," but rather the other half of a whole. Despite what appear to be growing similarities between the sexes during this time of burgeoning androgyny, and despite all lingering differences imposed by cultural, sexual, psychological, emotional, and philosophical considerations, it is probable that, during our lifetimes at least, our culture will continue to mandate that men behave in special ways. This is a complicated need on our parts. In this world it also becomes all too easy and convenient for us to forget that compassion, integrity, honesty, self-respect, and sportsmanship are male ideals along with strength, control, grace under pressure, success, and winning. Not for a moment will this book take the position that there is anything wrong with being strong or successful, but it will point out the terrible human price that many men pay for winning or achieving as a compulsive end in itself. We can begin to defuse our obsessions by humanizing our goals. The need to *feel* manhood will no doubt continue. The need to *prove* it to ourselves or anyone else may not.

Given the depth and intensity of our cultural conditioning, the cards seem stacked against us now, but the process is just beginning. First, we can start by understanding that we can unlearn many of our more stifling male patterns without witnessing the wholesale disintegration of our way of life, without shirking responsibilities and commitments, and without suffering emotional or sexual catastrophes. We must begin somewhere! The single most important prerequisite in undertaking this journey is nothing more than the desire to make life a little better, a little more honest, perhaps more real, and finally more human, until we are all quite a bit more free.

Despite the confusion, this is still an exciting time in which to live. Men and women now have great room—and opportunity—for personal growth. So far, the changes in men have been slow, but we can at least discuss these issues with each other now and risk nothing of our manhood in the process.

1

Genesis: In the Beginning

AH, MEN! We think we are free, but everywhere we are in chains. We believe we are masters, but we are slaves. We are bound by a tradition of male dominance and unconscious animosity toward women. We are enslaved by a mystique of masculinity, a complex of attitudes, cultural expectations, and behaviors that define the role we must play.

Men tend to blame women for their predicament. That is a mistake. The drives for women's liberation and equality are only the most recent phases of a struggle that has been called *the longest war*. The battle is old, probably as old as human society. Its source is the estrangement of men and women.

To many the phrase "estrangement of men and women" will seem absurd. Men love women. They always have, or at least did until women forgot their "proper" roles as wives and mothers.

But men have always looked upon women with a mix of desire, awe, and hatred; and to understand the origins of the male's dilemma we must first go back several millennia, to a prehistoric time when men and women existed in primitive societies based on the hunting of wild animals and the gathering of wild, edible plants. Then, men stood in awe of females for their power to deliver new life, not realizing, as men would not realize for thousands of years, that they, too, played a role in the reproductive process.

Artifacts, especially the female fertility figures, the so-called Venus statues from as early as 30,000 years ago, stand as eloquent testimony to primitive man's reverence for the female's power and for her apparent unity with nature. Early men equated the mysteries of pregnancy and childbirth, in addition to the other natural phenomena they witnessed, with lightning, storms, earthquakes, and volcanic eruptions. Men's earliest creation myths told of an earth mother from whose loins, unassisted by any male deity, all life had sprung.

But men's early reverence for women and their power of reproduction began to change, probably at the beginning of the cultural transition from gathering and hunting to settled agriculture. It was at this time that men began to realize that they, too, were a necessary part of reproduction. The result was an eclipse of the female's status. Men redrew creation myths to reflect the male's new sense of importance. New religions, including, much later, Judaism and Christianity, spoke of a male creator, God the Father, who acted without female assistance. Men finally denied that women played any role at all in reproduction, other than to act as receptacles and incubators for the male's already complete seed. The pendulum had swung in full arc.

Although we have come to terms with the knowledge that men *and* women are necessary for reproduction, the sense of wonder that early man attached to the process of creation remains—a wonder that not even the explanations of modern science have been able to dispel. Many people continue to think of the capacity to give birth as a magical power. To many women it is the most intense experience that life can bring; while to men it is a mystery they can never truly share. Thus there is a chasm between the sexes that not even close male participation in preparation and final delivery can ever overcome. To many men, in the past and in the present, it is a source not only of wonder and awe but of a sense of inadequacy, envy, and even hatred of the opposite sex.

Because I wanted to understand more fully the male's contradictory feelings toward women, his attraction to and reverence for them, on the one hand, and his envy, hatred, and subjugation of them, on the other, the opposites that help create the dilemma for him today, I spoke at length with the anthropologist Ashley Montagu, author of more than fifty books, many dealing with the questions at hand. I asked him if, in his mind, there was a direct link between men's estrangement from the process of childbirth and men's attitude toward women.

B.A.: Do you think that males feel alienated from nature by the exclusive association of women with childbirth?

A.M.: I would say so. You see, men also want to have children. Of course, the desire of men to have children is so repressed that it seldom reaches the conscious level and therefore is always denied at a conscious level. There are derisive and understandable roars of laughter among men upon hearing this. Nevertheless, men were and still are jealous of women's capacity to have a baby, even to menstruate. But they have not been content merely to transform women's capacities into disabilities to explain women's continuing subordinate role.

B.A.: This sounds as if the male is afflicted with a kind of schizophrenia. On the one hand, he needs women because he knows that women are his link with nature, but on the other, he feels a fear and perhaps a hatred of them.

A.M.: Yes, that's a very good word to describe it. It's a portmanteau word, schizophrenia, a catchall for many things. But in the sense that it is a split, such that one part of him fails to recognize the other, this is almost deliberately effected by the culture. For example, among the Australian Aborigines, there is no understanding of the relationship between intercourse and childbirth, and the fact is that while they understand such a relationship in other animals, it is entirely denied for human beings. They believe that women do not really participate in the process of reproduction at all. The significant point about this is that they deny that women have anything to do with childbirth. Now, you ask, how can this be when you see where a baby comes from? Well, they feel that a woman is an incubator. The Greeks held the same view—that woman is simply an incubator in which the child grew. But it was the father who was responsible. The Australian Aborigines say a spirit baby enters the woman's womb and that it will only do so when she is married to a man of the right moiety and clan membership. The father has to tell the woman that this is about to occur, otherwise it won't. And that's how you know it's his child. Of course, he can dream this, too, so he doesn't have to be there; and he doesn't even have to tell her. He can be away for three years and return to find a newborn baby there and know that it's his child. Women don't have babies. They are simply a residence until the child's ready to be born. The woman's role is entirely demoted here. Intercourse doesn't have anything to do with it. Father and mother can have as much intercourse as possible, but that has no relationship to childbirth.

B.A.: You mentioned menstruation, too. Would you elaborate on that?

A.M.: Well, menstruation has long been regarded by many peoples as the female's method of ridding her body of evil humors. Menstrual blood is therefore unclean, harmful. Many cultures have taboos against contact with women during menstruation. They are considered unclean and are separated from the tribe and punished if they fail to remain apart until menstruation has ceased. Nevertheless, men have copied women's natural means of cleansing their bodies, which they believe menstruation does, so some groups, such as the Australian Aborigines, perform a ritual operation on adolescent youths, at their second initiation, which is called subincision. This operation consists of slitting open the urethra on the underside of the penis. A stone is placed into the slit to keep it open permanently. Then, often at ceremonies and initiations, the slit penis will be incised again to make it bleed in imitation of the female's menstruation. Since the male has to attain by pain and suffering to himself what the female does naturally (although often also with pain and suffering), the subincision ceremony serves as a further ground for resentment against the female.

Montagu also described "infibulation," an operation that some primitive tribes perform on females at puberty, in which the clitoris and both labia are cut away. In a North African variation on this operation, the vulva is sewn up, leaving only a small hole for menstruation and urination. "Here," according to Montagu, "the jealousy of the male has gone so far as to limit virtually completely the female's capacity for pregnancy and childbirth." But when the girl marries, the sewn orifice is enlarged to allow entry of her husband's penis. Later, at the termination of a pregnancy, it will be opened by incision, only to be resewn after childbirth.

Should one be tempted to dismiss this as just another example of uncivilized behavior, Montagu has a ready reply: "People objected when I said in *The Natural Superiority of Women* that I suspected many surgeons and gynecologists performed hysterectomies out of hatred for women, out of jealousy. They said, 'How can you say such a terrible thing?' Well, it was not so long ago that American surgeons were performing clitoridectomies by the hundreds. Today, they are 'castrating' thousands in a way. We have plenty of cases and actual records of this and where it is done—cases where there was nothing wrong with the women. When I say actual cases, I mean not five or six or twenty or a hundred but thousands." When I suggested that it might have been done for avarice, Montagu said, "Oh, yes, but when one understands the fact that it is a man who is the gynecologist, one can't believe that he's lost all sense of what this means to a woman, to be told that she has to be dewomanized, hysterectomized." Male envy, hatred, and need for dominance carried to its logical conclusion?

Whatever the precise balance of men's feelings for women today or in any historical period, at no time has the relation of power been altered. Males have been dominant in all societies and cultures. Although there have long been theories, some recently resurrected by ardent feminists, about a "golden age" of matriarchy in which women were the dominant social and political force, anthropologists have searched in vain for over a hundred years for any evidence that any society has been truly matriarchal. They have found none. From the most distant past to the present, males have always filled virtually all positions of effective leadership and authority in social, religious, economic, and political institutions.

The patriarchal organization and patriarchal attitudes that define our society and prescribe the primary role men must play are the products of biology and culture. Even now, many probably still believe that males and females are genetically endowed with characteristics that predetermine behavior, in the way that genes are responsible for more body hair for males, a broader pelvis for females, and so on through numerous observable differences. This belief is not completely unfounded, though it is prone to exaggeration. There is enough evidence for biological influence on some sex-typed behaviors that is intriguing enough to merit consideration.

The sex of normal offspring is set at the moment of conception by genes in the male sperm. In humans, the female ovum and the male sperm each contain twenty-three chromosomes, slender threads made up of genetic material. The successful penetration of the ripe ovum by a single sperm creates a fertilized egg cell of forty-six chromosomes aligned in twenty-three pairs. Only one of these pairs is responsible for the sex of the new embryo. From the mother comes an X chromosome and from the father either an X or Y. The sex chromosome in the father's sperm determines the sex of the child. If it is an X, the embryo will have two Xs and will be a girl; if the father's sperm contains a Y chromosome, the child will have one X and one Y and it will be a boy.

Anatomical and physiological differences between males

and females develop during the nine months of pregnancy. Actually, until sometime around the sixth week after conception, the genitalia of males and females are indistinct. Both have a single opening which leads to the bladder and internal genitals. Each has tissue that can develop into either a penis or a clitoris. Then, suddenly, in some still unexplained manner, the Y chromosome transmits a genetic code which causes the indistinct genitalia of the male embryo to develop into testes. From that point, the testes begin to produce excess androgens (the male hormones), especially testosterone, which completes development of the male's sexual organs.

The male sex organs also affect the developing brain, especially the hypothalamus, a region deep inside, which when fully matured acts through the pituitary glands to bring about the characteristics we associate with adult manhood, such as facial and body hair and regular sperm production. The operation of androgens on the brain also predisposes males toward greater aggressive activity from early childhood. Because of their hormonal balance, males will engage in far more rough-and-tumble play, will tend to wander farther away from the confines of home and parent than will females, whose hormones seem to produce greater nurturant behavior and, some would maintain, a greater passivity.

Because there remains strong disagreement on the precise mix between biology and culture, I asked Ashley Montagu about the biological basis of sex roles—if there is, in fact, any basis for the widespread belief that male superiority, that male roles are biologically determined.

A.M.: None at all, although there are still plenty of people —some with Ph.D. degrees—who claim this. There is even a book, written in 1973 about the "inevitability" of male dominance, and there are people like Lionel Tiger and Robin Fox who believe this. But the fact is that all these roles have very little to do with biological factors.

B.A.: How do we derive particular sex roles, then?

A.M.: Well, the fact is that the roles that many believe to be biologically determined are socially determined, culturally determined. These are gender roles. Masculinity and femininity are required, learned roles, and maleness or femaleness are biological. These are genetic, but they shouldn't be confused with sex roles.

B.A.: How does this confusion arise?

A.M.: The confusion arises from the fact that most people don't understand that these aspects of maleness and femaleness are biological facts. When a baby is born, they look at its external genitalia and they say 'This is a boy' or 'This is a girl.' That is biologically determined. Of course, they may be wrong about that, too, for one can be born a biological male and, by behavior, be feminine, or the reverse. But on the average, appearance is indicative of biological sex. It is not, I must stress, indicative of a particular pattern of behavior, of a particularly defined role in life.

The culturally determined sex roles to which Ashley Montagu refers arose thousands of years ago, most likely in the Upper Paleolithic period among hunting and gathering societies. These groups divided the tasks of providing particular types of food according to sex—males hunted larger animals, often leaving their primary group for several days, while women stayed together with the children, venturing only a short distance from camp to gather edible plants that grew wild nearby. Females did occasionally hunt small game near the main settlement, but the task of supplying animal protein was largely left to males.

In recent years, some feminists have challenged the view that a division of labor according to sex was the direct product of biological differences. They argue that women were strong enough to hunt, just as they were and are strong enough in many societies to bear heavy burdens and do difficult agricultural work. Moreover, they say neither the menstrual cycle nor childbirth would prevent women from participating as hunters. Rather than adapt work to fit sexual or reproductive cycles, reproduction is usually adapted to fit the type of work expected of women. Often, primitive women space pregnancies by means of extended nursing. But it was no doubt difficult, if not impossible, for pregnant women or women with small children to go on the long treks that must have been necessary to bag sufficient game. It would have been far more sensible for these women to engage in the crucial tasks of gathering, from which Paleolithic groups acquired over two-thirds of their food.

I asked Montagu if there might not have been some aspect of male/female biological differences—the male's tendency toward greater aggression and the female's toward greater nurturance—that might have influenced roles.

"Oh, yes," he replied. "It is mainly because the male has

always been physically more powerful, rushing around, exhibiting muscularly greater power, which has enabled him to impose his ideas upon the so-called weaker sex. Of course, females are actually stronger constitutionally than males, but muscularly they're not as powerful. One shouldn't confuse one with the other. It's the muscular power which gives the male his social power over the female. This is the basis of the politics of sex. In evolution of humans and the development of hunting, it was to the advantage of the group to have males who were faster and more powerful than the females."

It was also an advantage to the Paleolithic group to have a sufficient number of strong, aggressive males for protection against predatory animals or against other human groups. There is one theory, the "combat hypothesis," associated with anthropologist, Marvin Harris of Columbia University, which holds that it is the male function as combatant that produces male dominance. According to Harris, any group that did not have a large number of aggressive males, trained in the use of weapons, or that allowed women to use weapons in hunting and fighting, would be at a disadvantage and would most likely suffer extinction.

Harris, who is a strong advocate of women's liberation and rights, believes women lacked the musculature to match men in the hand-to-hand combat that dominated warfare, and still does, even in our age of nuclear weapons. The woman's wider pelvis also inhibits running ability somewhat, potentially enough to put her at a serious disadvantage in any direct contest with a male warrior. In matters of life and death, then, it was the necessary reliance on males for protection, based, in the first instance, on their strength and speed and, in the second, on the experience gained in hunting, which led to male dominance and to the establishment of certain roles as a male preserve.

Ashley Montagu also commented on this function. "Of course," he told me, "it was to the advantage of the group to have males, to protect it from animal and other attacks. Lions, for example, won't attack a group of baboons or apes; they will attack solitary animals. So the advantage is not only in being individually more powerful but being a member of a cooperative group, and that's a very important point to understand. Muscular power alone isn't enough either for hunting or protection, but has to be considered in relation to the human group. Our evolution has not been solely as individuals, as some biologists believe. The group is extremely important in considering evolution as we see it."

I asked Montagu if our life style today, which certainly seems competitive rather than cooperative, is a throwback to primitive societies in which the man who was the quickest, the strongest and the best hunter derived the greatest rewards, sex and status; whereas today the man who is the successful man, the powerful man, will also enjoy high status and attract many women. He denied this.

"It's certainly not! Living primitive societies that we have any knowledge of, those peoples who correspond to our earliest prehistoric ancestors, have no chieftains. They live in small populations seldom exceeding thirty to fifty individuals. There are no people who are superior to others by rank.

"What is most valued is wisdom in each of these cultures. And it doesn't matter how young or old you are. Anything that has to be decided is decided by the group as a whole. Justice and equality are characteristic of these societies very much more so than they are in our own societies.

"The competitive behavior you mention is not a development of something we carry within ourselves as a biological potentiality, but is a result of the fact that when we moved out of the food-gathering, hunting stage of development and into agriculture, we could control the reproduction of plants and animals. We stayed put in one place instead of moving in a small group all over the place and then increased the amount of food to whatever limit we wished and thus increased the number of individuals that could be supported. We now had larger villages. This only occurred about twelve thousand years ago. First large villages grew into towns, and towns frequently merged with other towns. It was here that you got the accelerated development of the traits of predation and intergroup violence.

"Distinctions developed between peoples. Formerly, only thirty to fifty people lived together, each one of whom knew everyone else. Then love and cooperation were the dominant principles by which everyone lived. But now, in the larger settlements, you could pass people on the streets whom you had never seen before and whom you didn't know and whom you didn't care about, who were now engaged in specific occupations—silversmiths, diggers of ditches, agriculturalists, foremen, surveyors, priests, chiefs. Here for the first time you got the development of power.

"Individuals began for the first time to envy the possessions of other individuals. They began to compete with each other for the first time. We have cultures in which we can see this process going on right at this moment—where whites have introduced themselves into New Guinea in very cooperative societies and have started to teach them competitive games. You can see how they're changing from cooperation to competition. They're extending the competition of games into their daily lives."

Settlement also increased the amount of intergroup violence, of aggressive behavior toward others, of war. Of course, there was always some warfare. Only a handful of gathering and hunting societies seem not to engage in some sort of warfare today, though they most probably did so in the past. Nevertheless, primitive warfare, though fatal to more than a quarter of any group's male population, was often more symbolic than real, and it was rarely if ever accompanied by an effort to destroy another group totally.

After settlement, however, men began to envy the possessions of other groups. Now there were permanent houses; there was food-processing equipment; there were villages with a deep sense of territorial identity. There is no question that the scale of combat increased, that war became far more destructive than it ever had been before. Villages often remained enemies of other villages for generations. Each would repeatedly attack and plunder the other, each attempting to rout the other and to chase the enemy inhabitants from their homes and possessions. Conquest and expanded settlement became important concerns as populations increased and as the needs of each growing group expanded.

Warfare continues to this day, almost entirely as a male preserve, but its causes—along with the general nature of human aggression—remain uncertain. Ashley Montagu believes after his detailed studies of aggression and violence, and of societies which refrain from this behavior, that this aspect of human behavior, especially of male behavior, is also "culturally determined." As he told me, "There are cultures in which absolutely nothing of warfare is known. Zero! Nobody marches; nobody engages in war; nobody engages in conflict; everybody's in cooperation with one another." He further concludes that although we do have specific pathways in the brain which facilitate aggressive responses to certain kinds of stimuli, these responses, too, are largely learned.

As a result, I asked him if there was a danger in the public's acceptance of the view of writers like Konrad Lorenz and Robert Ardrey, who maintain that human males have instinctive drives of aggression and dominance.

Montagu feels that "no respectable psychologist" can any longer subscribe to the concept of aggressive human instincts. "The danger of the instinctivists and innate aggressionists is that they tell you that we are all born with an instinct of aggression and dominance. That is to say we're all born with drives which are oriented in the direction of inflicting injury upon other human beings, even to the point of death. That we are born murderers. That's what Lorenz says, and the notion is very appealing to people who want to explain to themselves why they are so ornery. It relieves them immediately of a sense of guilt that they have been carrying around for being as ornery as they are. Now they're told that it's the way they were born. It's just there; that's why we will always have wars, and we will always have conflicts and so forth.

"The danger of all this is that it sidetracks our attention from the real causes of aggression and hostility, and these are not inborn. These are, for the most part, learned, and as we know, human beings are capable of learning anything. They're capable of learning to be terribly aggressive. They have within their brains cellular arrangements that can be readily organized to function as anything you wish them to function as. Man is born with a 'polymorphous educability.' In other words, he's structured in such a way that he can learn anything. He can learn not to be aggressive; we have plenty of cultures of this kind. But we're told by a playwright like Ardrey and a man who studies ducks, Lorenz, that human beings are instinctively aggressive because that is their opinion. Now I don't know anything about ducks, and I'm perfectly willing to say that I will absolutely refuse to deliver an opinion on how ducks behave towards one another. But Lorenz isn't willing to admit that he's wrong about anything about human beings, anymore than Ardrey is."

Nevertheless, Montagu does believe there has been a definite association between males and violence from the earliest times, though he maintains this was an acquired behavior. "In gathering-hunting cultures," he told me, "it was the male who was familiar with the bows and arrows. He was and is the hunter; the woman was and is the food gatherer. The male is the more active for reasons we've already gone into. He's physiologically and hormonally different, muscularly more powerful, taller. As the civilization developed and wars grew in intensity and frequency, these males were the soldiers. The man who was, and very often still is, valued and admired was the hunter and the soldier. This was and is a prestige fraught with profound consequences for society."

Because of their value and importance as hunters and warriors, males were the dominant force in all hunter-gatherer societies. Thus, patriarchy, with its attending male dominance and its attitude which devalues women, stemmed originally from anatomical and physiological differences—greater musculature, strength, and predisposition for aggression among males; menstruation, pregnancy, childbirth, and predisposition for nurturance among females. Groups purposely encouraged and welcomed the birth of large numbers of aggressive males for combat. They often practiced female infanticide to keep population at a level consistent with traditional living standards. And finally, some groups tended to reward strength and aggression among males with sexual access to the group's females and to sanction the forcible sexual possession of women from other groups.

Later, evolving social and cultural systems incorporated perceived differences between the sexes into strict legal codes and institutional regulations. Men wove male dominance into myth, with male deities first joining, then replacing, an earth mother as creator of all life; into organized religions in the East and the West; into the Roman, English, and American systems of law, with their explicit subordination of women to the will of fathers and husbands; indeed, into the whole fabric of societies throughout the world.

However, in each society in the past as well as in the present, though male dominance has remained a constant, the precise role, the precise behavior deemed appropriate for each sex, has been and is defined according to a complex mix of heritage, tradition, and innovation. As a result, the precise roles men and women are expected to play are defined differently in different societies and cultures. A masculine role in one may turn out to be a feminine role in another, and the reverse is equally true. In the United States, as in many other modern western societies, the male's role is identified and delineated by a specific type of behavior, one that conforms to an ideal termed masculinity, another source of the male's dilemma today.

2

Perspectives on the Male Role

WHAT IS the male role and what does it mean to be masculine in American society today?

Until recently, only a few writers thought of these questions. But the rise of the women's movement in the 1960s changed all that. The realization that women played definite roles in the United States raised the obvious question of whether there was a male counterpart, a male role. We now know there is.

Just the word *role* should give us pause. The term itself, resurrected in recent years by feminists and social scientists to describe the female condition, is derived from the language of the theater, from the French *rôle,* or roll of paper containing an actor's part. In current social science jargon, a role is defined as any pattern of behaviors that is encouraged for an individual in a specific situation or that the individual has been *trained to perform*. The concept at once seems to rob us of our free will and reduces us to mere players, even if it is on the largest stage of all.

If the concept of male and female roles is new, the roles themselves are not. At the core of the male role are patriarchy and male dominance. In the United States, the male role is also linked to a long-held tradition of manhood. Our current idea of masculinity has its roots deep in America's frontier experience, in men's interaction with and adaptation to the new wilderness environment. Manhood, as derived from the nineteenth-century tradition, was a badge worn proudly by males who waged successful battles with the environment and with themselves. Pioneers, farmers, mountain men, hunters, trappers, soldiers, cowboys, and, later, businessmen—these were the heroes of the American pantheon of manhood. No one bothered to list the virtues that defined the ideal; they were understood. But we can look back through history and literature and see that men valued simplicity of manners, rugged individualism, strength of character as well as of body, the belief that the actions of "real men" were central to an unfolding drama in which it was necessary for each male to prove that he was of sufficient merit to warrant the ultimate accolade, "There goes a man!"

The embodiments of the nineteenth-century ideal and its twentieth-century analogue still flash before us on the movie screens. It is William S. Hart struggling against the forces of lawlessness in the silent classic *The Great Train Robbery*. It is Humphrey Bogart, cool and imperturbable, fighting crime in *The Maltese Falcon* or defying the Nazis in *Casablanca*. It is Gary Cooper's marshal, standing alone against three killers in *High Noon* while hardy but cowardly males hide behind closed doors. It is John Wayne in countless westerns and war movies from *Stagecoach* through *The Sands of Iwo Jima* to *True Grit*. It is Alan Ladd as Shane, riding in from nowhere to clear up a corrupt town and save a widow in distress. It is the ideal lover as seen in Rudolph Valentino's Sheik, in Clark Gable's Rhett Butler as he sweeps Scarlett O'Hara into the bedroom, in James Bond's numerous, and usually loveless, conquests.

One also sees the male ideal in literature, and no one has captured its essence better than Ernest Hemingway did in his novels and short stories. In virtually all of his major fiction, Hemingway disdained femininity and all things associated with women. His was a world of men and male pursuits, a world in which women were mere adjuncts or bothers when present at all. It was a world of manhood and the need to prove it over and over. It was the world of machismo, the Hispanic notion of men proving they have *balls* to themselves and their fellow men.

Many of the people I interviewed spoke of Hemingway and the male's ideal of masculinity. But none caught his spirit better than the political satirist Art Buchwald.

"I met Hemingway," Buchwald told me, "and he was probably the most macho of all machos. It was late in his life in Paris. He was acting the role of Hemingway, and he was a sort of parody of himself. The first question he asked me, really the first thing he said to me, was 'Have you ever wrestled a bear?' I said no. And I laughed. And later he told someone he thought I was a little shit."

Buchwald laughed. "It didn't bother me, because, you know, if Hemingway says you're a little shit, at least he remembers who you were."

Hemingway was one of the "bulls" of American literature. Our current "bull" is Norman Mailer, in many ways Hemingway's counterpart *manqué*. Many who spoke of Hemingway talked about Mailer, too, for he revels in the same ideal of masculinity as Hemingway. Gore Vidal, one of America's top novelists and Mailer's sometime sparring partner at Manhattan cocktail parties, noted that Mailer's subject matter and themes were the same as Hemingway's. He told me: "Mailer set out to be exactly like Hemingway. He also wanted to break the stereotype of the Jew as being nonviolent—you know, the fat little boy with glasses and violin case who gets beaten up by the tough Irish and Italian kids. He wanted to break that stereotype, so he was going to be a drunk, which Jews are not supposed to be; he was going to have a lot of wives, a lot of children, just like the macho Hemingway. But it didn't work for Hemingway, and it hasn't worked for him. It's a mistake to try to be something that you are not. Hemingway shot himself at the end—or was that really Hemingway he shot? Maybe he shot the drunken, impotent braggart that had taken his place in the mirror of life. Mailer's mind is better than Hemingway's was, and he tries very hard to justify the imposter in the mirror. His views on sex, women, and life are to the right of Anita Bryant. I liked William Gass's phrase about Mailer in the *New York Review of Books:* 'A little fascist rooster, flapping two right wings.' "

So far, only Mailer's public reputation has suffered as a result of his macho image. But Hemingway was destroyed by carrying the world of fiction into his life. It is now argued that Hemingway fought all of his life against a softer, more feminine side of his personality. In the end, the battle was too much for him and he committed suicide, thereby admitting that his life was a failure. But "inevitably," Leonard Kriegel writes, "one wishes that Hemingway, for one moment before he pulled the trigger of the most famous shotgun in American literary history, had paused to pen a sentence in which he told us what he has learned of the failure of *heroism,* the inadequacy of *courage,* a sentence into which he managed to put all that he knew about the terror of not being a man, of not bearing up."[1] Perhaps we will get the sentence from Norman Mailer.

Destructive as it can be on the individual level, the machismo we see in the overbearing masculinity of males in the fiction of Hemingway and Mailer becomes a particularly dangerous model when it defines the actions of men in power. Modern

politicians, especially those at the top, have a power to destroy humanity. On at least one occasion we have been close.

I asked Buchwald if he saw an obsession with masculinity affect the behavior and policy of American politicians. Lyndon Johnson is often mentioned as an example. "Yes," Buchwald said, "Johnson was concerned, but I think that's true of everybody who is in the White House. And I think one of the reasons you get all of these goddam terrible wars—the Vietnam war is a perfect example of it—is that the macho thing came into it. I think it came into it with Kennedy, and I think it came into it with Johnson, too." I asked him if he could give me some examples of things that they had done. "Well, if you want to simplify things somewhat, after the Bay of Pigs, Kennedy felt he had lost his masculinity or something, or he was considered no longer tough or something. Then the next show that came along after the missile crisis, which should have been satisfactory, was the damn Vietnam war, and he was again trying to show the Russians that he was tough."

Gore Vidal has observed the same process. While we were speaking about Hemingway's and Mailer's obsession with machismo, I asked him about the same obsession in politicians like Kennedy and Johnson. "You have a very interesting situation," I commented.

"Diabolic," he answered. "You have your war situations. That seems always to have been the case. One good point, however, is that you never get anything from the bureaucracy that can be good, nothing useful, but you also don't ever get a war out of the bureaucracy, which includes the Pentagon. Generals do not particularly like wars. They are very messy and you can get into trouble. You can even get hurt. They like large appropriations and they like war scares, but they do not like wars.

"No, it's the politicians showing off, especially on television. It was Jack Kennedy trying to offset all the bad publicity over the first time around with Cuba at the Bay of Pigs. He was getting ready for the congressional elections of 1962, the off-year election, so he pulled that missile crisis, which just about could have killed everybody. That's dangerous, that's sick, that's predictable."

"So he was trying to assert his manhood?" I asked.

"Oh, yeah . . . and he knew that would have been highly appealing to the dumb-dumbs across the world, and it was."

Art Buchwald also saw this attitude continuing after John

Kennedy. "Then Johnson," he said. "Every time Johnson thought about getting out of the war or quitting while he was behind, I imagine that macho spirit came in and he said, 'I'm not going to let the Americans lose a war; I'm not going to be the first president to lose a war.' I think those were his words, or something to that effect."

"Yes, and Nixon said the same thing," I pointed out.

"I think they all have that macho spirit when they get in the White House," Buchwald said. "I mean the high point for Gerald Ford was the Mayagüez incident. When he rescued the men, it made him feel very manly."

Manhood, machismo, masculinity . . . The attributes we find in films, in novels, and in the behavior of ordinary men as well as political leaders are, as Dr. Harvey Kaye put it in *Male Survival*, "the embodiment of heroism and courage, aggressivity and aptitude."[2] They are the ideals of heroic action, though they certainly pale in comparison with the classical tradition of Heracles, Hector, and Achilles. Still, in its present setting, American men can see themselves as, and expect themselves to be, heroes, studs, providers, warriors, empire builders, and empire savers. Though their ideal is a phantom of literary imagination and tradition, it exerts a profound effect on the American man's life.

Actually, the heroic ideal and the notion of manhood have been tempered by industrialization and technological advance in the twentieth-century United States. The trials of manhood that we can still see in the surviving primitive societies and, it must be said, in some subcultures of our own, are less possible for those most nearly modernized. Gore Vidal caught this aspect of the male dilemma perfectly in *Myra Breckinridge*. "Today," he writes, "there is nothing left for the old-fashioned male to do, no ritual testing of his manhood through initiation or personal contest, no physical struggle to survive or mate. Nothing is left him but to put on clothes reminiscent of a different time; only in travesty can he act out the classic hero who was law unto himself, moving at ease through a landscape of admiring women. Mercifully, that age is finished."[3] Not completely, though. For we still see its remnants in the daring of balloonists attempting to cross the Atlantic or in the mock-heroic buffoonery of the daredevil.

We also see remnants of the heroic ideal in literature. Nowhere have we seen it better recently than in James Dickey's novel, *Deliverance,* the story of four urban men, bored by their everyday lives, who seek adventure on a wilderness river. I asked Dickey if their trip was in any way a quest for manhood. "Yes," he replied, "very much so." Dickey's characters feel they are "lesser men than men used to be," and I asked Dickey if he thought a lot of men felt that way these days, since most of the traditional landmarks by which men used to measure themselves have changed or are not as obvious as they used to be.

"Well," Dickey said, "I remember my late friend, the American poet John Berryman, saying to me that in this culture everything and everybody is insulated against harshness and danger. 'Jim,' he said, 'a man can live his whole life in this culture and never know whether he is a coward or not. And I think he should know. Don't you?' And I said, 'I sure do.' I also remember that the French writer Henry de Montherlant said one time, 'If you are ever bored with your life, risk it!' That is my character Lewis's type of thing. And that is the story, the dramatic involvement, of *Deliverance*. It is about three rather hesitant men with different qualities who go on the river with Lewis because they are bored. Lewis is bored in a fierce way; the others are just kind of languidly bored. Nice men. Honest fellows. But they go just to get a change of environment. To get away from the nine-to-five days at the office. To get away from worries about household bills. To get away from having to cope with grocery shopping with their wives. To get away from church on Sunday. All of that. For them it is a way of charging the spiritual batteries by a change of scene. That is why they go."

Dickey's book shows—as does the film based on it—that man tampers with forces of nature at his own peril. The wilderness "is not something to fool around with," Dickey says. "The rocks in the river are real. The rapids are real. The men who attack the rapids are real. And the rapids don't care about you at all."

Some men try to emulate the heroic image. Dickey says many men have endeavored to duplicate the river trip he described in *Deliverance*. And many of them died. Most men, however, have had to remain satisfied with only a pale shadow or merely a dream of the bygone heroic role. For them, the role survives only in the shared mystique of masculinity. The code of masculinity nonetheless gives men a primal bond with one another. It defines the conduct and behavior according to which men must live. It molds the image that individual men present to the world. For many, it is the cement that holds their identities together.

Of course, we all know what it means to be masculine. We see it on film and we read about it in novels and in male magazines. We don't have to define the concept anymore than nineteenth-century men had to define manhood. We can tell at a glance who fits and who doesn't. A certain bearing, a certain carriage, a way of doing things instantly marks one male as masculine and another as falling short of the ideal. Dan Wakefield caught the essence of the matter perfectly in his 1970 novel, *Going All the Way*. "You had to have some quality that was hard to pin down, a certain kind of confidence, a little swagger but not in a boastful way, an easiness, a style, an air of casual good nature, of leadership that wasn't sought but seemed to come natural. You couldn't pin it down, but you could see it in a person."[4] Tom Tryon, a bestselling novelist and former actor, identifies this bearing with the kind of guy "who's so afraid of his own masculinity that he has to walk around so he can hear his balls clanging all the time. God knows in Hollywood I've met a lot of them. They're just so uptight."

In more exaggerated form, similar swaggering postures and gaits can be seen among wild male chimpanzees and baboons. It is also observed among the strutting male gang members in our cities and in the posturing of male peasants in southern Europe and a number of other societies.

But masculinity is more than mere posturing, and just as Dan Wakefield found the concept "hard to pin down," so might we. Masculinity seemingly refers to traits and behaviors and occupations unrelated to one another, except that they are instantly recognized as legitimate male pursuits. If we list masculine endeavors, for example, we would probably all agree on professional athlete, explorer, soldier, auto mechanic, truck driver, businessman, playboy. No problems there. But few of us, I think, would consider listing ballet dancer, even though dancers are at least as athletic as (and in far better shape than) most athletes and far more coordinated than all but a fraction of us. What is wrong? Clearly, dancing, at least as a vocation, is considered by men to be a nonmale activity, something unsuitable for a "real man." That is not true in other societies, but for ours, it is a real demarcation between masculine and nonmasculine behavior.

One aspect of masculinity should be clear at once—a legacy

of our patriarchal tradition. The aversion men often feel for male dancers should suggest that part of the essence of masculinity is an aversion for things feminine. There is a strong antifeminine bias that lies at the root of masculine behavior. In its most extreme form, in the machismo that characterizes Latin societies and which is present to some degree in our own, there is a visible contempt for women that exists despite the professed, and probably genuine, reverence in such societies for the mother.

This has been noticed. Tony Randall, who understands the actor's concept of role and who has thought hard about the male role and masculinity in American society, told me in a recent chat that he sees a very strong anti-intellectual and artistic bias that arises from widespread identification of intellect and culture with women. They are pursuits fit for women or for men who are not truly masculine. Arts and the intellect are both somehow "effeminate."

Randall further noted the popular identification of talent in the arts as a sure sign of effeminacy and the popular notion that artists in all the creative fields tend toward homosexuality. A peculiar result of this prejudice is that many homosexuals presumed they were talented simply because they were homosexuals, so they went into the arts. "Americans are getting over that," he commented. "If you look at an American ballet company and a Russian ballet company, there's no question which is more virile. The Russians are, because being a ballet dancer has always been a respectable job for a man in their culture. We're changing; we're getting over that kind of inferiority complex. We have our Eddie Villellas today. People like that."

Randall further observed that one aspect of masculinity is its contrast with femininity: "It's all a matter of contrasts, light and shadow. And so masculinity depends in one sense on the amount of femininity around. A man isn't a man by himself; a man is a man in relation to women."

That is true to a point. But we also find that masculinity is defined by a man's relation to other men. For the macho, this is most important, more important than his relation to women, a relation taken for granted as being that of a superior to an inferior. As the psychiatrist Anthony Pietropinto puts it, the male "gets his primary validation by being a man-among-men, respected in the eyes of other males." In this view, then, a man's relationship with a woman is successful not for itself alone, but for the enhancement the man derives in the opinion of his fellow men.

Beneath the permutations in meaning and behavior associated with masculinity, there are a few basic themes that have been identified by sociologists Robert Brannon and Deborah David in their widely used text *The Forty-Nine Percent Majority.*[5] In their view, four themes pervade and identify the male role in the United States today. First, they find, men must be "sturdy oaks," conveying to all an air of manly toughness, of extreme confidence and self-reliance. Second, there should be "no sissy stuff," nothing that can stigmatize a man as feminine, including the full range of stereotyped feminine characteristics, like openness, emotion, and vulnerability. Third, men must follow Harry S. Truman's injunction to "give 'em hell," even to project an aura of potential violence and aggression. Finally, men must be "big wheels," demonstrating to the world that they have success, status, and importance in their careers.

Gore Vidal describes the male role in America without the sociologist's jargon. "What is the male role?" he asks. "Well, it's knocking people down, behaving like Norman Mailer occasionally does at parties. It is an impossible role. Most American men are fat and soft, and weak prisoners of their jobs. They have about as much autonomy and as much power over their own lives as a Russian working on an assembly line in Minsk. Contrary to this, to keep them reasonably contented or at least to keep them from revolting, they are fed, through television, an image of themselves which has no correspondence with reality. The Marlboro Man, if he ever existed, has been dead for many generations."

"You have a male population which has been trained into docility and order so that it will fill up the assembly lines of Detroit, which is as close to hell as you can get in real life, by keeping them slightly drunk on beer, bombarding them on television with pitches for guns, telling them about the enemy that ranges from women's lib, the lesis, the fags, to the commie weirdos.

"Men define themselves as men by what they are fed. First, by the school system, which isn't very good. Second, by television advertising, which is godawful. Third, by the whole buzz of the culture, which expects these fat, soft men, who are mostly happy watching strong, tough men play games on television, to be content when they are not.

"There is a very good book called *The Working Class Major-*

ity by a young man who actually worked on the assembly lines, and he was talking about the blue-collar worker. He said, 'You know, they are much criticized and they are mocked because they don't know how to talk to women. They whistle and behave at the age of thirty like they are still fourteen years old.' He said, 'How can they behave in any other way, since they are never allowed to really meet women?' They go to work very early in their lives; they are kept on the assembly line; and when they get off it, they are worn out. They just pass out. So all they have is Friday and Saturday night to get drunk and misbehave, behave like schoolboys and have no relations with women at all, not even a whore, which is certainly not a very interesting way of meeting somebody, or with the woman who is trapped into looking after their household.

"The thing that makes an economic system like ours work is to maintain control over people and make them do jobs that they hate. To do this, you fill their heads with biblical nonsense about fornication of every variety. Make sure they marry young, make sure thay have children very early. Once a man has a wife and two young children, he will do what you tell him to. He will obey you, and that is the aim of the entire masculine role, as it has been defined in this society. It is done to keep the man really *caponized* so he will do whatever job people want him to fit into. And knowing that he isn't very content with that, giving him sordid TV dreams of people knocking other people down, people shooting other people."

For those outside the working class, success in career and making a larger and larger salary add to the man's image of himself and, he expects, in the eyes of others. Tony Randall agrees, adding, "In America, there is no question about what makes you a big guy. Money!"

"Money is God?" I asked.

"Yes. Money is God. Everybody absolutely worships together without one dissenting voice. And the man who has money is the most virile. Because he controls power."

"But what happens to those marginal men who can't accumulate a significant amount of money?" Are they emasculated by it? Do they look to validate their masculinity in other ways? To men it seems that many find another way in violence and another in sex."

"Sex and money are the same thing," Randall observed. "Women are attracted to power."

Power . . . the ultimate aphrodisiac, as Kissinger says. Though he detests women, the man wants them sexually, and for himself he wants the characteristics of masculinity he thinks attractive to women. His code of masculinity directs that he be a walking phallus, preferably an erect phallus, ready and always willing to do battle at a moment's notice and never, as is too often the case, for a moment's duration. He is primal man again. And with his identity secure, he can relive the male fantasies of an age gone by.

3

Frogs, Snails, and Puppy Dogs' Tails: Learning to Be a Man

ONE THING must be made clear at the outset; males in our society have to learn the male role and what it means to be masculine.

Most evidence points to the conclusion that the roles people generally believe to be biologically determined are really the products of society and culture. As Ashley Montagu put it in our conversation, masculinity is a "required, learned role." His colleague, the late Margaret Mead, agreed, arguing on the basis of her study of primitive tribes that "many, if not all, of the personality traits which we have called masculine or feminine are as lightly linked to sex as are the clothing, the manners and the form of headdress that a society at the given period assigns to either sex."[1]

The enormous variety of cultural experience that Mead and other anthropologists have found throughout the world indicates that peoples have always had the ability to adapt particular sex roles to particular circumstances, a characteristic of cultures which suggests that there is no single pattern of sex-role behavior that is innate or permanent.

To be sure, every culture has had concepts of masculinity and femininity. But these concepts have varied so widely that it is virtually impossible to specify a role or a behavior that is universally and unquestionably male or female. The human body is not "a straitjacket for personality."[2] Sex-linked behavior must be learned.

Sex roles for both males and females are learned through a process termed socialization. Almost immediately after birth, the parents and other adults begin to project their expectations and assumptions onto the infant. Usually, the doctor's first words to parents in the delivery room are "It's a boy" or "It's a girl." If the father is outside, pacing nervously in the waiting room, he is soon informed that he has a "fine, strong, healthy, and good-looking son" or a "beautiful little girl." It is immaterial that both male and female babies are equally pink, cuddly, and delicate. A girl is typed as beautiful and the boy as fine and strong.

In most cases, the parents have chosen a sex-linked name for the child. Hospitals continue gender identification with treatment that supports a particular sexual identity. Blue and pink blankets wrap the respective males and females, and bright pink ribbons often adorn the female infant's hair. No blue ribbons for the boy, however . . . too feminine . . . too sissy.

Most parents will deny that they perceive children according to stereotypes, but the evidence affirms that they do. From the beginning, parents rate the appearance and behavior of their newborns according to preconceived notions of what is appropriately male or female. Infant girls are described as "softer, more finely featured, smaller, and more inattentive"[3] than boys. Fathers go to greater extremes than mothers, describing their daughters as "weak and delicate"[4] and their sons as "firmer, larger-featured, better coordinated, more alert, bigger, stronger, and hardier."[5] Both parents will invariably find differences between male and female personalities. This at an age of less than twenty-four hours when objective observers can find no dissimilarities between the sexes except for genitalia!

Already committed to specific stereotypes, parents are the primary transmitters of appropriate sex roles, a process that begins seriously after the first few months. During the first few weeks the newborn is simply an object to be pleased, to be protected from pain. There is little if any give and take to the relationship between infant and parent. The infant at this stage is even unable to differentiate the sources of its pleasures and pains. Within a few months, however, it recognizes that its parents—those familiar faces and voices—are the sources of external stimuli. The baby soon learns that it must give something back to those images and sounds.

Quickly the child is taught the behavioral rules. The parent's reward system is simple: affection for "good" behavior, punishment or withdrawal of affection for "bad" behavior. At an early age, by the simple admonitions "good girl" or "good boy," parents forever implant gender identity. True to form, at three or four, the child will state firmly, "I am a boy" or "I am a girl."

To the mother, who is most often at home and in continuous intimate contact with the newborn, falls the chief responsibility for the infant's earliest gender conditioning. During the first six months, mothers tend to talk far more to a daughter than to a son, but they give their sons more hugs and caresses. At about the age of six months, mothers seem to cuddle boys far less than girls; in fact, they discourage boys from seeking accustomed physical contact. On the contrary, they distract boys' attention with a variety of objects in the firm belief that it is more important for males to develop independence and autonomy.[6]*

These efforts soon pay off, for by the age of one, boys look for and call for their mothers far less than do girls. Further, they are able to play longer without the mother's presence.

This encouragement of independence later has a rather critical impact on the boy/girl differentiation. For instance, it has long been thought that boys naturally had a better ability to perceive space and distance (close correlates of the male's generally superior analytical ability).[7] But in reality, it is mother's willingness to allow her son to be adventurous and work problems out for himself, to allow more for mistakes than she would with girls, that accounts for the male's superior ability in this area.

Parents also encourage a specific male attitude by selecting certain clothes and toys for boys. Of course, the choice is partially made for them. A brief walk through the children's department of any large store reveals immediately that manufactured clothes are sex-typed. For girls there are frilly nightgowns, dresses, and pants and shirts that are far more elaborately decorated and brightly colored than those for boys. For boys, even small boys, it's football jerseys and cowboy, Superman, or Zorro costumes or T-shirts adorned with pictures of current sports heroes. Could any boy exposed from infancy to the face of Joe Namath, Bruce Jenner, or Steve Garvey not wish to emulate them and what they represent? As he grows older, the boy's shoes are rugged, sturdy, geared for rough play on dry land, ankle-deep water, or just plain old mud!

Toys follow the same pattern, no matter what parents may think. Along with his blue blanket and the train or sports-car motif of the wallpaper in his room, the growing boy will be deluged with balls of all sizes, especially those used in male sports. Toy trucks, cars, airplanes, trains, pistols, blocks, and marbles litter the closets and floor.

* For a review of evidence that finds some ambiguity in these results, see Carole Offir and Carol Tavris, *The Longest War: Sex Differences in Perspective* (Harcourt Brace Jovanovich, 1977), p. 173, note.

Little girls, of course, get dolls, dollhouses, nurses' uniforms, miniature cookware, stoves, and tiny replicas of domestic appliances to make her comfortable with the future. If a boy should ever cross the line and, heaven forbid, request a doll or a tea set, his horrified parents will quickly remind him that such toys are for little girls, that only boys who are "sissies" play with dolls and the like.

The terror felt by parents whose little boys want to play with "feminine" toys is indicative of yet another aspect of parental psychology that directs a particular sex role. Parents do not treat boys and girls equally when it comes to play associated with the opposite sex. Far more flexibility is granted to girls, at least until puberty, when they, too, more than at an earlier age, must overtly conform to a specific sex role in preparation for their life's duties as wife and mother. Until puberty, however, girls are permitted to engage in rough games, although the spirited, exuberant girl will be labeled a tomboy. She may play aggressively, though her clothes are often not designed for it; she may play with cars, trucks, and blocks rather than dolls. There is little fear that she will somehow become unfeminine because of the early connections.

Not so the boy. Parents worry that any display of a preference for feminine play is a sign that the boy is a sissy, that he might turn out to be unmanly or, worse still, a homosexual. Masculinity is regarded as far more precarious than femininity, and it must be guarded lest it be overcome.

Fathers, none of whom wants a "queer" in the family, are especially concerned about the behavior of their sons. They react strongly and negatively to any sign of deviance from the ideal. Parents try to give their sons a sense of masculinity that hinges at an early age on not being like girls.

In most cases, parents are successful in directing their sons toward a male psychology. The pattern is set by the age of three or four. Walk into any preschool or day-care center, and you will most likely see three- and four-year-old boys engrossed in play with blocks, cars, and trucks—they are rarely at the art table. They spread out over the available floor space, building cities and highways, leaving no room for girls who just might wish to play with the same toys and chasing away any who might venture over to play with them. Clearly, the boys have already internalized some feeling of what it is to be male, and they now harbor some animosity toward the other sex. They have a sense of what it is to engage in masculine activity. The boys will immediately choose toys that are suitable male toys, rejecting those and any activities which interest most of the girls. Outside, the boys will emulate masculine behavior by racing their "big wheels" or "green machines" as if the schoolyard or playground were some sort of miniature motocross. If you talk to the typical four- or five-year-old boy, you will find that he also has a firm sense of what will be expected of him as an adult man, of what occupations and roles are approved for his sex. Mother and father have done their jobs well.

Although boys remain largely in the care of females—their mothers and, later, teachers—a significant change commences at the age of five or six. By this time, boys begin to feel a far deeper, more sexual sense of love for their mothers. This places the boy in direct competition with his father, a competition accompanied by fears of destruction and castration. The boy is expected to surrender, to abandon his mother to his father, a process that leads to feelings of frustration and loss. At the same time, the father begins to make more insistent and forceful demands that the boy renounce any "feminine" or "babyish" traits for behavior that is tougher and more manly. This additional demand compounds the boy's frustrations and anxieties. The boy is asked to give up a great deal, especially by the demand that he trade his mother's seemingly unconditional love for the promise of love from his father—love that must be earned as the boy proves, by conforming to some, as yet, unclear and difficult standard, that he possesses real worth as a male. The boy's unconscious surrender is an act of fealty by which he admits his father's superior strength and worth.

The transition to the father is eased somewhat for the young boy by his feeling that identification with his father and everything the male role represents is far more desirable than his earlier association with females. The strong, initial close contact with females has, however, created a serious continuing dilemma for the boy by the time he is psychologically weaned away from them to be cast forever in the shadow of his father's role.

During the early years, while under the direct jurisdiction of women for all his waking hours, the boy learned that as a member of the male group, he was to avoid anything characterized as girlish or womanly. Yet he has learned these lessons of independence, self-sufficiency, the disdain of all things sissy, from a woman who in fact represents the dependent role. No wonder that when he is older, his "self-conscious hypermasculinity,"[8] as Philip Slater calls it, is challenged by any contact with females, as though femininity were some sort of contagious disease. Simply put, for him, girls are like Mother, and Mother taught him to be a man, so is it any wonder that as a conditioned reflex he immediately assumes the role of the male stereotype when he comes in contact with a woman?

In contrast, according to psychologist Ruth Hartley, Father looms very important in the boy's world. He appears independent. He does what he wants to do. He's boss in the family; his word is final. He works to support the family. He fixes things in need of repair. He seems bolder and more restless, like the young boy himself. Like him, too, Father tends to "mess up the house." Although he enforces obedience and "gets mad a lot," Father seems able to make children feel good. He laughs and makes more jokes than women do. Boys feel that, compared with mothers, fathers "are more fun to be with; they are exciting to have around,"[9] to be friends with. The boy understandably wants to be like his dad.

Despite the conflicts, the father now becomes the most influential hero in the boy's life. But the message that the father transmits and the lesson the boy learns from him are mainly the negative one of what a man should not do. Although they may be fun and exciting, fathers also turn out often to be mechanical and tense with their sons. Following the behavior they learned as children, fathers often tend to camouflage their most tender feelings toward their children, especially their sons. They refrain from affectionate gestures (except, of course, with a daughter before she reaches puberty and becomes a sex object in her own right). Fathers greet their sons with a mock punch rather than a hug, never a kiss, limiting their play to some form of roughhousing or masculine sport. The lesson is clear: According to one psychiatrist, Jack O. Balswick, if the boy "never hears his father say 'I love you,' never feels his father's arm around his shoulder hugging him, if he never sees his father cry, it confirms his impression that these are things men don't do."[10] With this lesson reinforced throughout his growing years, the boy reaches manhood determined not to show his true feelings. He is emotionally constipated, regardless of how deeply he actually does care about his own situation or that of his family and friends.

However, in most cases a boy simply does not see much of his father, who is often away from the home. Either he works all day and comes home too physically exhausted or emotionally frazzled to get involved with his child, or he is separated or divorced and the mother has custody. As a result, one major means by which sex roles are learned—identification with the parent of the same sex—is available only minimally to the young boy. Most fathers are just not around the house enough to serve as complete models of male behavior. Boys do learn some things from fathers, but most of their lessons about what it means to be male come through trial and error, vicariously through identification with male substitutes, whether peers, older boys, sports stars and other male heroes, or characters in movies and on television. The young boy has to master an image of the male role, a role that is culturally defined. Since nearly all males in the culture have gone through the same process, the image tends to be stereotyped; there is little exposure to the range of possible or potential male roles developed in other cultures.

Unfortunately, the information he gets from other boys is often distorted, since his peers and older boys have no better notions of masculine behavior than he has. Boys have to pool the various impressions and anxieties each has derived from his earliest years. But, according to psychologist Ruth E. Hartley, the pictures boys draw of the male role are "oversimplified and overemphasized. They're pictures drawn in black and white, with little or no modulation, and they are incomplete, including only a few of the many elements that go to make up the role of the mature male."[11] Boys are expected to show greater physical strength and better athletic skill; they avoid almost completely any expression of emotion, tender feelings or nurturance, the acceptance of responsibility for those who are weaker. It is an imperfect blueprint, drawn by children, and it is hardly sufficient.

Through its schools, society helps in molding the male identity. Preschools, no matter how well intentioned, complement parental direction of masculine behavior. The teachers, who for the most part are women, further transmit sex-role stereotypes to the young children. Boys and girls are treated differently, with profound consequences for each. Later, in grammar school, the stereotypes learned in preschool are reinforced by the materials most schools use.

In preschool, teachers usually respond differently to the boys and girls.[12] Girls receive attention from teachers when they sidle up to the teacher, hover, and behave dependently. Teachers reply with a pat on the head or some other affectionate reward. If a girl has trouble doing something on her own, the teacher will most often do it for her rather than let her figure it out for herself. Should a girl be disruptive or very aggressive, the teacher will react in a low-keyed manner, with any reprimand issued softly, and the incident is soon forgotten.

The teacher's relationship with male students is quite different. Teachers tend to give boys far more attention, whether the boys are nearby or across the room, whether they are misbehaving or not. When a boy asks a question, the teacher will respond with a longer, far more detailed answer or explanation than she would with a girl. Teachers, like mothers, encourage boys to work independently, to work things out for themselves when the assigned task is difficult. When the boys are successful, the teacher praises their independence and resourcefulness. Finally, teachers encourage male aggressiveness by their response to it. If a boy hits another, for example, teachers respond loudly with a stern reprimand and a scolding, responses which only reinforce, through the attention the boy receives, the very aggressiveness that caused the incident in the first place.

In grade school readers, the boy has until recently encountered a world in which certain traits and behaviors were clearly preferred. Male-centered stories and biographies far outnumbered those featuring females by at least two to one and by as much as six to one. Boys and men in these stories had a monopoly on the traits that American culture has traditionally regarded most highly—ingenuity, bravery, perseverence, achievement, and sportsmanship. Boys and men make things, often for girls and women, who are unable to do so for themselves. Boys and men use their wits to solve problems. They, far more than girls and women, are clever and adventurous. From these stories, boys learned, too, that girls—whom they have learned never to emulate—are incompetent at most tasks, are fearful in new or dangerous situations, require men to solve most of their problems, and "typically react to a crisis by dissolving in a puddle of tears."[13] That this feminine behavior is undesirable for boys is reinforced by parental injunctions that boys don't cry, boys are brave, boys are not afraid to take chances, to face danger.

Television, which now monopolizes most children's evening and weekend morning hours, reinforces the stereotyped male behavior learned from schoolbooks. Psychologists Carol

Tavris and Carole Offir note that the young boy sees, even if he is not completely conscious of it at the time, that a vast majority of the leading characters in prime time shows are males, be they cowboys, cops, soldiers, secret agents, or spacemen.[14] Men play important roles for themselves, their families, their community, their nation, their world, or their planetary federation. For the most part, women have no meaningful role outside of the home and family, although there are some exceptions. But even when women are shown as having demanding occupations, they are most often dependent on a man for support and protection. Whether it is Police Woman's strong male partner or the unseen Charlie directing the destinies of his Angels, males are pictured as authoritative and competent. And while leading female characters are nearly always young and beautiful, leading male characters may be fat, bald, old, or even paralyzed from the waist down. In all cases, the men are aggressive, constructive. They depend on their intelligence and their wits to pull them through successive weekly scrapes.

Thus the young boy's character traits, which are relatively fixed in childhood, are the products of a wide variety of sources. Nonetheless, anthropologist Ashley Montagu reserves most of his venom for parents. As he told me, "Mothers and fathers and everyone else in the culture condition boys to know that a boy, when he falls down, doesn't cry. Only sissies cry. He is taught that. All the snide remarks that are made about females by males reinforce his conditioned belief in his essential difference. This difference between the sexes becomes part of his psychology. All this is acquired, and it is very bad indeed. I define the American home—well, most homes—as institutions for the systematic production of mental illness in each of its members. Most children would be far better off without any parents at all, because the parents visit their follies and their sins and their inadequacies upon their children. What do they want children to be? Adults like themselves? Nothing could possibly be more insane than that."

Absurd? Overdrawn? One might think so. And yet the product of American society and home that we have seen so far compels us to give credence to Montagu's indictment. Parents—and particularly the father—instill in the young boy the values and behaviors that they accept. Why? Parents will tell anyone that they do it for the boy's own good, to make it easier for him to make his way successfully through a hostile world. Many times, however, as Montagu indicates, a father may project a behavior and a role that is modeled on the behavior that brought him his "success." In other cases, the father's demands might be designed to compensate for some earlier failing in his own life. A son gives a father a chance either to relive his youth or to rectify his own mistakes.

Gradually, both subtly and overtly, the male child is nudged by parents, peers, and the society at large toward the role considered appropriate for him. What is expected of him is not defined clearly at first, yet he is expected to conform to social notions of what is manly. These demands come far earlier than complementary demands on girls, who are allowed more freedom and more time to experiment. For the boy, however, the demands and pressures come at an age when he is least able to understand either the behavior itself or the reasons for it. Moreover, the demands that parents, peers, and society make on the young boy are strictly and harshly enforced. The boy is impressed with the danger of deviating from his assigned role, even if he still does not fully comprehend what the role will be. As he grows, he learns what not to be, for if he transcends normal bounds there are threats and punishment, often from those closest to him. Outside the home, epithets like "scaredy cat," "coward," and "sissy" are drummed into his ears along with the ultimate put-down that he is behaving like a girl.

Not being like the other sex also means that boys must repress their emotions and deepest feelings. According to Dr. Harvey Kaye, the small boy receives a clear message: "Vulnerability is a vice, emotionality is odious, and stoicism connotes strength."[15] From early boyhood on, the boy is conditioned not to express his feelings or emotional needs to anyone else. He learns that it is unmanly to be dependent on another, just as it is unmanly to be frightened, even if there is real danger. He learns that he must never cry, only babies and girls do that. He must never ask to be held, never allow himself to be hugged or kissed. Such behaviors may be acceptable for a girl, but they are incompatible with the boy's goal of being tough and in complete control of himself.

Throughout his youth, the boy has had to confront and overcome contradictions in the messages he received. He has faced countless dilemmas over the ambiguity inherent in the training given to him. The contradictions began early, with his mother, who alternated between letting him run wild, jump on the furniture, and so on, and admonishing him to be careful not to break anything. By the time he is eight, however, the boy perceives that parents expect him to be somewhat naughty, to play outside much more than girls—in short, to be a "real boy." But he has also received other messages which tell him not to behave like a wild animal, to settle down, to act grown-up, to control himself—all at an age when he probably enjoys being a bit destructive.

When he does behave like a "real boy," attempting to emulate one of the roles he thinks approved, he may find the sanctions against too much freedom strong and instantaneous. In grade school, for example, around other boys who feel the same need to be active and loud, he is forced into a constant conflict between his own restlessness and activity (masculine attributes) and the teacher's insistence that he be quiet, submissive, and passive, behaviors he already associates with girls. In light of this, it is easy to agree with one observer of the male scene, Herb Goldberg, who concludes that "the 'blessings' of being a young male in our culture are extremely mixed."[16] The dilemma is indeed painful.

Of course, not all boys respond equally well to expectations that they develop appropriate male behaviors. Differences between individual boys make it difficult if not impossible for some to fulfill the male role. Boys between eight and eleven realize that they are expected to be able to fight and to be athletic. They must run fast, play rough games. They need to be smart, able to take care of themselves in any situation. They have to know things that girls don't—how to climb, make a campfire, use tools. Most important, they know they must never do anything the way a girl does it, like the way she throws a ball or the way she runs.

In adapting to the male role, smaller, weaker, less coordinated boys are especially vulnerable to the opprobrium and ridicule of other males. But even a boy with better than average abilities and strength can suffer if his endowments and interests tend toward activities excluded from the culture's definition of what is masculine. No matter how coordinated he is, no matter how strong, a male ballet dancer, for example, is likely to be considered insufficiently masculine by other males.

The pressure on boys is most intense during their teens. By then, boys understand the prescriptions of the male role. Should they fall short of the ideal, they may be the objects of degrading epithets, with the result that many a boy is driven, as Goldberg notes, into "senseless self-destructive, even crazy behaviors and risk taking in order to prove to himself and others, over and over again, that he is a man and that he isn't afraid,"[17] but most of all to prove to himself and others that he is not like a girl. The demands of rapidly budding masculinity reach their height for the boy in high school (perhaps earlier now), where the laurels of success adorn the competitive athlete, the masculine ideal. (Schools often seem geared toward elevation of athletic endeavor over all activities, including academic achievement.) In high school, boys find that only those who fit the ideal male image, principally through sports, are able to achieve another conquest of growing importance for adolescents reaching adulthood: the attraction of beautiful, desirable females.

During adolescence, boys who find the "mainstream"[18] masculine role impossible may simply give up and resign themselves to being hopeless cases. The vast majority, however, is adaptable enough to learn what the culture dictates. Even boys who are by nature shy or passive will realize that their personalities are considered unmanly, and they will try to cultivate more masculine behavior, to change or compensate for their deficiencies. Most boys succeed and are able to approximate the approved male role by the time they are adults.

By the time he is an adult, the male has learned the masculine role. He realizes that this role must be earned anew every day. He knows that every move he makes will be judged, that he must constantly be on guard about his mannerisms, deportment, and demeanor. He must choose his play and recreation carefully. He must be cautious in spontaneous moments of conversation and in casual comment. He must be wary in any situation in which he might be measured against the ideal male standard. He must be strong and healthy, and whenever illness strikes he must not complain. A "real man" never gives in to bodily ills or injuries unless the results are completely debilitating. He must project an air of invulnerability and of independence. He has learned that a major indication of his manliness is to be able to say, "I can do it by myself. I don't need anybody's help."

He has also become, over the years, a fierce competitor in all aspects of his life. While he must remain loyal to the code of his fellow males, identify with them, and protect their interests, he has been taught to seek in any situation his own position of power. He is expected to compete within the group while still remaining loyal to it. For him, as for all men, rivalry and comradery must go hand in hand. As Goldberg says, "He has learned to value himself in terms of his achievements, successes and victories."[19] He has learned throughout his life that when he runs faster than anyone else, speaks with more force and effect, wins at anything he does, gets higher grades in school and college, or does anything to demonstrate that he is not only masculine but superior to other boys, he will receive the admiration and affection that is the just reward for success. The die forever cast, out of the mold comes the stereotype complete with the imprint "Socially Acceptable Male." Sensitivity blurred, feelings masked, he is ready to do battle with life as he perceives it through the veil of conditioning. As an adolescent and then as an adult, his attitudes and his behavior inform all aspects of his life, especially as he tests himself in the chief arenas of masculinity—in sports, in career, and in bed.

4

Winning and Losing: Sports

IN AMERICAN society, and perhaps in many others as well, there is an intimate relationship between budding masculinity and sports. Boys learn from a very early age that they are expected to engage aggressively in a wide range of athletics. The reason is simple: our widespread belief that sports are valuable beyond the immediate experience of playing, that sports build character and prepare a young man for life.

Robert F. Kennedy spoke for a generation of men when he said: "Except for war, there is nothing in American life—nothing —which trains a boy better for life than football."[1] Most men would undoubtedly agree. But when I asked George Plimpton, author of books and articles on the world of sports, for his comment on this quote, he replied: "Nonsense! It doesn't prepare for the experience of life. Football? Why should it?"

"Well," I said, "many people agree with Kennedy. We read all the time that football and other sports prepare young boys for a competitive life in a tough world. It teaches them to get along with others, to pull together as a team."

"Sure," Plimpton replied, "I know the arguments; you learn teamwork; you learn the merits of individual effort; you learn training; you learn toughness. Well, you can learn these things being a grocery boy. You can learn them studying history. I suspect you learn far more about 'life' studying for and taking college entrance examinations than you do down on the football field running a post pattern. I would be inclined to agree if Senator Kennedy had suggested that football was the best training for war.

"I guess the main thing sports teaches you is to face an immediate, palpable challenge. You become involved in a situation that is obviously competitive. And there is no doubt that life is very competitive."

Psychological studies do offer confirmation for Plimpton's

view. In one study of nearly 15,000 competitors at all levels, psychologists found no empirical support for the notion that sports build character.[2] On the contrary, they found that sports actually limit growth in some areas. The Catholic philosopher Michael Novak, an ardent fan of competitive sports, puts it somewhat differently. He argues that there certainly is some "transfer between sports and life," and he notes that "every participant in sports feels certain increases in mental and physical powers, even in the self-confidence that comes from a well-prepared body." Still, he feels this kind of argument should not be stretched too far. "Sports are lovely for their own sake," he writes. "We should not be naive about how much of their value is transferable to the rest of life."[3] Being a star athlete does not mean that one will become a purposeful, ethical, civilized human being.

In fact, the results of organized competition might be harmful to the individual and to society. For one facet of organized sports, especially football, is the inculcation of a rigorous belief in team loyalty, of unquestioning obedience to authority and profound hatred for the opposition. Many of the revelations about sports and their effect on children led one critic, Jack Nichols, to charge in his book *Men's Liberation* that "Little League players are tomorrow's big league goose-steppers, hoping for a win and following the coach's directions. The entire circumstance turns a man away from self-regulation and puts his body at the service of the team, in the rough and tumble of authoritarian, if not totalitarian, training."[4] This aspect of athletic regimen as practiced at many major universities prompted James Michener to observe that "if the militaristic type of leadership evidenced . . . is what sports idealize and sponsor, then our democracy is doomed."[5]

There is no doubt that games do provide an outlet for the energy of growing children. For boys, however, there is also an early perception that games and the organized ritual of athletic competition (such as "Pop" Warner Football and Little League Baseball, to name a few) are introduced at earlier and earlier ages as part of the process of becoming a "real man." Physical strength and athletic excellence are quickly seen as important measures of masculinity. Throughout their early years, boys rate themselves against their peers. In psychologist John Gagnon's words, "They see themselves as stronger or weaker than other boys, more skillful or less skillful in physical pursuits."[6] As he grows, a boy's physical development and athletic attainment are twin sources of his sense of self. Success or failure at this early test of manhood adds to or detracts from his self-esteem.

Parents, especially fathers but not exclusively so, also believe that success in sports is a sign that a young boy is coming along all right, that he is not a sissy. As a result, many parents drive their sons into athletic competition with great zeal. When he is not competing, the boy is expected to sharpen the skills he will need to compete successfully. Sports become compulsive and, as Marc Feigen Fasteau, author of *The Male Machine,* notes, "the mandated center of their lives."[7] When the boy is successful, when he wins or does well to help his team win, the parents lavish praise on him. When he loses or does badly or lets his team down, the parents may heap scorn upon him, punish by withholding affection or, in some cases, by hitting him—parental reactions that are known to have driven some children to attempt suicide.

Of course, parental pressure and coaching are not prerequisites for athletic success. I asked Bruce Jenner, the 1976 Olympic decathlon champion, if he came from a very athletic family. "Was there a lot of motivation from your home situation, a lot of identification with sports, that kind of thing?"

"No. I would say we were a very competitive family; we did compete all the time. But my dad wasn't the type of guy who told me, 'Go out there, Bruce, and throw that ball,' or 'I'll throw it and you catch it,' or 'You've got to work on this, you've got to work on that.' No, he never did anything like that.

"I think where my family helped me out the most is that they were always interested in what *I* was interested in doing. If I was in sports, if I had a game, they would be there—and when you're young and your parents show an interest in what you're doing by showing up, hey, that's a reinforcement of what you're doing. They're going to come out and you're going to work hard at it because . . . you know, here they are, the people who taught you everything, and they're showing their approval of something you're doing. That's going to spark your own enthusiasm, because young people want to please their parents."

It is true that children desire to please their parents; but parents' demands can be constructive or destructive. Jenner's parents encouraged *his* interests, not theirs. Too often, however, it is the boy's father's interests that are encouraged. And all for what? We know that for every boy whose father forced him to practice pitching, fielding grounders or fly balls, batting, or passing, receiving, placekicking, or shooting baskets, only few survive the intense competition beyond their high school years. Many do not even make it that far. For too many, there is already a sense of failure in a life that has hardly begun.

The essence of a boy's early physical activity and athletic endeavor is competition. Boys constantly strive against other boys, either alone or as part of a team, to see who is the stronger, the better coordinated, or the best. Probably, some form of limited competition is the norm of existence, no matter how much we might like cooperation to take its place. James Michener, certainly no extremist on the desirability of competition, puts it this way in his book *Sports in America:* "I find competition to be the rule of nature, tension the structure of the universe. I believe that normal competition is good for a human being and I am sure that flight from it hastens death."[8] Nevertheless, Michener joins others in condemning "fanatical competition or senselessly prolonged tension." These are unnatural and undesirable and, he believes, should never be foisted upon youngsters as the norm of life.

The spirit of competition, the desire to strive against someone else, the desire to beat someone else, is deeply ingrained in us. I have noticed a sense of aggression that comes out in a lot of men when they compete. One watches them playing, or just watching, and senses an aura of aggression that becomes very active. I asked Bruce Jenner if he had ever noticed that, too.

"Oh, yeah," he replied, "I notice it in myself when I'm competing. What a turn-on to go out there on the track and just beat every person there. Hey, I'm a male just like everybody else. Men have the desire to conquer. That's been going on for millions of years, with wars and everything. It just so happens in sports we don't war . . . but we have Olympic Games, and you sort of go to battle on the battlefield out there. And your job is to go out there, which is what sports are all about. There's only one guy who can win, and there are thirty-two guys who want to win, or they wouldn't be there. It's a physical turn-on to go out there and come up with the performance you need to do it. Some of the greatest highs of life come that way. It's a tremendous feeling."

"Something a marginal man never knows," I added. Jenner suggests that what the marginal man doesn't know is how to test himself—how to discover his own limits. "The marginal man never knows how far to push himself; physically, he doesn't know how to push himself. Take the Olympic Games as an example. In the 1,500 meters, the last event of the decathlon, you get to a point where you get tired. You feel the fatigue coming on a rise, and you think, 'I'd better slow down.' But you just have to keep going like that, like you're going to go on and on, even though it feels like you're going to die. Well, not really. But the pain comes on, rises, and it goes to a peak and then levels off. You can sustain a tired feeling and very heavy breathing, and you can sustain that for a long period of time until all of a sudden it starts to subside.

"Your body can take a tremendous amount of physical punishment; there are times when your body actually feels as if it's burning from the buildup of lactic acid. Now, the average person, the marginal man we mentioned, he would never push himself that far. He would have quit long, long ago. But you can push yourself that far. You can push yourself a lot farther than you would ever imagine."

Jenner emphasizes competition against oneself for its own sake, as a means of learning more about oneself. Most Americans, however, would put the emphasis on competition against someone else; and thus the prime need is to defeat another, to prove that you are better, more manly. Americans are not alone in their desire to win; no one could seriously claim that. But although the Englishman also likes to win, although he plays hard, too, the national ideal in England is still "It's not whether you win or lose but how you play the game." In the United States, the ethos that has guided athletes for years—though only recently codified—was Vince Lombardi's dictum "Winning isn't everything, it's the only thing." Winning thus becomes a total obsession that lends an unhealthy tinge to competition that should be primarily for enjoyment, substituting anxiety for pleasure.

Along with many other observers, Jenner sees this emphasis on winning as an outgrowth of our American system. "The whole capitalistic system in the United States is based on competition," he says. "It's the most competitive society in the world. A lot of times, people think that the only ones who are really competing are the athletes, that it doesn't spill over into the big world. That's not so."

George Plimpton agreed that this terrible pressure to win in sports is a reflection of American life in general. "You don't learn how to lose," he said; "you learn how to win. And you're supposed to win. And if you're a professional player, you'd better win, or you're going to get fired. But for those of us who aren't professionals there are other aspects. I went to an English school here in New York where we were taught that the good life was not simply a question of winning, but rather of doing the best you can—and to learn to have fun, and compassion, and be gentlemanly and graceful about losing. We had a football song: 'There's naught to choose 'twixt win or lose, the game's the game for all.' Heresy, in those days! The funniest damn football song. 'We do not mind the winter wind, or weep o'er summer's bier, nor care a jot if cold or hot, so long as football's here. . . .'

"Sport is supposed to provide pleasure, not anguish, and the pleasure should not be so totally committed to winning. I like to win as much as anybody, but the best part of a game is to think that you've really done the best you can. You come off, and you say, 'Gee whiz, I had a good time doing that. I got beaten, but I didn't play badly.' "

Most Americans don't react this way, however. For many, losing is a disgrace. Far too many accept Lombardi's dictum and its corollary, stated by football coach George Allen, that "when you lose, you die a little." A competitor feels he has to be number one. Anything less makes him a lesser human being. As a result of this pressure to win, competitors will often do anything to win, even to the point of trying purposely to maim an opposing player. Thus, the violence in sports becomes a necessary part of the drive to win at all costs, to avoid the contact with defeat, degradation, and the brush with death that Allen speaks of.

Much has been written recently about the violence of American sports, but this is not a recent phenomenon. Early in the twentieth century, football became so violent—eighteen college players died of injuries in 1905—that President Theodore Roosevelt felt he had to intervene to save the game from itself. Roosevelt called representatives from thirteen colleges to the White House, insisting that the colleges themselves take responsibility for debrutalizing the game, threatening federal intervention and legislation if they did not. Although the violence decreased after 1905, there still remained much deliberate viciousness.

Ashley Montagu related the following story to me: "It was in 1928 when the captain of the Columbia University football team told me about the last game they had played with Yale. There was a Yale player who was the best tailback Yale had ever had. The Columbia coach gave his team orders that on the very first opportunity they were to go out and sit on his knees and get him out of the game. They did, and they busted his knees. They considered that sport. I was appalled. I had just come from England, where you would give an opponent every break possible—no pun intended—and would avoid ever coming in contact with his knee. If it wasn't cricket, you didn't do it."

Why the violence? There is a belief that sports, particularly the contact sports like football, satisfy modern man's need for physical contact and at least the potential for violence. This view is prevalent among those who hold that males have an instinctive drive for aggression. Konrad Lorenz argues that this instinctive aggression should be redirected, and he maintains that "a simple and effective way of discharging aggression in an innocuous manner is to redirect it at a substitute object."[9] Lorenz thinks that sports are akin to fighting, that their primary function today is as a cathartic discharge of aggressive drives. The psychiatrist Anthony Storr agrees that sports are a most efficacious means of redirecting aggressive impulses, and he even dreams of annual competitions between nations—for example, to see which nation can produce the most effective mental hospital.[10]

Many of the thoughtful persons with whom I spoke agree that sports are a good outlet for aggressive urges. For example, I asked James Dickey, "Do you think that as the rivers and the forests disappear, as men get more and more urbanized, they develop a whole other set of values about what it is to be a man and how they define and envision themselves?"

"Oh, yes," he answered, "I do think so. And I think that's channeled into sports like football. It's what my great idol, William James, called it when he said that what we need is a moral equivalent of war. Or as Robert E. Lee said after the Battle of Fredericksburg, 'It's a good thing that war is so terrible as it is. Otherwise we might get to like it too much.' You do need a moral equivalent of war."

George Plimpton sees football, with its abundance of physical contact, as satisfying a vital need, but a need that is vital for only a part of the male population. "You know, about sixty percent of the people are supposed to truly like to hit people. It's something that goes back to self-preservation, I guess, or authority, or gaining territory, or any of the old Ardreyan territorial imperatives. The other forty percent don't like to hit or be hit. They rely much more on their brains. It doesn't mean that they don't have courage; it just means that they become wide receivers rather than interior linemen. Or they become tennis players. Or secretaries of commerce. Now, this doesn't mean that tennis players don't like to go and watch football. But I think they may have a faintly different attitude about watching it than the hitting sixty percent. The sixty percent like to watch the centers and the tackles; they applaud a great tackle and go 'yay!' and they have a much greater empathy for the people playing the interior line, especially when they get to a running back and smack him down. The tennis players may watch the wide receivers, or they talk tactics . . . or they stay in their seats at halftime and watch the band. I think everybody brings along a slightly different attitude toward a game."

Despite these and other claims, there is far more persuasive evidence that sports do not serve as an outlet for aggressive tendencies. Rather, sports seem to reflect aggressive tendencies. If they did serve to discharge aggression at all levels, one would expect to find the United States a far less violent society both at home and abroad. We know this is not the case. America has been involved in military actions throughout the century—about one every 2.7 years. At the same time, there seems to be an increase in domestic violence, murder, rape, and mugging—and the perpetrators are predominantly male. Even the world of sports is not immune, as attested to by the epidemic of serious violence among fans. It is, sportscaster Howard Cosell recently noted on national television, "one of the most disturbing phenomena on the American scene," and it shows little sign of abating. In truth, violent, aggressive sports and violent, aggressive individuals and societies seem to go hand in hand.

There does seem to have been a noticeable increase in violence recently, beginning in professional sports but spreading to fans who go overboard in support of their favorites and youngsters who emulate their sports heroes. I asked George Plimpton if he could relate masculine notions of machismo and aggressiveness to the popularity of contact sports in this country.

"I don't know the answer to that," he said. "I wish I did know. You know, I spent some time with the Boston Bruins and played with them. I didn't really know very much about the physical aspects of hockey—I mean I had skated as a kid and played it a little, but I don't ever remember the body-checking or high-sticking. . . . It always seemed to me more of a game of skill. The year before I joined the Bruins I remember the Soviet team came to the U.S.; they had all that fantastic skating ability and passing, and they damn near beat the Canadians. Then they came down and played the Philadelphia Flyers, and the Flyers, the Broad Street Bullies, really went after them; they physically destroyed this Russian team and kept them from doing anything on the ice. The Russian coach threatened to withdraw his team. I remember watching that on television and being disgusted. I hated the way the crowd was cheering this body-checking and violence. It turned my stomach. In fact I think I even wrote a letter to the Philadelphia *Bulletin*.

"Then I went and played with the Boston Bruins and found myself playing a game that I'd only been sitting in the comfort of a chair criticizing. I always thought that the violence in hockey was really more a show for the fans, that it had little if anything to do with the game, that if they were playing hockey without any fans, the players probably wouldn't be so violent. Actually that turned out to be absolutely wrong. The violence and intimidation are essential parts of professional hockey. Players talk about having to 'muck it up' when the puck is headed into a corner. You go in there after it, and the guy who's the stronger, the more physical, and the more intimidating, is going to get ahold of that puck, control it, and center it out where one of the wings or the center is going to be able to take a shot at the goal with it. And if you back away from that confrontation, you're lost.

"So knowing that changed my opinion about violence—at least controlled violence like a stiffly delivered body-check. If the Russians want to play their careful, precise type of game, they've got to take into consideration that they can be checked, because that's part of the rules. The founding fathers of hockey realized that if you can knock a man off the puck, you've got it. They condoned that tactic. And control of the puck is the essence of winning in hockey."

I then asked Plimpton if this contact, the body-checking, had a special attraction for the fans.

"Well, I'm rather disturbed by the attitudes this brings out in some fans. I have sat next to so-called fans who don't believe that hockey players should wear helmets. They shout out to them on the ice and call them cowards and sissies. There was something awful about people shouting about that, because it makes it seem as though what they really hoped to see was some indication of the fragility of the human skull, snapped in some way, people damaged, noses smashed in a fight.

"I would like to think that people go to see games to enjoy skills, or because they have a chauvinistic sense of wanting to see the team bearing the name of their city win; perhaps they go because they have a bet down. I don't think they go to see the violence. There may be one or two kooks there for that reason. Actually, most sports aren't set up to provide violence. Heavens, if you just wanted to see people crashing into each other and suffer, you could provide that. But no one would go."

I felt that there was some ambivalence in Plimpton's mind, that he wanted to believe the best of people, despite his gut feeling that they might in fact enjoy the violence immensely. So I asked him more about this sense of morbidity among fans, especially among the male fans. "Those same fans go to automobile races. They really don't go there to watch that race, do they?"

"They damn right do," he shot back without hesitation. "The racing fan likes to see the drivers go right to the edge, but not over. That's what racing skill is—to go right to the limit."

"But," I asked, "do they really want to see the skill of the driver or do they really want to see if somebody gets killed?"

"I suppose there are lunatics, a small group who hope subconsciously that something really 'exciting' is going to happen —a crash. Everyone else certainly wants excitement. But you'd have to be a raving psychotic to think to yourself, 'Boy, I hope I see someone get killed out there in a car.' No, almost all the people who go to Watkins Glen to watch the Grand Prix are racing buffs: they love the machines; they love the drivers; they love the skill; they love to see the machines going at incredible speeds. But they don't come to see anyone hurt, and they don't leave the racetrack fretting that there hasn't been a fatality. In fact, the clear, good feeling that comes with watching a good race is important because death has been conquered."

The fans are there, then, for the vicarious thrills that sports provide. The fan can experience at a distance all the feelings of success and failure as he watches skilled athletes perform. Bruce Jenner has thought a lot about this aspect of the spectator's mentality. "Do people want to live vicariously through you?" I asked him.

"Oh, of course they do. Exactly. That is why sports are so big. People sit there in their room and they have a can of beer, they've got friends with them, and they're watching the football game and they're thinking, 'God, wouldn't that have been something to catch that pass. If that were me out there, I would have." And they want to live that experience. They want to know what the athlete feels like and what he goes through. That's why people watch; that's why they love it. People really live through sports."

For many, being a spectator may be the only real contact with sports that they have. It is an important contact nonetheless, for sports, whether played or watched, are the "single most important male rite in society."[11] Sports provide fans with a common ground on which they can come together, even if it is ultimately to disagree. "The great thing about football," Art Buchwald told me, "is that you can have a brother-in-law that you have nothing in common with, and you can talk to him about football. It seems a common ground for guys to talk about. You use football and other sports as a way of opening up a conversation with people you don't even know. And you don't have to get personal with them."

George Plimpton sees this aspect of athletics as important to the athlete, too. "For many players," he said, "the great thing about teams, the one thing they really miss when they have to give the sport up, is the camaraderie, the sense of fraternity, the sense of manhood, of going out after a victory and celebrating, and all that. It goes back to the medieval period, with knights clanking their tankards after a jousting tournament. It's being part of a small, elite group of skillful performers. If you ask former pros what it is they miss, they don't say that it's the games, or the practices, or the training periods. They miss that fraternity—that macho fraternity."

Many men, particularly those who have played on teams at some time during their lives, try to continue contact with athletics as long as possible.

If they don't, or if they can't participate in competitive sports any longer, men sense that something profound has gone from their lives. They have lost an affirmation of their masculinity. They have lost an important relationship, a bond with other men, based on vigor, strength, and competition. With the loss of this avenue of male expression, one for which watching can never substitute, many men channel their energies into another area, their careers. Here the same values pertain, the same bonding with other men prevails. Just as they either won or lost in athletic competition, they now either win or lose at work.

5

Tote That Barge, Lift That Bale: Work

"WITHOUT WORK," Albert Camus once wrote, "all life goes rotten. But when work is soulless, life stifles and dies."[1] For many men, work seems a never-ending drudgery. Joseph Heller brilliantly caught the essence of this situation in his novel *Something Happened:* "We come to work, have lunch and go home. We goose-step in and goose-step out, change our partners and wander all about, sashay around for a pat on the head, and promenade home till we all drop dead." To the question of whether this really is the most one can expect from the few years of life one has, Heller's protagonist, Bob Slocum, always answers, "Yes!"[2]

Of course, some men do find satisfaction in the work they do. They enjoy it and look forward to its challenges. Many of these men are craftsmen, following the same tradition as artisans of preindustrial society. However, for far too many men, work crushes the mind and annihilates the spirit. The worker, to use the young Karl Marx's term, is "alienated" from his work and separated from the human essence of his being. Some men make a deal with themselves; they will do their time, take their pay, and retire on their pensions. This is the sum of their existence, for they are often as numbed at home as they are on the job. Songwriter Paul Simon noted this aspect of the modern worker's existence perfectly when he wrote, "We work our jobs/ collect our pay/ believe we're gliding down the highway/when in fact we're slip-slidin' away."*

But although we complain about our jobs, we seem to be a nation of workaholics. I brought this point up in a discussion with Michael Korda, a bright, perceptive analyst of modern-day business mores. His three books, *Male Chauvinism, Power,* and *Success,* open the door of insight into the unchartered world of business. He is himself a success in the publishing jungle, wearing the mantle of vice-president and editor in chief of Simon and Schuster—a "natural" to delve into the question of work and its meaning for modern man.

"It has been my impression that people work hard, harder in fact than we generally give them credit for," Korda told me. "A lot of them don't work efficiently. A lot of them are stupid, and their work has to be done over by someone else. A lot of them do work which is by nature boring or involves long pauses. A lot of them just do make-work. What I find incredible is the astonishing number of people in this nation who hold down more than one job. They're workaholics!

"You know, half the people on the police force have two concurrent jobs," Korda said. "It doesn't really matter how hard they work at those jobs. What is important is that they're putting in a sixteen-hour day. We always hear how hard businessmen work. They complain when they put in a twelve-hour day and say, 'You know, I'm a workaholic.' Well, half the cops on the force are putting in what really amounts to six days a week. Four of them are tours of duty, but of those days almost half are in the pursuit of double jobs. Half the force is moonlighting, half the industrial workers hold two jobs, half the women who work in industry are also keeping house, which is really a double job —they raise children and cook and so forth. This is a country where double effort is perfectly common for ordinary working people. We talk about the typical eight-hour day or forty-hour week, but they put in a twelve-, fourteen-, fifteen-, sixteen-hour day.

"Sure, it may be a day full of pauses where they don't do anything. But basically even that is not true, certainly not true in manufacturing. Have you ever been in a steel plant or a car assembly plant? Well, I don't know that I could physically do a day's work in that GM assembly plant I recently visited in New Jersey. I don't think I could do it! The noise . . . I could never get used to it. I think I would rather do anything else."

Most of us would probably agree. We, too, "would rather do anything else." Why do men do it, then? Why do we work? Why do we go on working the way we do?

For most men the answer is simple. They must work to survive. A job equals money. The family needs money for its support, to acquire the necessities of life and a few of the luxuries, and, it is hoped, to achieve the security that all desire for themselves and their loved ones.

Because of this, the worker runs scared most of the time, for his position at work and in society seems precarious. Art Buchwald puts it this way: "Most guys in this country are afraid. Most everyone works for someone else; somebody else is in charge of his life. He can get laid off at any time; his salary stops but the payments don't; everyone is in debt up to their ass; and the man feels this. He lives in deathly fear of losing his job, losing his livelihood. He fears he won't be able to provide his family with all the things he is told they must be supplied with. It's tough. Sure, there are a few independent souls in this country, doing what they want, able to say 'Fuck you.' But there aren't many."

Certainly, money seems to be the most compelling reason for men to work. Still, the need and, at times, the craving for work, even at a job one dislikes, seem to be stronger than they would be if work were simply a response to the need or expectation of material recompense. Money is important, but there does seem to be a psychological dimension to men's desire to work that goes to something basic, to the very core of each man's conception of himself and to his being as a male. He is driven ever onward by the values he has been taught are intimately bound to our notions of masculinity.

For one thing, men have learned that work gives them their male identity. Men are expected to be the breadwinners in most families. Today, more and more wives also work. Men still resent this trespassing onto their domain, especially if the wife makes more money than the husband. Work for men is too intimately bound up with their sense of worth as a male, since the male must be the provider, responsible for his family's well-being. But even more than that, the man tends to value himself and his fellow men according to his and their ability to perform, achieve, and produce. No wonder that for most men work becomes the most important element of their lives, more important than sex. No wonder those who find themselves without work, often through no fault of their own, judge themselves less than men. Feeling deprived of the approval and esteem society grants to the successful breadwinner, the jobless suffer severe psychological depression, often losing all sense of their own worth as individuals.

Work for the adult male, like sports for the youngster, is a means by which each man can reaffirm his identity as a male. Through work he validates himself. Through work he measures his masculinity relative to other men. Work, in Marc Feigen Fasteau's words, "is the area of life into which 'masculine' traits are thought to fit best and is the principal adult arena for proving one's masculinity."[3] The metaphor "principal arena" suggests that work is closely related to the sports that the male played as a boy. As Jack Nichols puts it in *Men's Liberation,* "Money becomes a substitute for muscles."[4] The adult male's primary interest has shifted to a different arena of competition—the workplace.

This should not surprise us. The competitive drive has been drummed into males from an incredibly early age. As we saw in our discussion of socialization and sports, the virtues of aggressive competition are enshrined with almost religious fervor and devotion. Early on, children learn the ideal of competition, as parents and other adults reward every triumph of one boy over another. Losers, as we have discussed, are taught to feel the sting of humiliation. The best grades, the best athletic performance—these are the achievements we come to value instead of learning, curiosity, or athletic endeavor for its own sake. Margaret Mead noted this attitude as early as 1948 in her study *Male and Female:* "It is not that the boy learns interest in defeating others, but that he fervently hopes he can beat enough others to be counted a success; the others are incidental, not so much rivals to be worsted as entrants to be outdistanced. His upbringing permits him no admitted glee in open battle, and later, in a competitive world that demands harsh and sometimes savage competition, he takes little pleasure in the game itself."[5] (As we shall see, this last aspect is changing and has been for some time.)

The competitive attitude had been indelibly imprinted in the American mind from the time of John Locke and, later, Adam Smith. The lesson Americans learn is that competition and self-interest are the bases of economic success. History tells us the lesson was learned. Witness American business in the nineteenth century with its robber barons, monopolies, and labor violence. The nineteenth century was the dawn of Darwinism, which quickly perverted into Social Darwinism. Business adopted the notion that those who were successful were necessarily the most fit. Human values—"consideration, friendliness, and charity,"[6] as Dr. Harvey Kaye identifies them—were "deemed little more than naive notions indulged in by 'failures' and fools."

No one wants to be a failure or a fool, so each man strives

in his work to achieve some measure of success. "In America," Ashley Montagu said, "the supreme value is success. And success is realized through competition—being first, top, the head, the best, et cetera." Success means different things to different people. Not all men know what it is they want out of life. In the past, men may have had firm goals for their lives, but this does not seem to be so today. In an interview, Joseph Heller put it this way: "We don't know what goals to achieve. Very few people want to be a J. P. Morgan or a John D. Rockefeller anymore, very few intelligent people do. Maybe there are people going to the Harvard Business School who have firm goals in mind, but I doubt they really do have a plan for their entire life. They merely want to be successful at business; and how do they know they are good at business if they don't keep taking over more and more companies? The goal is never reached."

For some, success simply means security. Men seeking a secure place at work and in the world can be fierce competitors, but for them competition does not mean they are trying to climb to the top of the corporate ladder; it may in fact mean, as one writer notes, "making one's particular rung as safe and plush and comfortable as possible."[7] Whether one ever reaches a plateau of security is open to question. It may be, as Jack Nichols suggests, that "a quest for security, no matter of what kind, is actually a search for the unattainable. An ultimate security cannot be guaranteed."[8] Even a sense of security, though it may be ephemeral or illusory, exists only when there are no challenges to and for one's position. But there are and always will be younger men, just starting their own climb, whose own goals may be far different and whose methods and tactics may be far more ruthless.

This mass of men who seek security above all else fall within Michael Maccoby's definition of the company man, which Maccoby discusses in his best-selling book *The Gamesman: The New Corporate Leaders.*[9] They identify with the company, are loyal to it. They are William H. Whyte's organization men who see their success depending on the overall success of the company. They go on, year after year, at mid-management levels, providing that measure of stability so necessary to the continuity of any business. These men are not always quiet and passive, though at their worst, they may be excessively submissive. Rarely are they tough enough to rise to the highest levels; they are far too afraid to take chances, as a corporate leader must. At their best, though, the company men are the most in tune to the needs of others within the business organization. They emphasize teamwork and cooperation, attributes that are necessary to balance the excesses of other executives. For them, rising to the top is less important than having security, for it is security that makes them feel a success.

How we define success remains problematic. Michael Korda offers some useful comments that might help clarify what success is. He describes success as the achievement of some goal, no matter how modest. In fact, he believes each person should begin his productive life with modest rather than grandiose ambitions. For him, success becomes "a journey, an adventure, not a specific destination." Korda believes that goals can easily change during a lifetime, that one's initial ambitions may at some point be superseded by other, perhaps larger goals. Not comfort or security—though success can certainly bring material rewards and a degree of security—but going farther than one at first dreamed possible is his measure of personal success. Korda himself exemplifies this definition. Starting as a low-paid assistant in publishing because he couldn't get work at anything else, then rising by the dint of good advice and hard work to the elite of the publishing world. The best we can conclude is that success is a relative state.

For Korda, true success is "public recognition" that one is good at something. "I think that is what drives many people," he told me. "Money is secondary. I don't mean that money is unimportant, and I don't mean that people would necessarily trade money for recognition. Very few people would say they'd rather have recognition than money. But the driving motivation for many people is recognition. They figure, not incorrectly, that money will come with recognition."

Perhaps. But there are many who would disagree that money is as unimportant as Korda suggests. For a large number of men, success means having the monetary wherewithal to purchase those things that set a man apart from his fellows—things that give him immediate and conspicuous status in the eyes of others. According to Ashley Montagu, "Success is measured in terms of external validations. No matter how good you are—whether you are the best, the top, the first, or the most—unless you can show other people, your success isn't complete. Remember the advertisement that says that when you drive up to someone's house in *this* car, they don't have to ask who you are

—they *know* who you are." Unfortunately, it is all too true that most men are inculcated with the notion that possession of certain objects of "status" means that they are successful.

Men do feel they should show their success. At a certain point, money becomes valued for the luxuries it will buy and the status and prestige they lend to the possessor. Most modern advertising plays directly to a man's desire for status, encouraging him to buy certain items because of the apparent status they confer. Men's magazines extol not only the inherent hedonism of our modern culture but endlessly reinforce the status value of specific products and objects. Successful men are portrayed drinking only the best scotch, wearing the currently prestigious loafers, carrying conspicuously monogrammed luggage or briefcases, driving the "right" car, escorting only glamorous and beautiful women. These are things that money can buy, these are validations! So men go on striving for more money long after all rational needs are met.

At the upper reaches of business, we see the analogue of this in the perquisites that business bestows on its leaders, at that level where salary, already enormous, no longer has intrinsic value. Just the trappings of being "on top" are often far more important than the money. Michael Korda illustrates this point with an anecdote about one executive who told him: "When I get into the limo on a rainy evening in December and look out the window, it isn't the speed I think about. For God's sake, the subway would be faster. No, I say to myself, those people out there are getting cold and wet and I'm in here, warm and dry. I had to go through a lot of shit to get where I am, but when I look at people waiting for a bus in the rain, it makes it all worthwhile. They know I've made it. I know I've made it." Then he is at peace, at least for the duration of the ride home.

But moments of peace for those in business are few and far between. For much of modern business is less concerned with production and marketing than it is with individual contests over positions of power within the organization. Korda believes that it is the drive for power that keeps most people going within the business organization. He writes, "What we are offered is no longer the opportunity for unlimited wealth, but the chance to acquire limited power."[10] To Korda the typical corporation serves as a "broker" that gives those who covet power a degree of power and a number of employees over whom they are able to exert it.

These modern power seekers are the counterparts of the nineteenth-century robber barons. Michael Maccoby calls them "jungle fighters," men whose drive to dominate others transforms life, especially business life, into a vicious, aggressive contest in which normal human relationships are distorted beyond recognition. To the jungle fighter, business is not simply a contest with winners and losers but a battle of life and death in which he seeks to destroy his opponent. In Maccoby's words, "Jungle fighters tend to see their peers in terms of accomplices or enemies and their subordinates as objects to be utilized."

Maccoby believes that jungle fighters can be divided into two types, "lions" and "foxes." In his view, foxes are cunning and sly, operating by "seduction, manipulation, and betrayal." They are able to find a place within the corporate hierarchy, mask their goals and their methods, and move up through the organization by "stealth and politicking." Lions, on the other hand, are often as wily as foxes, but they dominate through the force of their personalities, their ideas, their courage and strength, and perhaps (though Maccoby doesn't say it) through the aura of aggression that surrounds them. Lions are the empire builders; others follow them because "they are feared and revered." They act like medieval kings, rewarding loyal subordinates with fiefdoms of their own, though careful to see that no one acquires too much power of his own.

In his book *Success,* Michael Korda accepts the Maccoby division into lions and foxes, and he writes that it is "the secret of every successful person . . . to combine both qualities *in the right proportions.*" When I asked if he would describe himself as a lion or a fox, Korda said he was "probably half of each." He said this with a slight twinkle in his eye, as though it were some sort of joke. But there is in his own writing a far harder edge than one would suspect after talking to him. He extols the power game—though his own methods may temper it, that I don't know—but he can argue without qualification that "if we believe in anything in the last quarter of the twentieth century, it is in the extension of power, the drive to dominance. Not to reach for power, in the contemporary view, is to limit one's potential, to set a limit to one's consciousness." Echoing the realization many have shared, that after the death of God and the reality of Auschwitz, all of humanity's traditional anchors are lost, Korda says: "There are no longer any plausible substitutes for success and fulfillment in this life, nor any comforting belief that failure here below will be rewarded in some way above. We have no alternative to present apotheosis; stripped of our uniqueness as human beings by Darwin, exposed to our own inadequacies by Freud, compelled to live with the knowledge of our immense potential for violence and irrationality by history itself, we are left to fabricate our own substitute for immortality. Power—'the ability to bring out our desires'—is all we have left."[11] If so, heaven help us.

Whether lions or foxes, jungle fighters are men whose masculinity has been perverted in the extreme. The virtues of competition and toughness have been blown out of all proportion to their intrinsic worth. The cult of toughness was particularly attractive in the early 1960s during the administration of John Kennedy and the first months of Lyndon Johnson's presidency. Men had to prove they had balls, and it was not uncommon in business to prove it by especially ruthless behavior that demonstrated to all that one was truly a man.

In fact, one French businessman has characterized his American counterpart as "a man caught in a stereotype. He is limited by a role definition obliging him to be supermasculine, supertough, supersufficient, and superstrong. It allows him that very little mixture of strength and weakness, independence and dependence, toughness and tenderness that is the essence of being human."[12] I asked Korda if that rang true.

"No, it is not true," he said. "American businessmen are not stereotypical; there is no such thing as 'an American businessman,' and we all know it. Some enjoy duck hunting or ecology or eighteen holes of golf, and they're still very good, shrewd businessmen; they're no less human than anybody else."

"But," I asked, "don't you have to play roles if you're in a large corporation?"

"But all life is role playing," he replied. "The question is: Are they roles we're suited for? Are they roles that are functional? Are they roles that are beneficial? I don't think that businessmen are particularly inhuman or that the human element is lacking in American business at all. I do think there is a political stereotype, yes. I think American businessmen—particularly in the Midwest and particularly in manufacturing industries—are probably stereotyped into a kind of Republican reflex mechanism which has become second nature for a lot of them. But this isn't true of *all* businessmen. Cyrus Eaton is practically a fellow traveler. Armand Hammer, the legendary leader of Occidental

Petroleum, has been doing business with the Soviet Union since well before the United States recognized that nation. Charlie Bludorn, chairman of Gulf & Western, has got a foundation that is doing God knows what in terms of educational and public broadcasting. There's Henry Ford, a kind of old-fashioned tyrant, yet the Ford Foundation is largely his baby, out there doing all sorts of things which he probably doesn't approve of, but which he recognizes a large corporation ought to be experimenting with and trying. No, I don't think any of them are *inhuman*. That is an absolutely untrue thing.

"The criticism I *would* make of American businessmen in general—if you remember that I said that I don't think you can make generalities easily about them or anything else—is that they are hard put to recognize the extent to which their passion for business overtakes the rest of their lives. But I don't think that that is so terrible either. Soldiers think about war, women think about beauty, and businessmen think about business."

No one believes current writings about business. The business world sees the changes. One major change that has taken place among executives is that it now appears more desirable to be liked than to be known as a son of a bitch. Of course, as Michael Maccoby notes in *The Gamesman,* there still are some corporate jungle fighters who "are exceptionally hardhearted and sadistic," but Maccoby finds that "on the whole, the modern corporate executive is much less so and is more concerned about being liked than the empire builder of the past." Maccoby traces this trend to the evolution of the modern corporation, where much of the ruthlessness of the past is no longer needed. Of course, there are times when all managers and executives still find it necessary to overrule their soft hearts to ensure that the company runs efficiently and effectively.

Korda finds no set pattern among executives, though he, too, identifies hard- and soft-hearted individuals among their numbers. I asked him to consider the humanistic aspect. "Can you be popular and effective at the same time in the halls of management?" I asked. "Or are the two mutually exclusive?"

"It's a very general question," he said. "You have to define what is popular."

"To be liked by your colleagues."

"By *which* colleagues? It's impossible to be liked by everybody. I think it's a meaningless question. If you have an effective grasp of what you're doing and an effective grasp of your own area of operations and an effective way of presenting yourself, then whether people really like you is not terribly important. If you want friends, you should go *find* friends. You shouldn't look for them where you're working. That is not to say that you should be a hateful personality. Charm, good fellowship, good nature, the ability to get along with people, all those things are very valuable in management situations. But they're valuable without necessarily *meaning* anything.

"Another point is that people may like you and be fond of you and think you're an absolutely terrific person—and still fire you the next day. I don't think it's a meaningful concept. I don't care whether I'm *liked* at work. I care whether I'm respected, effective, and rewarded.

"Of course, people who are likable find it much easier to get along in business situations than people who aren't, unless they're extraordinarily talented or extraordinarily powerful or extraordinarily knowledgeable, in which case it no longer matters at all. For several reasons, Harold Geneen of I.T.T. is not reputed to be a very likable person. The question is whether he would have gotten to the top quicker if he were likable. I doubt it. There's a certain kind of superenergy in power which has nothing to do with likability.

"David Mahoney, on the other hand, is one of the most likable, attractive people in the whole world, and he has been chairman of the board of Norton Simon Industries for years. He is a very powerful executive and highly liked even by people he's canned. I think it's a question of style.

"People who succeed probably feel in their bones and in their guts which of those two things they are and know better than to step out of character. Geneen probably knows better than to try to make people like him, and Mahoney probably knows better than to try to act like a corporate monster. I think there's some quirk in the nature of your personality that you have to follow."

Many of the most successful corporate leaders today, however, are what Maccoby terms "gamesmen." The gamesman is interested in competition, in challenge, much in the same way that an athlete is. He, too, wants to be a winner. But unlike the jungle fighter, he does not seek to destroy his opponent. He is often a mass of seeming contradictions, a team player but also a loner who wants to shine, detached but driven to win. He seeks riches and power not for their own sake, but as part of a game he can win, a game that will give him "fame, glory, the exhilaration of running his team and of gaining victories." The worst thing for him is to be known as a loser. Though he seems more humane than the jungle fighter, the gamesman's preoccupation with winning, with successful team effort when that is necessary, leads him to discard others as soon as their value to the team diminishes. Few, it seems, except perhaps the corporation man, are immune from the effects of excessive competition and the drive to win.

But what of that mass of blue-collar workers crouched behind those ever-clicking machines that seem to enslave them throughout life? Why and to what ends are they driven? Is it martyrdom, dreams of sacrifice for something better to bequeath to their offspring, a world built of opportunity—the Horatio Alger myth become reality?

This transfer of hope, of success, of the opportunity for yet a better life for one's children makes "sacrifice" bearable. This would seem to be the motivating force. Yet is it? Or is it desperation? Is it the basic need just to survive? Or is it fundamentally an accommodation with life, with that dream, to make it all bearable? It is, as we all know, a little of each.

No matter what a man works as—laborer, craftsman, company man, jungle fighter, gamesman—there are enormous costs to the individual. As Jack Nichols puts it, "As he struts toward the pinnacles of success, too often he forgets the whole spectrum of rectitude and integrity which should, hopefully, line his avenue to the top." Ashley Montagu also sees the costs. "Learning to be a human being—that's what you are supposed to be doing," he said. "That is what you are, what you were created for. You know, we have the most remarkable of all the traits on this earth—educability, the capacity to learn anything that can possibly be learned. That's what human beings have, and the first thing you have to learn to be a human being is to be loved. But the average male is brainwashed. He cannot love. He has lost his emotions. He has adopted the notion that emotions and the competitive drive for success are incompatible. And so he has shunted aside his emotions and his emotional life."

I asked Michael Korda if a man was at a distinct disadvantage in corporate life, especially if he wanted to reach the top rungs, if he could not in some very vital ways repress feelings, emotions, and sentiments that might be a nuisance in day-to-day dealings—or whether emotions could be put to one's advantage in some situations.

"Well, anything can be put to your advantage and feelings and sentiments more than anything else, I suppose," Korda replied. "But I don't know that it's necessary to repress sentiments; I don't think that they do, particularly. What you're saying is that businessmen have feelings, sentiments, and emotions —yes! Does it prevent them from pushing you up against the wall and robbing you blind? No! But that is the nature of the human animal, right? I mean your own father, if he could find a way of cheating you in business, probably would. History is full of that in everybody's family. The first thing Howard Hughes did when he was seventeen and gained his majority was to steal the entire Hughes estate away from his own grandfather, who was his favorite person in the whole world. That's the way people are. I don't think you can beat that."

But even if he rises to the top, the individual man's personal life is often disrupted. Part of this is due to those very masculine drives that motivated him in the first place. Work is at the very center of his existence, and often everything not directly related to work and success is slighted. For many, sex is secondary, except as a symbol of power and success. The man has a wife and children, but these are often only necessary adjuncts to the man's image and to corporate success. Many men work late or on weekends or on vacation days as a means of avoiding the close emotional ties that marriage and parenthood require. Some men feel guilty about liking their work more than their families, and many stress their disenchantment with work, with the long hours and the numerous trips out of town, to mask the real enjoyment and satisfaction they derive from their jobs. At home, as at work, they have lost the feelings of tenderness normal to human beings of either sex. They monitor themselves constantly until their emotions and their feelings are only pale shadows of what they might have been.

6

Wham, Bam, Thank You, Ma'am!: Sex

THE COMPETITIVE spirit of sports and career spills over into the male's pursuit of women. Why do men want success in sports and in their careers? Why do they want big cars and big houses? *Penthouse* creator and publisher Bob Guccione answers, "To attract women. That is why they do many of the things they do. When a man goes and buys a car, he wants to attract a woman with it."

"But," I said, "he is also trying to impress his fellow men with his masculinity, with his prowess in attracting women. Wouldn't you agree?"

"Exactly," Guccione replied. "It is much like young boys fighting not over a particular female but just to show their physical power, to demonstrate who is the better male. But they are also competing for a prize—for the prize itself—*and* to demonstrate that they are the best men."

The desire for an image of sexual prowess inheres in almost all males, no matter what their income or social position. In business, the image of sexual prowess gives one the reputation of being the kind of man one can have trust in, a man who can handle matters of importance. In the shop or on the assembly line, it takes the form of sexual banter as each man tries to one-up the others. As one auto worker describes it, "Each member of the group seems concerned mainly with exhibiting sexual experience and competency through the competition. Past sexual history is described and compared in some detail."[1] And all members of the group want to be winners.

Sexual conquest is an essential part of the masculine persona. Sexual prowess, or at least the image of sexual prowess, is the goal. Sex is part of a game men play, much like the games they played as boys. The aim is to score. Once they won on the field of play; now they score and win in the great pastures of prurience.

Marriage does not necessarily bring the game to an end. As an old saying goes, "Before marriage, boys will be boys and girls will be virgins; after marriage, boys will be boys and girls will be faithful." The male seems to be an eternal voyeur and an eternal chaser after sexual conquest.

In this, he is like the protagonist in François Truffaut's film *The Man Who Loved Women*. Truffaut's man goes to bed with a lot of different women. Yet he is never satisfied; he has this voracious appetite for more and more. But his affairs are all superficial, and he is lonely. Fearful of intimacy with women, he constantly tries to insulate himself from the real emotional commitments that people must make if a relationship is to progress beyond the physical. That is his tragedy.

Every day men look at women and lust after them. Many times they will settle for temporary, impersonal encounters that provide momentary release and enjoyment. They may be serviced by anyone from a casual pick-up, the chambermaid in a hotel, a masseuse in a massage parlor, or a woman in a whorehouse. Some men prefer sex for pay, for they don't have even to feign involvement. So even in our age of liberal sexual mores, droves of prostitutes wander the streets of our major cities; neighborhood massage parlors thrive on providing sexual gratification for a lot of men who don't want to get involved in a deep relationship.

If all of this sounds tremendously insensitive, cold and calculating, devoid of deeper feelings, it is! However, the reason men are often so insensitive to all but their own feelings and pleasures is bound up deeply in the nature of male sexuality, how it develops, how it is transmitted to young boys, and how they learn to express it. Males, too, are casualties of their own insensitivity.

Those with whom I talked agreed that the male, especially from his teens through his twenties, has a powerful sex drive. Albert Ellis, in fact, maintains that one of the reasons the human race has been able to survive is that "the male is imperiously driven toward sex and will to some degree, when he is young particularly, strongly desire to screw almost any woman in sight. Biologically, at least centuries ago, this would lead to impregnation and to the perpetuation of the species."

But Anthony Pietropinto, a New York psychiatrist and author of the provocative book *Beyond the Male Myth,* adds a note of caution: "I think men's sexual nature is basically different from women's," he told me, "insofar as a man requires a degree of arousal. We have the men's and women's liberationists who say things like, 'Well, why does it have to be intercourse? Why does a man have to have an erection? A man without a penis can be a good lover.' Men can't buy that. Sex for the male is penis-centered. The penis has to be aroused.

"It's fine for a woman to say, 'Why can't a man accept me even though I am fat, sloppy, ugly, and dirty?' The reason is that most men would not be aroused. A woman can physically participate in sex regardless of what she feels for her partner; but if a man is not aroused, if he is not turned on in some way by a woman, he is not going to respond. Unfair? Maybe it is unfair. But nevertheless, you have to be turned on.

"Men can say, 'I don't really care about her that much, but I'm going to do it anyway.' It's impossible to put male sexuality on a strictly cerebral level. Women can't say, 'Why can't he turn on to something other than my body? I want him to think of my wonderful mind and get an erection.' Men just don't do it that way. They have to be aroused."

It does seem that many men are quite capable of having sexual relations without emotional commitment. Some men have terrible marriages, can't stand their wives, and yet manage to continue sexual relations with them anyway. There is a compartmentalization in the man's mind which enables him to accept that somehow he is just screwing another female object. Some men are capable of having sex with almost any woman. They're able to turn off all the unpleasant aspects and turn on to that which attracts them, even if it is only a depersonalized vagina.

Women, on the other hand, are by their very nature more personal about sex because they're invaded by the penis, a foreign object, which is not so readily accepted by the woman. She integrates the man and his penis within her if she is receptive to him sexually. She does not want a disembodied penis. A man, though, will take a vagina, any vagina, without a woman. In fact, many prefer it.

To shed more light on this aspect, I asked Pietropinto: "Do you know the expression about the penis that has no conscience, about men being ready to get it up under any situation, under any circumstances? How true have you found that to be? Is it a myth?"

"I think it mainly depends on what phase of life a man is in, what his emotional state is," he replied. "It is certainly a myth insofar as it surely is not true of all men. And I think you would probably find that most men really can't relate quite that easily and that impartially. However, I do think that during the early phases of a man's sexual life, in his youth, his teens, a lot of men are very capable of having sex with prostitutes. Many enjoy that. They may manage on any given night to pick up any sort of woman and engage in sexual relations. They may even relate sexually to women who are not that attractive to them. To do this, however, the man really has to compartmentalize his feelings and relate to the woman merely as an object.

"The biological sex urges in the early teens are quite strong—any man can tell you this. Sometimes you get attacked by women who argue that this is cultural. This is why boys have strong sex drives and girls don't—because girls are told it is taboo, and so forth. But this is nonsense. I've talked with many women, not only patients, but friends, and they admit that in their early teens they never related to anything genitally. They may be quite active now and will talk about being horny, but they don't have the same type of development that a boy does. Suddenly he is having erections without any apparent arousal. He is not sure what is happening. It's a tough thing to come to grips with."

"Has anybody done a study, for example, of teenage girls to find out if they get horny much as teenage boys do?" I wanted to know. "Do they have sexual dreams, nocturnal orgasms? I've never seen any research."

"They do. They may even have sex early in life, as they do in many cultures. But again, this doesn't really seem to be related to lust, but rather in terms of what the group is doing, and what they want to do. It just doesn't seem to happen the same way as it does for boys. And I don't think it is strictly a cultural thing.

"Their fantasies are different, too," Pietropinto continued. "Women have fantasies right from the start, that they are going to meet their one ideal dream man, fall in love, and get married—the initial female adolescent dream. The adolescent male doesn't wake up in his teens and say, 'Boy, do I want to get married.' His feeling is 'I want to have sex.' He thinks, 'Boy, there are a lot of desirable girls out there, and I want to have sex with a lot of them.'

"One of the things my publisher wanted me to address in

Beyond the Male Myth was the question of whether men were 'naturally more promiscuous.' Now, that is a very loaded, very difficult question, especially since we are using the term 'naturally.' Again, my feeling is still yes, because first of all I think men are far more capable of giving themselves on a strictly physical level, getting physically aroused, of relating to women as objects, as bodies. Now, if I interpret 'natural' as meaning 'normal psychosexual development,' then men can and do relate, especially early in life, to women as objects, as bodies. Women don't seem to do this. They have no psychological need to do it, whereas men must defend themselves more against incestuous feelings. So I still see men as naturally more promiscuous."

Traditionally, then, men have been penis-centered. Men have had the feeling that the moment their cocks were hard, they had to stuff it into something. And that came from men's fear, a fear that antedated the women's movement, that if the penis didn't go into something shortly after it got hard, it might turn soft. Men have feared they would look impotent. A corollary of this penis-centeredness has been the assumption that sex is largely for the man's pleasure. Sex is something a woman provides to please him.

The penis was made to go into a vagina and therefore, the moment it got hard, that was where it had to go. That was the right place to put it. And far too many men got the entire sexual encounter over with as quickly as possible. One woman spoke for many when she said this about her partner to psychiatrist Avodah Offit: "He has no subtlety, no finesse. It's like going to bed with a computer. Three minutes of rubbing and kissing, one minute on the clitoris, and then he gets in and pumps away until he comes."[2]

Some of the male's speed in a sexual encounter may be the product of his early experience with masturbation. The young man masturbates quickly, furtively, behind the closed door of the bedroom or the locked door of the bathroom, hidden from the gaze of disapproving parents, who generally punished masturbation as a violation of some particularly solemn and holy prohibition.

I asked Albert Ellis if the speed with which some men engage in intercourse might be traced to this early experience with masturbation.

"It could be," he said, "but then anything could be. In masturbation, a man might want to get it over faster, to get the sensation of orgasm. He focuses intently on exciting images, and since there is no reason to delay, he may want it quicker. Lots of people do—just as they eat fast, they bolt their food down. So a man may train himself to get quick pleasure, and then he gets used to it that way. Later, when he is having a sexual relationship with a woman, he may fall into the same pattern. On the other hand, he may have just the opposite reaction: He may actually take longer in intercourse because he is not focusing so intently. There are many possibilities."

Two of the most impressive sex researchers, John Gagnon and William Simon, trace much of the problem of adult male sexuality to the young male adolescent's experience in masturbation, but they stress different aspects.[3] During adolescence, the increased flow of male hormones produces a sort of chronic irritation in the boy, causing him to have frequent erections that direct his attention to his penis. The boy begins to experiment, fondling his penis, stroking it, until at some time he experiences orgasm and ejaculation. At first, masturbation is a purely physical experience completely detached from any feelings or emotions toward the other sex. Boys often engage in group masturbation as a game, without feminine stimulation, or perhaps later in chorus, to a magazine centerfold. Sex is perceived as a physical act, like the experiments with masturbation—something the boy will do *to* girls when he gets the chance.

Traditionally, sexual encounters that followed his early masturbatory experiences were characterized by a superior-inferior, dominant-subordinate dichotomy. Men took the initiative in moving a relationship into the sexual arena. Men did the first hand-holding. Men made the first move to kiss. Men did the first caressing, the first genital touching. This was something they *learned* young; they still do; there was and is nothing genetic about it.

Boys are taught early on that they should take the initiative in their relationships with girls. A girl might learn some ways to make herself more attractive to boys, or to some particular boy in whom she is interested, but it is up to the boy to make the first move. As two psychologists put it, "The social hierarchy was clear; the initial impetus to heterosexual relationships was male. A girl sat home by the telephone until a boy asked her out."[4] It was the boy who decided what they should do. He provided the transportation. He paid for everything. And for what?

The boy's goal was usually some form of sexual conquest. For the younger boy, it might be simply a kiss—a "French" kiss, with his tongue deep in the girl's mouth. Or his hand might be cupped over her breast, outside her sweater. These were prized victories, and the boy regaled his male friends with detailed accounts of his exploits. Through a long, slow but anxious process, the boy gradually upped the ante.

Dan Greenburg recalls how it was in the 1950s. "Dating in those days was really something. You would ask a girl out five or six days in advance to go to a movie and have a bite to eat afterward. Perhaps you would borrow the family car. And maybe by the third date you would try to kiss her good night. And if things went well, maybe around the fifth date, you might try, perhaps, a little fondling, above the waist outside the clothes. If you were really serious, in a few months you might get below the waist outside the clothes. Don't forget, we're talking about dates with 'good girls.' "

For older teenage boys and young men, dates were the necessary preliminary to get a girl into bed. Every facet of the date was calculated with one goal in mind. It was the ritual of conquest. The male sought to impress his date with his worth, his accomplishments, perhaps his intellect—all so she would succumb easily to his physical advances. Every penny spent was designed to aid the impression of his position, his attractiveness, and to put the female in his debt, a debt that could be repaid only one way. There was little relaxation, rarely any real interest in her worth, no sense that her desires might be as important as his. A girl was merely an object, designed to lie on a man's bed with her skirt up and her legs spread.

All too often, of course, the man failed. His efforts went unrewarded. All too often he complained, as in Marc Feigen Fasteau's words: "I took you to the Four Seasons for dinner and to a forty-dollar Broadway show and you're throwing me out after a cup of coffee and a peck on the cheek?" However, for many men this was enough, for it gave the illusion of conquest, an illusion which was in many cases as important for the male ego as the reality of success.

The male was able to fulfill the role he was expected to play. He knew what he was supposed to do. He was, as *Cosmopolitan* publisher Helen Gurley Brown told me, "supposed to chase girls, he was supposed to make passes, he was supposed to be horny twenty-four hours of the day.

"But women knew what they were supposed to do also.

They were supposed to refuse. They were supposed to resist. And if necessary, they were supposed to run away. Somehow it didn't impugn a man's reputation for virility even if she did get away. The man was expected to chase girls, so he could chase them knowing that he wouldn't really get them. But he got credit among his peers for chasing. He could go running around making a lot of noise, chasing, chasing, and he could talk to his buddies and say, 'Oh boy, did I give that girl a run for her money, and I almost got her.' Or he could even lie and say she did succumb when she didn't really. The man was able to maintain this tremendous façade of virility. He was horny all the time, and he was after girls all the time. And if he didn't score, that was O.K. He wasn't really supposed to, because good girls weren't supposed to do that sort of thing. Only a few girls really were the kind you could get to."

Whatever the façade, whatever the reality of men's sexual encounters, successes, or failures, the male sex drive was constantly portrayed as a raging energy, a force that men were usually unable to control, a force that was, perhaps, impossible to control. And yet, the truth was that the façade masked a lot of insecurity. Dan Greenburg recalls that there was a "lot of ambivalence and lying. You tried to get laid. But you did it in ways that would defeat you. You really didn't want to get laid in many cases, because you were afraid you would be refused, afraid you might be impotent, afraid you wouldn't know how to fuck, afraid you would be laughed at. There was an enormous amount of ambivalence and unease about the whole thing. Some youngsters managed to fail at every attempt they made until they were adults or married."

Men were pulled in different directions by contradictory feelings. On the one hand, they felt the pressure of their intense sex drives. They wanted sexual relations. They were also driven by the requirements of masculinity: Real men were conquerers. They compared notes and boasted openly of their success. On the other hand, however, men felt the constraints that a basically religious though increasingly secular society placed on sexual activity outside marriage. Religions taught that indiscriminate sex was loathsome to God and a sure path to damnation. Sex was dirty for some, a necessary evil for others. The unyielding, puritanical American culture, further nurtured by the "Sex is sin" religious convictions of new immigrants, led to overwhelming cultural conflict for all.

Men were peculiarly affected. Society seemed to accept the

notion that men were slaves to their sexual passions. Society also believed that men needed many women. There was a tolerance for a husband's infidelity that was never granted to a wandering wife. There was no male counterpart of Emma Bovary or Anna Karenina. And there was a belief that any man could be undone by an "irresistible woman." It was generally believed, Anthony Pietropinto says, "that every man had his breaking point, that no matter how strong he was, how firm in his resolve, somehow or other there was always a woman gorgeous enough to undermine every defense he had ever built up against his passions." He had to fear that kind of woman and once he met her, every ideal he had was gone. As Pietropinto quotes George Bernard Shaw, "Nature just threw him into her mouth like a sailor throws a scrap of fish to a sea bird."

Men are attracted to "that kind of woman," a woman of some sexual experience. "Men traditionally related to women on two levels," Pietropinto told me. There were women—the so-called bad girls—with whom they could have sex, and the 'good girls,' the kind you married, the kind who was going to be the mother of your children, the kind you brought home for your parents to meet." All of this is part of the process of relating to women as objects. They were sex objects. Wife objects. Mother objects. Categories that are impersonal, unreal. And categories because they're distinct entities in the man's mind, which could cause problems for him in his relations with his partner.

Men seem to be hopelessly mired in this process of making women into objects, of categorizing them as either prostitutes or madonnas. This creates a kind of schizophrenia in the male's sexuality. Men have different needs and ideally they want to have them met by one woman—the combination of a \$500-a-night hooker and a schoolteacher, to borrow Lenny Bruce's phrase—or they look for someone else to give them what they're missing.

This prostitute-madonna complex was the subject of one of the most controversial parts of Pietropinto's book. I asked him to amplify a bit, to tell me if he found men actually to be schizophrenic that way. He replied: "You mean, do they tend to split off parts? Is there a duality, is there a split? My answer is yes. And my point about it is that it is not just a phenomenon we see in highly neurotic men. It is something that every male goes through as part of his psychosexual development. Men have a heck of a time ultimately resolving and integrating it.

"The danger in the prostitute-madonna complex depends on how the man resolves it. If he doesn't, he may be in danger of not being able to accept sex with the same enthusiasm from a woman whom he settles down with. However, I think because most men are really relatively aware of the fact that it would be great to have both qualities in the same woman, that is their ideal. If they fail to find the ideal, they may cheat on their wives or lovers. I think that basically men do have a need for one woman who is going to meet all their needs. If they can wrap it up in one woman, fine. If they are not satisfied they are likely to move on and try elsewhere."

The male, according to Ashley Montagu, is the "gadfly of sex; he'll mate with virtually any woman he encounters." Women, on the other hand, traditionally mated and married with the idea of establishing a home and having children. Men, Montagu says, marry largely "to assure themselves of an easy source for the satisfaction of their sexual needs." All too often, the male in our society confuses his sex drive with love and makes sex the basis of his relationships with women.

But sex is not enough by itself. Too many men select beautiful sex objects for wives. And, as Ashley Montagu says, this "is no basis on which to build a secure marriage. The sexual interest will fade if there is nothing else to the relationship. Interest is reinforced only if there is something else—the development of a respect for the partner's character, a liking for her. We too often confuse sex with love. You have to be a human being and relate to another human being in all matters, including sex." For too many couples, monogamy becomes monotony, and it is more commonly accepted for men to look elsewhere for emotional or sexual gratification.

When sex alone is the foundation for a relationship, there is little hope the relationship will endure. The problems of sustaining a relationship are difficult enough in any case. Even when couples stay together, they are often at each other's throats. "Some marriages," Dan Greenburg says, "are either a joke or are marriages in name only." Often the husband and wife will grow apart naturally, as he deepens his involvement in his career and as she deepens her involvement with their children. This can and does happen even among the most mature adults. But all too often, when men marry because of an intense physical attraction, they soon find they have chosen to share life with someone with whom they have no common interests and with whom they find it impossible to communicate. Immature to begin with, the male finds it easy to walk out, to blame his partner or the institution of marriage for a failing that is, in part, his own.

The main problem, then, in all of the male's traditional sexual experiences—his early experiments with masturbation, his fantasies, his later relations with real women—is his tendency to treat women as objects, his essential difficulty in perceiving the necessary interrelationship of sex and feelings, sex and empathy, sex and love. In the explosion of sexual information after World War II, men learned the technical details of new positions that provided diversion and excitement, new techniques for the seduction of reluctant women. Men's magazines like *Playboy* and later *Penthouse, Oui,* and *Hustler* went, as Ashley Montagu put it, "whole hog in the alleged interest of initiating men into an understanding of what sex is really about." But it was not what sex is really about.

Sex is what you make of it. It can be a dirty thing, a beautiful thing, an ephemeral release of tension, or a moving encounter between people, depending on the feelings within you. For too long, men have found it difficult, if not impossible, to have a deep, intimate sexual relationship with women that transcended the physical act. As Rollo May so aptly expressed it, we can "have sexual relations from now till doomsday and never experience any real relationship with another person."[5] For too long, women have been merely objects to be used for gratification and for proof of one's masculinity. Because men have found it impossible to confront their own feelings, they have been unable to understand the feelings of another. For too many men, sex is sterile, as it will be until its deeper meaning is discovered.

7 Feelings

GORE VIDAL told me a story that reveals much about American men and the way they are: "I saw a movie called *First Love,* about a boy's first love affair with a girl. They are both in a university, and it's a nice little movie. But at the end of it, I kept saying to myself, 'There is something odd here. Now, what is it?' Well, the director was a woman. But that wasn't it. Then it occurred to me that all of the boy's lines and attitudes were those that you would normally expect from a girl. The boy was the more sensitive, the more loving one of the two. He was overwhelmed by the experience. She was kind of tough, and at the end it is the boy who, holding back his tears, decides that they can't go on as they are, that she is merely using him as a toy.

"Now, I thought that this was an interesting reversal. The audience near La Costa was made up of marines from Camp Pendleton and they couldn't figure out what was going on. Nothing sounded like anything that they had been taught, or like anything that they had seen on television. So they were truly mystified." So would most American men be mystified by this vision of the male's softer, hidden side.

We have seen throughout the preceding chapters that men are conditioned from early age to internalize their feelings, to refrain from expressing their emotions. As they grow, they are taught what men—real men, masculine men—do and do not reveal to others. As a result, the adult male becomes, in Dr. Harvey Kaye's words, "anesthetized and robotized because he has been heavily socialized to repress and deny almost the total range of his emotions and human needs in order that he can perform in the acceptable 'masculine' way. In time, feelings become unknown, unpredictable quantities, expressions of which threaten him and make him feel vulnerable."[1]

This is not to say that men don't have feelings and emotions.

Many people think men are emotionally shallow, but what they perceive as an inability to feel is really the male's defensive shield, a protection against his own vulnerability. Nor is it true that men never show their emotions. Some emotional outburst is perfectly acceptable, as a man's open display of contempt, anger, hostility, or cynicism makes clear.

However, many men find it impossible to express their feelings. They keep things bottled up inside, even at the risk of endangering their own health. Art Buchwald commented on this when I asked him whether the pressures of his work, the deadlines, made him tense.

"It's possible," he said. "But they also tell you that as you grow older, it shows up a lot more. But I keep things to myself pretty much—that also contributes to the tension I feel. I never get angry, and I never lose my cool—outside. I keep it all inside. That causes hypertension as much as the pressure from work."

Clinician Albert Ellis, noted author of over thirty books on sex and sexual behavior, sees this holding in of emotion as a problem for both men and women. I had asked him whether he observed a reluctance to cry, for example, among the men he has examined over the years.

"Yes," he said, "but it's not only American men. It's American women, too. I see innumerable women who come to the Institute for Rational-Emotional Therapy in New York City start crying and immediately get apologetic. Maybe men are more ashamed because crying is defined as a feminine trait in our culture. Once tears are viewed as a feminine trait, and a man is not supposed to be at all feminine but a hundred percent masculine, we exaggerate the undesirability of giving in to them. But both sexes probably feel somewhat ashamed of crying, partly because it may inefficiently interrupt thought processes. So, first, people note their own crying and view it as a weakness. Second, they put themselves down—denigrate themselves as bad *persons* for having that weakness. And third, in a culture which emphasizes lack of androgyny, where one *should* be totally 'masculine' or totally 'feminine,' men make themselves feel ashamed of 'feminine' emotions, such as crying."

I suggested another possible side effect might be that feelings are seen as inconvenient, that they become more and more of a nuisance, because, as Ellis had mentioned, they do impede certain types of progress.

"Yes," Ellis agreed, "but that's changed, too. You see, that's one of the revolutionary things in some of our subcultures. In the old days virtually all Americans would put down a man's crying, but today if you are self-disclosing, if you cry easily, and if you show your feelings, then you get accolades in subcultures, like certain therapy groups. You don't get put down, but actually applauded!"

"You might get accolades in the subcultures, but you certainly won't in business," I pointed out.

"That's right! That's right! There are times and places that are quite different. In certain situations you'd better *not* cry—in the stock market, or something like that. You'd better be watching the tickertape and not crying, 'Oh my God, isn't that terrible! My stock is going down!' Because that won't help you, and the other people who are working with you, whom you are selling the stock to or buying it from, won't honor you for doing that. So there are lots of situations where superemotionalism will impede you. There are others, though, where it helps you."

"Do people have the capacity to differentiate between the two?" I wondered.

"Yes, they do it all the time. Quite definitely! You have a stiff upper lip on the ball field or the tennis court, and you don't have that stiff upper lip in many family and personal situations."

But the male seems particularly unable to express his deepest feelings in intimate relationships. Many find a deep relationship thwarted by their own inability to make an emotional commitment to another. They are imprisoned by their own egos. At some point in his life, a man contemplates marriage, but at the same time, the thought of intimacy, real intimacy, terrifies him.

Dan Greenburg agreed with this. "And I think that has always been the case," he said. "There is always something very scary about intimacy, and it doesn't matter what people, what class, what country you consider, you find they think there is something very scary about it."

The male's emotional condition has been portrayed in fiction, and nowhere has it been treated better than in Joseph Heller's novel *Something Happened*. Heller's protagonist, Bob Slocum, finds it impossible to overcome his sense of inadequacy, his inability to share his more intimate feelings and emotions toward his family; his inability to respond adequately to his family's needs. I asked Heller how he himself would describe Slocum's character.

J.H.: I would say his character is a composite. It's a very definite personality. He's a man who has certain failings, weaknesses, and obsessive strains in him which would not necessarily be universal.

B.A.: What are the obsessive strains?

J.H.: Well, I think he has four or five characteristics that I would think of as obsessive strains. He keeps reverting to them. They are stimulated by the various difficulties he encounters, largely as a result of his inability to deal with his relationship to his daughter, with his normal son, with his retarded child, with his wife, and with his own past.

B.A.: What is it in his past that so disturbs him?

J.H.: In this area it is his memory of relationships to his mother and his father and their effect on him as he tries to exist in a corporate executive position that is analogous to the environment of a family—except that he is far more comfortable in the corporate family than he is in his family relationships. His family relationships are too unpredictable for him; they can take unpredictable turns; they cannot be labeled, classified, or fit into organizational charts the way they can be in a corporation.

Now, of course, Slocum is not necessarily like all individuals in business. Among the people I knew when I was working for a company, many of whom are still friends, there was a diversity of character. There were many people who, with a great deal of calmness and almost no disturbance, could dedicate their lives to moving up in business, they could take a great deal of pride and satisfaction in achieving some goal—and yet they led normal (or perhaps abnormal), happy family lives.

I created a character, and my character is able to see farther ahead, indeed he has a compulsion to see farther ahead than most people have. He is more sensitive, with almost excruciating vulnerability, to tenderness, so much so that he *overcompensates* for it continuously. He uses hard language, a rough wit that is nothing like he is inside. In the early part of the book he has the ability to control his emotions; he can talk about his retarded son in a very callous way. But in time, all of his control, all of his defenses break down.

B.A.: There is another thing in the book that falls within the realm of emotions and feelings: Slocum and his feelings for his small son. Now, Slocum's son is certainly not a winner. He does not live up to the so-called masculine ideal that so many of us are conditioned with when we are small. And yet, Slocum's feelings for his son, his emotional side, his capacity for intimacy, are something that he knows is there. He feels it, but he cannot express it. And that very lack of ability to express oneself emotionally and sensitively is what seems to be destroying a lot of men today. Would you agree with that?

J.H.: Yes, although it is kind of a sweeping statement you make. But let me stay with Slocum, with the particular case. There are two times in the book where Slocum does try to respond with emotional honesty, both times with his daughter. He reaches out to hug her, though he knows what's going to happen. He knows she is going to mock him and make him feel like a fool. Nevertheless, he is able to overcome his foreknowledge, even though it is very important to him to maintain his status within the family. He comes forth to hug her, and she responds exactly the way he predicted. She sneers and turns away from him.

He does this twice with great effort. It's very hard for him to do that. But at those moments he is almost overcome with compassion and pity for her, because he loves his daughter, though he most often conceals that. On the other hand, he feels a great deal of disappointment about his son, and he conceals that, too.

Another aspect of Slocum's character, and the book dwells on this, is his feeling that the little boy he once was is still with him in the person of his son. This is also something that is very strongly embedded in all personalities and is something that people will not confess to as readily as Slocum does when he is presumably speaking in secrecy. This helps account for his extreme overidentification with his son.

I was amazed to learn the great psychological accuracy of Slocum's feeling. It goes beyond all I ever dreamed of. The accuracy is on a level I couldn't have expected. People of the Los Angeles Medical Psychiatric Association invited me to a seminar on the book.

Getting back to Slocum, though, he has taken his son and made him a part of his own psyche. When he hurts his son, he is hurting himself. When he is disappointed in his son, he is disappointed in himself. And when he destroys his son, he destroys a part of himself.

Slocum exists as an incomplete human being because he has managed to repress, or at least hide, most of his feelings. He exists alienated from a crucial part of himself, and he is subject to the psychological problems that result from emotional repression. However, for Slocum, the existence of his feelings also causes psychological distress, as it does for most men. To feel and to express these feelings is expressive of a side of human personality that men wish to disown, a side that becomes particularly disturbing to them in their relations with other men.

Despite much that has been written about male bonding and men in groups, relationships between men usually remain superficial. Men still suffer great discomfort and embarrassment if another man tries to get close, tries to confide. Men are suspicious of the man who makes an overture and of themselves if they are receptive to it. A man who weeps or shows dependence or any kind of "weakness" will most likely be considered unmanly by other men. Moreover, he will probably regard himself as less of a man. On the other side, most men will consider tenderness toward a fellow man or receptivity to his need to unburden himself of his deepest feelings as an affront to masculine dignity and as an example of feminine behavior. These attitudes lead to a further association, from the feminine to the homosexual. And both the man who recognizes his deeper feelings and tries to express them and the man who listens with sympathy are likely to harbor doubts about their own masculinity and to fear that they have latent homosexual tendencies. This is not unusual.

Heller has noted this problem and the male fear. "I think a tremendous part of Slocum's difficulty, and I think it a masculine difficulty, is the feeling that one is either being infantile or effeminate if one confesses to those very soft desires Slocum does have. Several times he talks about a wish to cry or of having a feeling akin to weeping, especially if he lets himself think about something personal, something to do with his relationships with his family. But his masculinity goes against this. I think a psychoanalyst would be familiar with something like this residing in all of us.

"Slocum is very much concerned with this. He has these fears; he dwells on the possibility that he might really be homosexual. Now, I don't think he ever feels anything that can be identified as a homosexual impulse, but the fear that he might be a latent, repressed homosexual is there with him.

"Many functionally heterosexual men will tell you they have

the fear. Many men will occasionally have an impulse which might be called homosexual. I don't mean desire—I mean just a certain impulse. There is one point in the book, when Slocum's talking with somebody—I think it is with Arthur Baron—and he just wants to reach out and touch Baron's hand. Now, that gesture may or may not represent a genuine homosexual impulse. It may simply represent a desire to touch a father figure, to be reunited with the father who died when he was a child. I think in Slocum's mind, he would want to avoid touching another man, because of his fear, his conscious fear, of having a homosexual impulse that would call his masculinity into question.

"There is a further aspect of this in that Slocum is also afraid that a homosexual impulse would mean that he has lost control, that he might go out of existence, just disintegrate as a personality. Now, that feeling of turning into nothing, of not existing, is also a real fear of many people. It is like the fear children have when the lights are out and the parent goes from the room. The child fears that if the parent leaves, the parent will cease to exist and the child will cease to exist, too. It is an ontological insecurity, which means a fear that you do not really exist or that you may cease to exist.

"Slocum expresses this fear in the novel when he is playing a children's game, when one says, 'Who am I?' He is talking about his daughter and he thinks, "I don't know who she is.' Then *he* asks who he is, and he finds he is not sure of his own identity. He is not sure because he is confused. He is unsure and afraid, because if he doesn't happen to know his own identity, he fears he will cease to exist."

If it is true that squelching emotional expression is a product of fears that one is not sufficiently masculine, it should come as no surprise that the expression of tender emotions is acceptable among those whose masculinity cannot be questioned. Soldiers can talk about fear before going into battle; they may weep openly at the death of a buddy. Athletes, too, are allowed a measure of freedom that most men are not. We have all seen star football players weep on national television after a game-losing fumble. We have seen the elation of their victories. But even for them, there is a constant battle to keep emotions in check.

I talked about this with Bruce Jenner, and he revealed some provocative facets of men, their battles with their feelings, and the direction they should take.

B.A.: Bruce, one of the things I have discovered in talking to people is that a lot of men, in order to gear themselves for success, have to somehow repress the emotional side of their character because it tends to be a nuisance sometimes. They start worrying about this and that, and it stops them. Did you have any problems with that?

B.J.: No, I really didn't. But ever since I've been very young, I always controlled my emotions tremendously. I don't know if it's because of athletics. I just always have controlled them. A lot of times even now I have a tendency to control my emotions too much. I was always trying to remain in control, never fly off the handle, and it's a hard habit to break.

My wife, Christie, is always telling me that I'm not showing enough emotions. I do think that's because of my athletic background. Whenever I was on the track or in the field I would gear everything to controlling my emotions so I could concentrate on my events. I had to do that. I couldn't let my emotions take over. I had to be thinking all the time.

I knew I had to do that to come up with the best performance. I can remember one meet where I probably did let my emotions take over. That was in 1975, just before the national AAU meet. I hadn't lost a meet in two years. I had been ranked number one in the world for two years. But in this meet, I went down the runway in the pole vault and I couldn't make the height. I couldn't even get off the ground in three attempts. As soon as I hit the pit the third time, I took the pole—remember, I usually never showed any emotion—and *foooooom!,* I winged that thing as far as I could. I almost hit a cameraman right on the head. I cussed, I said a few words I probably shouldn't have. I stomped out of the pit, ran right across the inside of the field, right outside the stadium, and sat underneath a big clump of trees and cried my eyes out about what just happened. And usually I would not show any emotion.

After it was over and after I had stopped crying, Christie finally came around the corner, and she didn't know what to do either. I went over to her and got some more things off my chest, and then I went back into the stadium and I felt fine. I felt like I had got it all out, and it didn't bother me. It wasn't like it was eating away at me anymore. It happened; I got it out of my system; it was over.

And I came back one month later—after really soul-searching myself when that meet was over; and I broke the world's record for the first time. But I think that bad performance had a big effect on the next meet. I was hungry. I was ready to go. Whereas up to this time, I'd been winning so many meets and doing so well that it didn't make any difference if I was psyched up or I wasn't psyched up, I was still going to be able to win the meet. But getting that loss and getting defeated, it all of a sudden had a big change in my whole attitude and I came back the next meet and I was hungry. I wanted it, but not because it had been taken away. I really believe, in a lot of cases, athletes do have to control their emotions an awful lot, and I don't find too many athletes who show their emotions that much. I don't know if it's because of the supermacho image, football players or something like that, they're out there to have a good time and they fool around and joke and play the jock role. But sometimes they don't really. In the last year or so I've changed tremendously in that area, and I think I've opened up an awful lot through the help of my wife. She's a very intelligent, very open person. She speaks her mind and I think she's bringing a lot of things out of me, but I still probably hold a little bit too much in.

B.A.: That's the natural discipline of an athlete.

B.J.: I think so. I saw the movie *Bobby Deerfield* the other night. It really struck me how nice it was when they were sitting in the car and they were talking and the girl was saying that it's nice to have a man who has some feminine characteristics. I thought that had a lot to it. And I think that's very true.

B.A.: Men are not allowed to show sensitivity.

B.J.: Right, right. I'm reminded of a friend of mine who is a lawyer. He has a law firm, he has fifty guys underneath him, he's very, very successful. I went to his house the other day, and there he was lying on the couch with his son lying next to him, and every time the boy goes out, he kisses his son good-bye. It seems like a very close, very warm relationship and I really respect the guy for that. Whereas, you know, how many fathers will lie down and have their son lie down with them, and the two of them lie there together and watch television? It just doesn't happen that often. That is not considered manly. But I really respected the guy for that; and like I was saying with *Bobby Deerfield,* I'm going through something like that. I'm trying to open up a little bit more, and I found that very very interesting.

B.A.: That's a fundamental issue in the book, this sensitivity, the ability to express feelings and emotions, to let yourself be yourself, with the barriers and defenses down, without having to worry about the masculine role and the image that you cast.

B.J.: I really agree with that.

8

Against the Social Grain: The Gain and the Pain

THROUGHOUT THEIR adult lives men look at themselves and say, in effect, "In order for me to validate myself as a human being, and as a man, I must achieve something, I must be somebody." That may mean anything from a successful corporate executive to a manual worker. But it also means being good at it and being recognized as good at it.

This striving toward a goal becomes the core of men's being, their main sustenance. It is more important than their sexual drive. But ultimately life becomes empty, because in pushing so hard for external validation, men allow their striving to negate so many other aspects of their lives, and of their characters. They have denied their emotional and sensitive side, their feelings. They can't disclose their feelings to themselves because that is an admission of weakness, an admission of their vulnerability. And to deny these is to deny their humanity.

For too many men this denial of humanity comes early in life. The tragedy of our times, Sterling Hayden says, is that most men seem to die spiritually in their early twenties. "They come out of the university and they look at the big, bleak, fucking horizon called the world, and they do the thing that somehow their life has told them they must do. And that is to join forces with some sort of an outfit, a corporation, a company, and they commit themselves to that company, and they now grasp their hands firmly on the lowest rung of the ladder, and they go to work. At that point they are dead. They merely delude themselves with the idea that when they are fifty-five or fifty-eight or sixty or sixty-five, they will live once again. Of course, when they finally reach fifty-five or fifty-eight or sixty or sixty-five, they are dead, just fucking dead! They can't experience life anymore. We see this all the time. It happens to anyone who invests thirty years in a career that kills him.

"I've seen it, out here, and I've thought about it out here in

Fairfield County. Especially at night. I lie back and I'm at war with myself. As we all are. I get going. I pace around all night. I've got the music going. And I think about all the men around me, all these men who will have to catch the train tomorrow morning at 7:27. There is the 7:27. This little Tooterville Trolley. Toot-toot. This little fucked-up train, you know? Heading in for Grand Central. But this is their security blanket."

Hayden had really struck a chord. It was years ago. I'll never forget how I once mortgaged my soul, became a commuter. I watched a faceless mass of humanity climb on a train in the morning, bury its nose behind the paper, sleep, and later get back on the 5:30 martini express for the run home. I woke up one morning, and I said, "Screw it!" I realized that I would wake up at age sixty or sixty-five, somebody would give me a gold watch, and I would have spent one-eighth of my life on the damn train—not master of my own destiny, not master of my own soul. I couldn't get off the train when I wanted to, I couldn't do what I wanted to do, I couldn't come and go as I pleased. And what would have I done with my life? I'd have thrown it away! So I quit—I walked into work that day and quit.

Fortunately, I was able to chuck it and break away, because I had the means to do so. Most people are trapped by circumstances. Some don't realize their plight; some don't want to realize it. And some realize it but can do nothing about it. I talked about this with Tom Tryon, who broke away from his career as an actor and ventured out to become a novelist—a precarious undertaking.

B.A.: Tom, one thing I sense about you, and it seems to be a very important part of your identity, is your great need for autonomy, for independence, for a sense of yourself as a free human being who can do what he wants, be the master of his own destiny. Do you agree with me?

T.T.: Yes. But I've fought a long, fifty-three-year battle for that. I haven't won yet, but I'm still fighting. I think the freedom of the individual has to be more highly prized than any gift a man could have. To be free to do what he wants.

B.A.: Isn't that what integrity is all about? But very few people have that integrity, or the luxury to have it.

T.T.: It really depends upon whether you can afford to have integrity. I think it is a lot harder for a man with a wife and four kids to have integrity than somebody in my shoes. But I think integrity is a very important value and certainly is something that people don't value as much today.

B.A.: Yes. You know, if you read a book like Studs Terkel's *Working,* you get the further sense that there is a great deal of violence, of browbeating, of dehumanization of all the good qualities like integrity that people need to elevate themselves. Men particularly fall victim to this. They identify with what they do, how much money they make. That is the only way they measure themselves. And there is a price, a human price that they pay, just for the lives that they are forced to lead. What brought about your decision to give up your acting career? Was it Hollywood itself, or something else?

T.T.: It was partially Hollywood, partially the assholes in power. It is very easy to lay waste to other people, to blame them. I arrived at a psychological point in my life that I wasn't even aware was coming, but when it came, I suddenly said: "Oh, yeah, get on with it." There was something else I wanted to do that meant more to me than acting. So I went and did it.

But I also happen to be of the live-and-let-live school. I didn't want—and I still don't want—anybody telling me what to do. I don't want to tell anybody what to do, and I don't want them telling me what to do. It's just too hard getting through life, just getting up in the morning, making it through the day is too fucking hard. Get off my back! Just get off my back! I didn't want any Hollywood asshole telling me how to live my life, and, thank God, I'm not obliged to anymore.

Now, if I'd had no success with it, you never would have heard about it. It just happened that my first book was enormously successful and very gratifying, which impelled me to do the second one; the second one impelled me to do the third, and so on.

B.A.: Were you always very success-oriented? As a young person, growing up, did you think about wanting to be successful?

T.T.: Yes. But it wasn't so much that you thought about wanting to be successful, you thought it was expected of you. I know it was expected of all of us—when I say "us," I mean my generation in the small town in Connecticut I came from.

B.A.: Do you think that attitude has changed in the last decade, that pressure on the male to be success-oriented?

T.T.: Well, I'm not totally cognizant of what goes today. I have to talk to someone young to find out where kids' heads are at today. I don't have a child of my own, so I'm not really cognizant of what their values are. I would say—as a surface judgment—no, they are not. They are much more willing to say, "Fuck off, leave me alone. Let the world go by." Not "Get out there, dig, plunge," and what have you. America, God knows, in the last century since the Civil War, has been enormously success-oriented, and compulsively so.

But why should this be true? I have not had a failure yet doing a book, but why am I not as entitled to fail as the guy who opens a vegetable stand down the street and it goes out of business? We should all be entitled to fail. We should not be expected to succeed. It is a terrible thing for parents to visit on their children—the sin of failure. I don't think there's anything wrong with failing.

B.A.: As long as you try?

T.T.: It depends so much on the circumstances and the person who is involved. Again, to go back to young people, if they cannot think what they want to do, it is wrong of parents to propel them into something they don't want.

After World War II, my father wanted us to go into plastics—just like the scene in *The Graduate.* Antithetical to any of my own interests or ambitions. Plastics! Or, if not plastics, advertising. He had a lot of connections in New York advertising. But there was something in my head that kept saying, "No, Tom, no. Hold out. Do what you want to do." When I went into acting my family cried, "Oh, no!" They really looked down on that. I was living in New York then on seventy-five bucks a month—which was the GI Bill—and I was trying to get jobs, and I was getting jobs. But it wasn't until the neighbors started telling my father that they had seen me on television that he woke up and started to watch. And as soon as I started to be successful, as soon as I was bringing home the bread, as soon as I started getting a reputation, then it became O.K. But before that, "Uh-uh," "Oh, no." It didn't fit the normal pattern, the normal role.

Sterling Hayden was another who found life on the neatly prescribed inside intolerable. At heart he was a wanderer, who at first chose what he thought was the way to security. But the path on the inside was rugged and treacherous. It endangered Hayden's soul. So he wandered once again, trying to find himself and the kind of life he could value. I asked him, "How did you first get into films? Knowing your background it seems incongruous, even though you have always had a lot of the artist in you. How did it happen?"

S.H.: Well, when the idea of going to Hollywood initially came up, it was half the expectation of attention and half the expectation of easy money. Recognition and ease. Somehow, I sensed something which I know is true—that acting in Hollywood led to a life of ease. I'd be the last man on the face of this earth to pretend that I don't love ease. I love a big beautiful bathtub full of hot water. If I have to go the other way, toward less ease, I guess I could now. I wouldn't want to. But when I was young, I used to pretend I wanted to go where it was tough. That was bullshit, you know. . . . So, Hollywood meant, in a way, ease.

B.A.: But it wasn't a question of glitter and glamour and stardom and all of those things?

S.H.: No. Not in the show business sense at all. I had never had an ounce of it at all. I did have—I'm trying to be as honest as I know how—I did have an awareness of the positive aspects of recognition. But in terms of the whole show business thing, to me it was just an easy way out.

B.A.: Sterling, you now have a special image—an image of someone playing the role of the macho intellectual. How did this happen?

S.H.: "First, I don't think I play that role. But I know what I represent to people—and that is the effort to be different. And they are right in perceiving this. I just don't relate directly to things that go on. I hold off and look at the culture. I'm not part of it at all. I'm outside. Different. Or at least I try to be.

Not that I've ever succeeded completely. Not at all. But I think people sense this role of the outsider in me. Often they come up and stop me, or a guy driving a taxi looks in the mirror and starts bullshitting or whatever. Now, a part of it is, when they look at me, they respond. Not because of films, not because of books, not because of the sea, not for any particular reason. I think they realize, "Well, here's a son of a bitch who somehow is trying to stay outside." And they want to know what it's like out there.

B.A.: Trying to be an individual?

S.H.: Yes. Sure. Trying to be an individual. But doing it so that, even though I might fail, at least I am out there doing it. I have not had to capitulate. I've been lucky in some ways. But, then, I know I could not have worked in an office. I knew that when I was eighteen. All my friends would go into the State Street Trust in Boston. Bull fucking shit! You know, an office, a desk—da, da, da, da. I would come off a schooner, my hands swollen and red. I'm cold and scared shitless. But I would think, "By God, at least I'm at sea. At least I'm not gonna sit here in your State Street Trust Company and do what you are supposed to do."

If you live outside the system, it's going to be easier in a way. In some ways it really is easy. The reason I was so enamored of the sea was that there was virtually no competition. Few young men were going to sea. When I went fishing out of Boston and Gloucester in the wintertime, it was the most terrifying thing I have ever done. Old fishermen wouldn't let their own kids fish, for chrissakes. They told them: "No, finish high school, get a job on land . . . in the post office." Never the sea.

B.A.: Was it a test of your manhood, somehow, to be able to measure up to the challenge of the sea?

S.H.: A test? No, I don't think so. I don't think it was that difficult. There was one big factor—the French have a wonderful word, *gloire*—glory, glory! There was and is glory on this earth. Yes, Jesus Christ, yes. And I found it when I went to sea—even before I went to sea.

I used to watch the sun come up, in Maine, where we lived on an island. We had a lot of what we called "townies," people from the middle-class world of suburbia. While they all waited for something to happen, I would get up to watch the sun rise. I would witness the majesty of it. And it moved me. It still does. When I meet other people, stuck in artificial worlds, who can't relate to this, I feel so alien.

So, when I was in films, we'd go to party after party. People there were always talking about film. I thought they were nuts. When they would say, "I went to see such-and-such film of Fellini's last night," I often wanted to say, "Well, I went to see a sunrise this morning, up on top of the mountain." One is a far more moving experience than the other.

B.A.: We don't often think of that. We often feel uncomfortable with anything that simple and pure. We forget all about it. We go on in our daily rut, playing our daily role, and we don't ever release ourselves.

S.H.: Now we're indulging ourselves in a bit of philosophy. At the time I was involved with the sea, it, the sea, was our philosopher. It taught us. It was really quite simple. It was simple in the sense that we were certainly terrified, no matter how romantic our notions. But we knew precisely what we might do to take care of our vessel and ourselves. And we did it! We did it very well. Then we just lay back and watched it go.

That's what we should do with life but don't. There is a point where their isn't much more you can do. At that point life is like the ship, she will take care of you!

It takes a very special kind of person to be able to just detach himself and accept the terror for what it is—to be able to allow himself in his faith to be free.

B.A.: Right. The fears are often ones we create for ourselves—things that we have to surmount. When you talk about rugged individualism, the will and the courage to be different, is there also a degree of pain that it invariably causes? The notion that it hurts to be different, because you must sacrifice much. You know the image of the wanderer in literature, an image that recurs time and time again—men aboard freight trains, sailing ships. It's an image of heroism, an ideal that all men might like to strive for, but a stance that is increasingly difficult to attain.

S.H.: Yes, and it is a very tragic world, that of the wanderer. We have a book in the house in Wilton called *Riding the Rails*. I read it only recently. It's very poignant. It's about men who are desolate, and their desolation is caught by the sound of the freight train, the sound of the big train, the main line of life.

S.H.: The world of the so-called wanderer. You know, the distance from the wanderer to the hobo is minuscule . . . minuscule.

And, of course, as one gets older, one finds that more and more true. You try to have the best of both worlds. I've tried to have the best of both—my family, my wife; and I also want the road, too.

In a way it's a form of hell, a still form of hell. Because even when I get away—and I don't mean get away just in terms of physical space—I mean, when I hit the road, I usually think, "Well, fuck it. That's the end of the marriage, of that life. O.K. or not O.K., but that's the way it's got to be." In order for me to be free as a man I've got to go, go, go. And so I go.

But! After maybe a month, going by motorcycle through Italy or Spain—I don't know where the hell I'm going—suddenly one night I'm in a little hotel. I start to think about my wife and what I've left behind. And then I'm gone. I'm just plain fucking dead gone. And then I fight as hard to get back as I fought earlier to leave. It's a duality of the soul, an incredible phenomenon. It's what I'm trying to write about now.

Sterling Hayden is not alone. A lot of men, perhaps all men, feel this duality of the soul, a yearning born of the energy they feel as men, countered by a diametrically opposed energy telling them to settle down, to conform to the social norm. It is almost like the duality between an instinct to flee and the instinct to conform.

It is a particular part of the male's being as he reaches his late thirties, a time that Yale psychologist Joseph Levinson describes as the period of midlife transition.[1] The male begins to long for something different. Sensing that his dreams of earlier years are not to be fulfilled, or realizing that the goals of his younger days were false, the male reaches out to the unknown. He creates new dreams and idealizes them just as he did before. In doing so, he fails to recognize the danger and the pain that will be his companion, even as he makes his way on the outside.

9 Women in Revolt: A Conversation with Elizabeth Janeway

IF MEN were once complacent about their situation, they suddenly went reeling. Not from the effects of the male role, which certainly continued to take its physical and mental toll on men, but now from women.

A somewhat organized feminist movement has existed for some time in the United States, extending back to the Seneca Falls Conference in 1848, the formal beginning of the women's movement in America. Although women achieved many of their civil and political rights, by the 1960s the hierarchy of the sexes remained intact. Men knew where they stood in relation to women. Outside the kitchen and the nursery, it was still a man's world.

Then, with the publication of Betty Friedan's landmark book *The Feminine Mystique* in 1963, women began to agitate ever more forcefully for fundamental transformations in society. The women's movement harbored some extremists, but it also drew ordinary women who were tired of the drudgery of homemaking and parenting, tired of the menial status of jobs available to them outside the home, tired of unequal pay for the same work as men, tired of being passed over when promotions were handed around, tired of being second-class citizens, tired of being patronized by men.

The women's movement has had many faces, from Betty Friedan and the National Organization for Women (NOW), through numerous groups on the left, to SCUM, a one-woman "organization" that advocated doing away with men. Like many other movements, the women's movement is often plagued by internal conflicts that are more vehement and more basic than the disagreements with its opponents. Within the movement there are those who see capitalism and the oppression of the property-holding class as the prime enemy of women. For them, as Peter Filene writes, "sexual inequality . . . is a byproduct of general economic inequality"[1] that will only end with a socialist revolution. Proponents of this view think of Betty Friedan and other moderate feminists as little more than female Uncle Toms. Actually, the moderates are much like labor leaders of the 1930s. They concentrate on bread-and-butter issues, on equal job opportunity, equal pay for equal work, child-care centers on and off the job, abortion reform. They work through legal channels, with lawsuits, legislation, and constitutional revision, as in the attempt to have the states ratify the Equal Rights Amendment.

Whatever their precise position in the spectrum of the women's movement, whether they scream their message to the unwilling listeners or communicate it in a whisper, individual women have told men, "I will no longer tolerate being a broodmare for your children. I will no longer tolerate doing only household chores as though they were some sort of exciting involvement. I will no longer tolerate being little more than your ego-massager. I will not do these things anymore." With these words women began to tell men that it was time to share power, something men had never before considered as part of a woman's natural birthright. Men were confused. Many still are.

Because women still speak with multiple voices, I thought it best to examine the women's movement and its goals with someone who could provide a broad overview. I chose Elizabeth Janeway, a novelist, whose two brilliant nonfiction studies, *Man's World, Woman's Place* and *Between Myth and Morning: Women Awakening,* mark her as one of the most intelligent and perceptive analysts of the women's movement and the male world.

We spoke at length in her New York apartment. I first asked her to delineate what, perhaps seven years ago, were considered to be the goals of the women's movement, the various different levels to which it addressed itself, and comment in retrospect as to what degree she felt those goals have been fulfilled or unfulfilled.

E.J.: In my view the women's movement is fluid, still fluid, and will continue to be so. It has to be seen as a process, changing within itself all the time. It's very hard to separate goals from each other. For instance, we hear a lot of people say that they can see the women's economic complaint, that they are for equal wages. Well, you're never going to have equal wages, you will never be able to deal with the economic side of it, until you deal with the social side of it. Women are not going to be paid equally as long as the society tells them, "Before you leave for the office, be sure the house is running all right and somebody's looking after the kids." Now, assuming you want to live decently, the house has to run reasonably well, and someone has to do it. More important, somebody has to look after the kids! But these functions are now laid on women and women alone —the woman is the person who does all this. Until you get a more substantial dual role aspect into family life, with both men and women sharing responsibility, you're talking nonsense if you are talking about equal wages for working wives and therefore for all women.

And even dual roles are never going to take care of all the things that have to happen to and with families, because we need community support, we need community linkage, we need all manner of other things done for children growing up than simply those done by parents. Children need more adult linkages to the larger community than the small nuclear family can offer. So that's it—those are my views, and to try to isolate different goals to me is falsification and self-deception.

B.A.: What about the whole idea of consciousness raising? Hasn't it been achieved, to a large degree?

E.J.: [laughing loudly] No, it hasn't. Again, it's a continuing process. It's very, very important. Women underestimate themselves, their talents and their reach. Above all, they still assume that men are more important than they are. They trivialize their goals and their aims, and because they think of themselves as less capable than men, they fall back into thinking that the way to get things done is to charm or manipulate a capable somebody—that is, a man. You cannot expect us to quit using this technique until we have had a lot more practice in doing things for ourselves, a lot more opportunity to control our own lives and to make our own decisions. Some of these will be wrong decisions, no doubt.

Well-meaning and helpful male allies worry about that. But all of us have to expect that wrong decisions are going to be made by women for a while. Decision making is a necessary part of the learning process for women, as it is for blacks. It is one way to find not only an individual identity, but a group identity. This has certainly begun. But this is going to be a much longer process than any magic seven years.

B.A.: I recall that Vivian Gornick, an author and a feminist, once said that the truly significant thing about feminism and about consciousness raising per se was that it was a new way for women to look at the world—to look at reality and to see themselves. This, to men, is a tremendous change.

E.J.: I want to tell you something else: It's a new way for *men* to look at the world. The new view is not just something that applies to women. There are a myriad of things women know about the world but have not yet put together into a structured and cohesive body of knowledge. Women are discovering what they know and beginning to articulate thoughts and putting them into behavior and action. But this is important for humanity, not just for women.

You see, a great many human assets got labeled "feminine virtue" and pushed off into the wilderness, out of the mainstream. It was as if they were in a repository, safe but out of the way. Men didn't have to worry about them for a while. Patience, humility, the ability to listen, a sense of process which allows for continuity and change, too—these are all good things. And consensus and collaboration are, I think, better ways of getting on than confrontation. These are human capabilities and techniques for social survival that are important to men as well as women. But we think of these as being feminine. They're not—they're universal, valuable for all.

B.A.: Do you think that more and more women are becoming nervous about the idea of eventual liberation? Is that what seems to be happening now with a lot of women who are opposed to the ERA?

E.J.: Oh, nuts. The people who are opposed to ERA are being used by strong networks of right-wing political groups, reactionary church groups like the Mormons and the right wing of the Catholic church. They have been subjected to a great deal of misleading misinformation.

B.A.: Such as? Please elaborate a little further. What, in your opinion, do women like Phyllis Schlafly represent today?

E.J.: There is no sense in trying to discuss Phyllis Schlafly's ideas on an intellectual level. I know people who have been with Phyllis Schlafly—she has backed down publicly, even on television—and then they have heard her make the same statement over again, on another occasion.

But let's talk about it seriously. What really makes people nervous about change is their personal commitment to the status quo—that's very understandable. If change comes along and you don't have a hand in initiating it, you're afraid, you're bewildered. This kind of confusion is true for men as regards changes in women's consciousness and behavior today—they don't know what's going on, they don't know how to control it because they don't know what to expect. Now, they could find out. Unfortunately, the last thing they seem to want is to listen to people who will try to tell them what's going on, something the women's movement has been interested in doing for some time. Women should try to explain themselves—but by the same token, men should listen—listen without the prejudgment which contributes to their own confusion.

What is important about the Equal Rights Amendment is that it says discrimination because of sex is against the law, the basic law of the land. It is a criminal offense. Therefore the burden of proof does not fall on the complainant. When the complainant says, "You are discriminating, it's against the law," and can offer reasonable grounds for the complaint, the government will have to take it on—as with any other instance of lawbreaking.

We do have some antidiscrimination laws now, but the funding to make them work has been inadequate, and also they are special, not universal. There is a big backlog of cases, and where the government does not act, the burden of proof falls on the complainant. There's been a backup of cases at the Equal Employment Opportunities Commission. Theoretically they should take the initiative, but they've been starved for money and staff. Put ERA through, and the whole legal arm of the government is on the side of equality and against sexist discrimination as it is against racist and religious discrimination. That is what ERA is all about.

B.A.: There is a tendency in American society for the forces of commerce and the media to come in and take hold of a particular phenomenon and try to market it. As soon as something becomes popular, someone out there tries to make it commercial. Do you think this has happened to the women's movement.

E.J.: Not particularly, although I don't think it matters if it does. The women's movement is much too big to have anything like that bother it.

The women's movement is a response to changed economic and social reality, not to propaganda from anyone. Thirty years ago there were six million working wives and thirty million working husbands. Right at the moment there are thirty million working wives and thirty-eight million working husbands—plus, of course, a lot of unmarried people; obviously this is not the total labor force.

That points up a major change; a change in quality, not in just degree. Women have always worked, but in the past they mostly worked at home. A great deal of work of productive value was done in the home. Some of it was for the family's own use. A hundred and fifty years ago there were clothes to be made, all the food was prepared from scratch—all the things that we send out for now originated in the home then. Some of the goods made at home were sold in the market, too, for cash. The family farm is a typical example, Well, this doesn't happen now.

Today's women make the same kind of economic contribution by getting a job in a factory, a commercial establishment, an office, a department store, or in a service trade. Economically, the motive is the same. What's changed is not the *fact* that women work, but the place—outside the home. This shift in the way people live is the fundamental reason behind the women's movement.

The women's movement is a response to changes in social and economic reality. These are things that have already taken place. A revolution has happened, you see. We are trying to catch up with it.

B.A.: You don't see the women's movement as being an initiator?

E.J.: Of course. The women's movement is an initiator of realistic responses to these changes, of creative, innovative responses.

As our talk continued, we turned to the doctrinal positions taken by some women on lesbianism and separation from male society—two areas that worry men. The press and hostile critics often attributed a great degree of lesbianism to the women's movement, and, indeed, the writing of women's luminaries Kate Millett and Jill Johnston made the charge seem plausible. Actually, the women's movement accepts lesbianism as part of the range of female experience, as part of the right of each woman to choose the sexual experience of her preference. Other women, not all lesbians, argue that women must get away from men and the male world, develop their own consciousness, de-

SUZANNE O'MALLEY

Dan Greenburg
"There is always something very scary about intimacy."

Ashley Montagu
"The average male is brainwashed. He cannot love. He has lost his emotions."

MARTY TORGOFF

Art Buchwald
"It didn't bother me because, you know, if Hemingway says you are a little shit, at least he remembers who you were."

MARTY TORGOFF

Alvin Toffler

"I would hate to see the masculine crisis laid at the door of the women's movement. That's a misunderstanding of it . . . a trivialization of it."

MARTY TORGOFF

James Whitmore
"There is a backlash already against sexual freedom."

CLAUDIA CAPOS

MARTY TORGOFF

Gael Greene
"The idea that power and success is very sexy and that a woman wants these is just so old-fashioned."

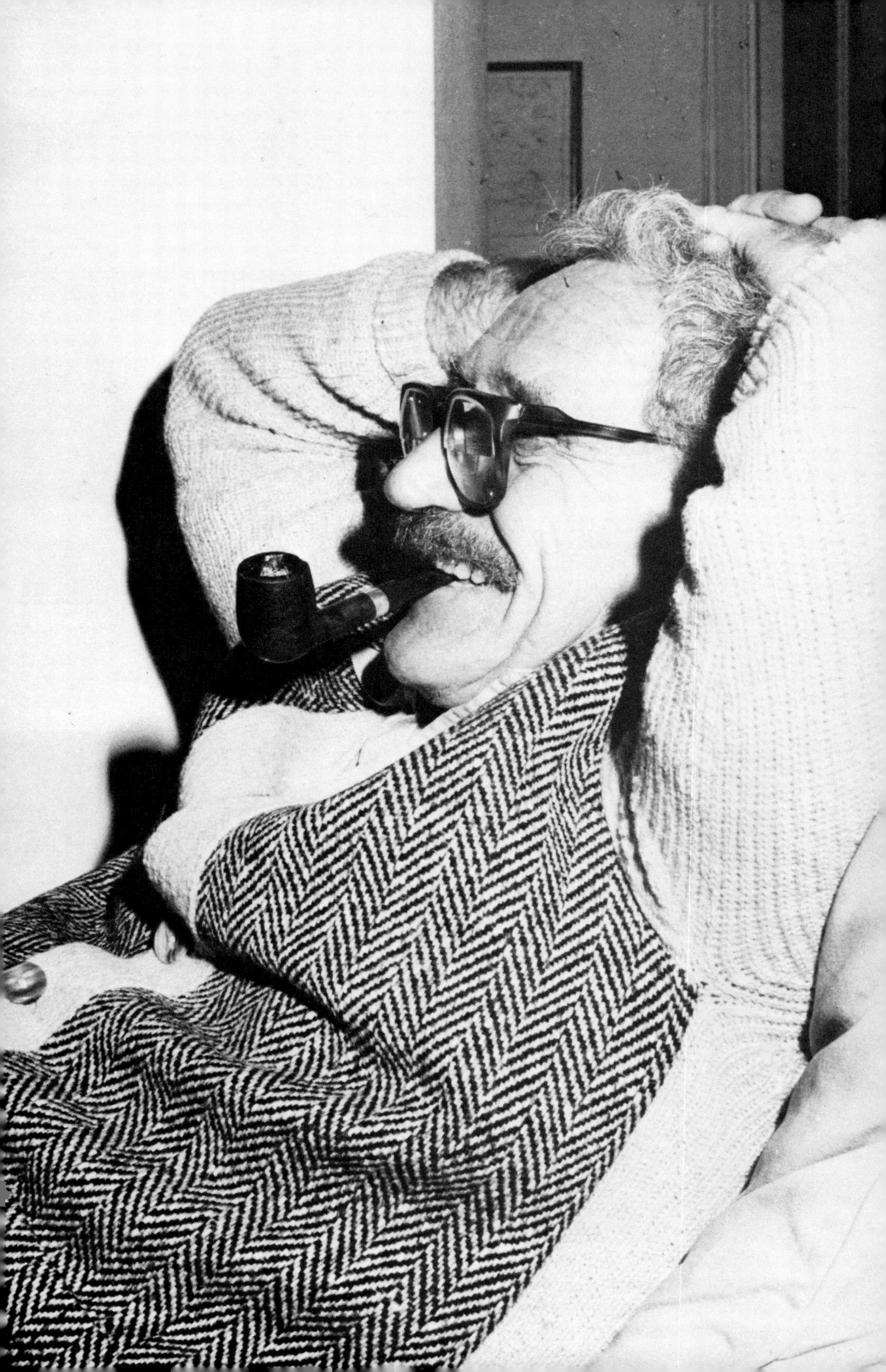

Tom Tryon MARTY TORGOFF

"A sensitive man? . . . I mean a guy who's not so afraid of his own masculinity that he has to walk around so he can hear his balls clanging all the time."

Albert Ellis MARTY TORGOFF

"The male is imperiously driven toward sex."

ARMEN KACHATURIAN

Helen Gurley Brown
"Women no longer demand that a man be steely, tough, and invincible."

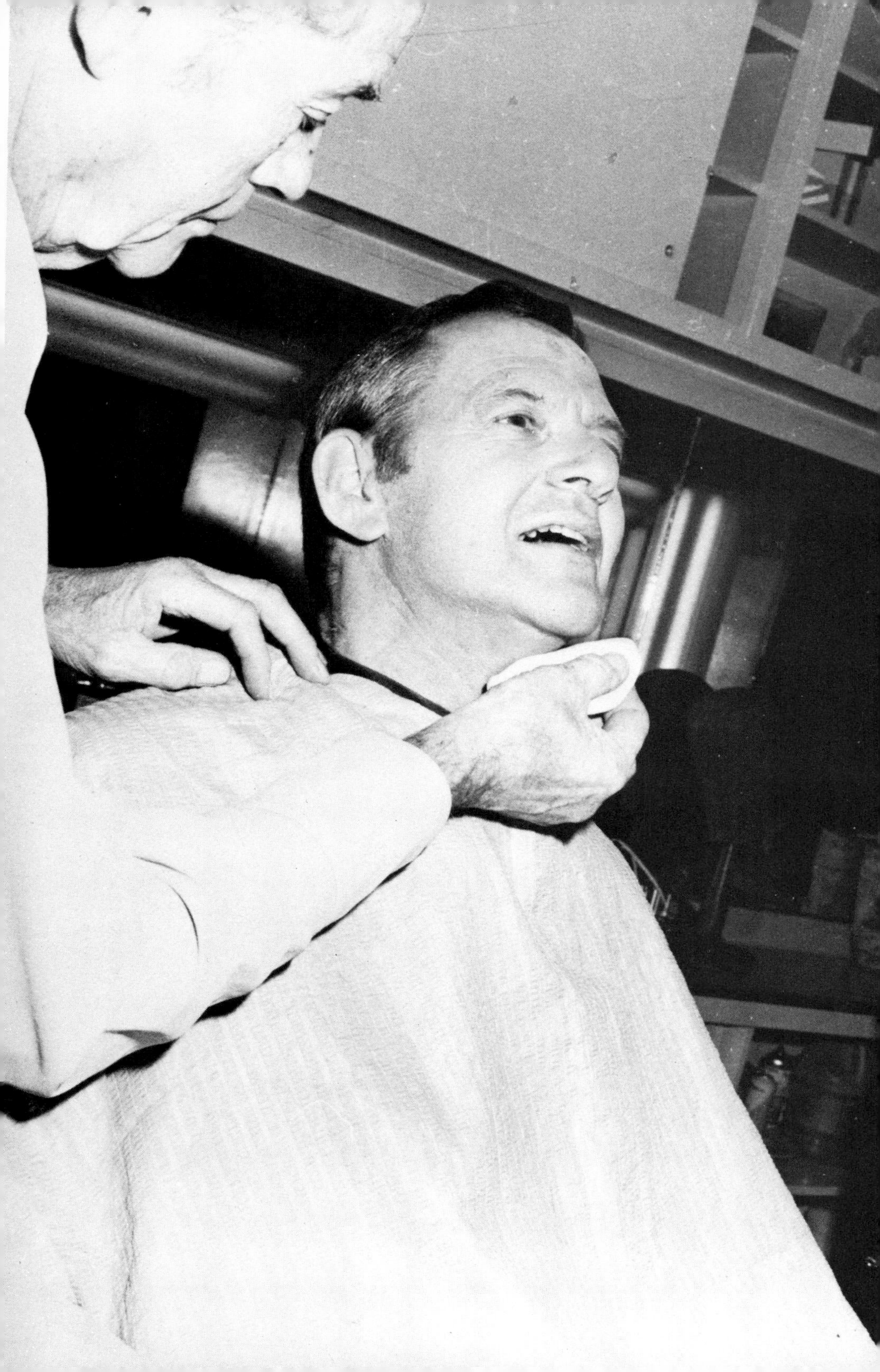

MARTY TORGOFF

MARTY TORGOFF

Anthony Pietropinto
"Sex for the male is penis-centered."

Tony Randall
"Yes, money is God. Everybody absolutely worships it together without one dissenting note. And the man who has money is the most virile, because he controls power."

Bob Guccione
"Why do men want success in sports and in their careers? Why do they want big cars and big houses? To attract women!"

MARTY TORGOFF

Gore Vidal
"What is the male role? Well, it's knocking people down, behaving like Norman Mailer occasionally does at parties. It's an impossible role."

MARTY TORGOFF

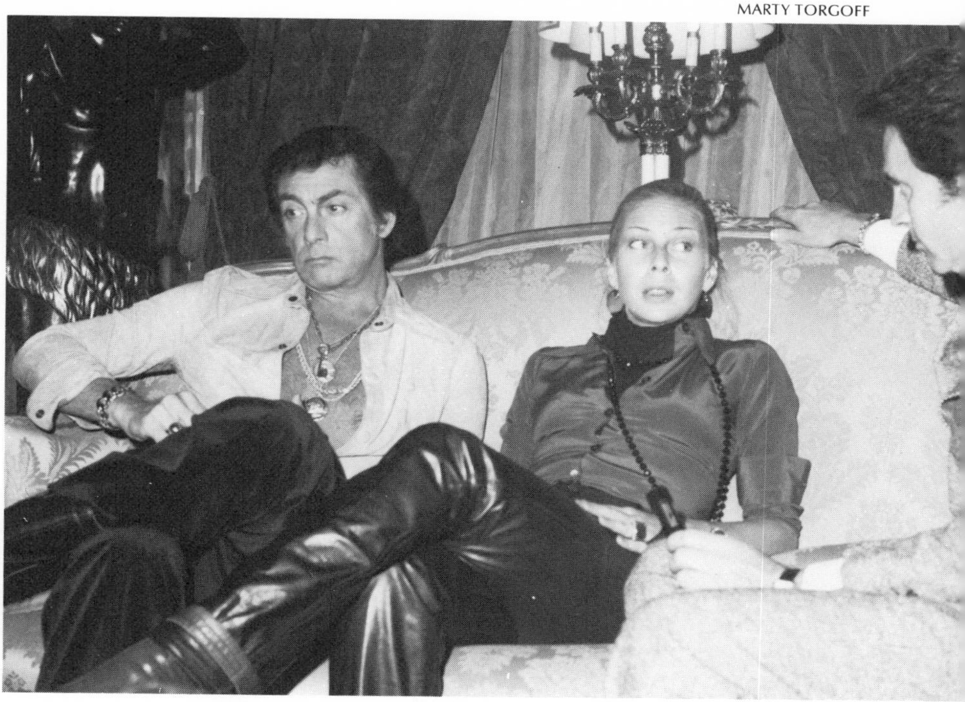

Bruce Jenner
"Ever since I was very young I always controlled my emotions tremendously."

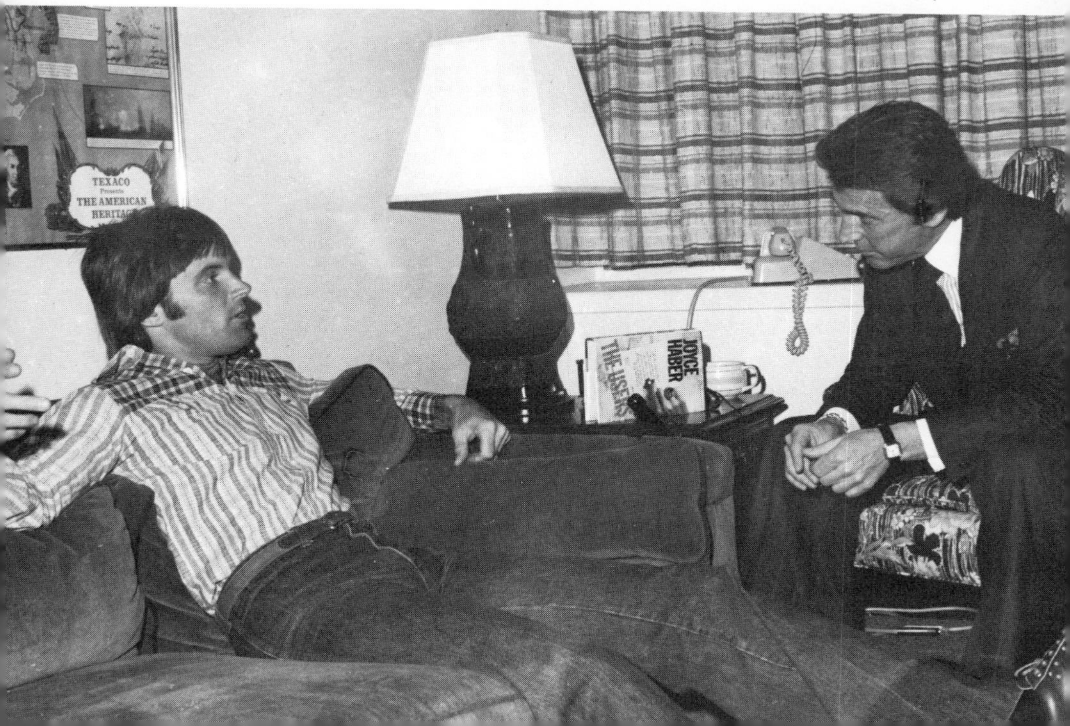

MARTY TORGOFF

Sterling Hayden
"Most men die spiritually in their early twenties. I'm at war with myself. All men are."

Elizabeth Janeway
"Women should try to explain themselves. Men should listen without the prejudgment that contributes to their own confusion."

Joseph Heller
"Many men will occasionally have an impulse that might be called homosexual."

MARTY TORGOFF

Warren Farrell
"Androgyny is the encouragement of every human being to be as individual as a snowflake."

MARTY TORGOFF

Michael Korda
"All life is role-playing."

MARTY TORGOFF

MARTY TORGOFF

George Plimpton
"You don't learn how to lose, you learn how to win. And you are supposed to win."

fine themselves as female humans. These women attack marriage and the traditional family as parts of a male-dominated world that must be resisted. Elizabeth Janeway, however, dismisses concern about this development.

E.J.: Well, the blacks said that about the whites, about "orthodox" social structures. Orthodox for whom? Certainly, some radical feminists have said that marriage as it has been defined by patriarchal society is wrong for women. Any movement can have a radical element around its fringe—indeed, it needs a radical element. There are always people who go to the edge, to try out new ideas—to see how far they will go, to test new hypotheses. There is a reason, one that has nothing at all to do with lesbianism, behind the effort of women to come together in sisterhood. It doesn't center on sex. Often sex comes in from the outside. What is primary, I think, is the idea of a truly equal relationship, a relationship free of the formal, built-in social inequity constant to most male-female attitudes in our society. Just as an ideal, that's exciting. Now, I don't believe in utopias—but intimacy that is equal, without fear or shame, signifies freedom and joy. And our orthodox sexual stereotypes don't make such equality easy between the sexes.

Philosophically, intimacy without fear, between equals, can imply same-sex affection for those who have suffered from macho domination. This sort of revolt against sexual stereotypes, I believe, accounts for some of the interest in and the exploration of ideas about lesbianism.

B.A.: What about the factionalism that seems to have risen within the women's movement over the past couple of years?

E.J.: How about the factionalism within any group? Political revolutionaries have disagreed violently in the past, religious movements have never been free from heretical challenges, and how about all those brilliant psychologists, those analysts, and their violent debates? Marxists argue with Marxists and Freudians with neo-Freudians, to say nothing of the followers of Jung. Any new movement is full of bright people who are excited about their ideas. You are bound to get some factionalism. I don't think it's particularly important, especially in a movement as broad and diverse as that of women, where people have differing priorities. It's surely much, much better than the kind of thinking that says there is only one right way to do things—one right way to do anything.

B.A.: I wonder if that's not attributable to the root of the women's movement itself. When you look back to the early sixties, you see people like Betty Friedan and yourself, both interested in raising very pragmatic aspects and issues showing genuine concern for the situation of women in society and culture and how they see themselves.

E.J.: I don't know what's purely pragmatic about that. How women see themselves is important in practical terms and theory. The two things work together. I'm thinking rather philosophically right now. I'm writing a book about power, a process of interaction among human beings, and what's wrong with our usual definitions of it. The experience of women is very important here, for women represent to me the central, the oldest, largest category of the weak. We know a lot about how it is to live as the governed class, what the social contact comes down to versus what it ought to be. I think the governed can exercise their influence. I think they do in fact have power; and part of the vision of feminism is our growing understanding of what that means both in fact and in theory. It's *also* wisdom that is of great importance for men.

B.A.: Men have been trying to classify women in the movement. For the last ten years, we were trying to get at the reasons why this should *not* be done.

E.J.: Well, the first thing to say to yourself is "Let's try to listen to women instead of making up our minds ahead of time."

B.A.: When you assume prerogatives, some responsibility must go with it. Some men feel that a lot of women want all the benefits but don't want to assume the responsibility. They want to eat their cake and have it, too. Do you think this is the case?

E.J.: No, I don't. I must say, I think women are just hellish burden-bearers. They go out and take on everything. I don't think men are right about that. I've traveled the country. I've just come back from a women's studies conference in Columbia, Missouri. The woman who arranged it teaches at the University of Missouri, but she's also married to a farmer. She lives sixty miles away and chooses to commute every day to the university, to her job. She has children, too, ages twelve and fifteen. She doesn't look as if she had children that old. She's perfectly charming. She seems to me typical of today's active women—running a women's studies program, off to the women's conference in Houston, lobbying for ERA, along with family, home, job. She does two or three different things, all the time. Naturally, she was a little weary when we met because it was the first conference she's run, organizing a conference on top of everything else. I think women are just bears for responsibility.

Now, there are women who have problems with the public presentation of themselves. There are women who don't really like to be seen out there competing . . . exposed. That's hard. There are moral commitments that say it's better that we do things as a group, together. That's also practically true. Women do better if they come on as a group, because any of those who aren't seen publicly as powerful can best show the clout they do have if they stand together.

You're never going to be perceived as anything other than a woman, unimportant in the old historical context, if you don't have group strength. Getting ahead alone is not enough. You're still abnormal. The men you work with are not going to think of an able woman as their brilliant young executive. They are going to think of her as their brilliant young *woman* executive. Exactly the same way they think of someone as their brilliant young *black* executive. Whether she likes it or not, a woman is perceived as part of a group. Consequently, there is an extra effort for such a person in taking on a public role. Some women just don't have the time or the energy to do that because of the extra social demands laid on them still, the ones we talked about first —the need to be sure the house is running and the children are looked after—the need, for instance, if you have a demanding husband and young children, to be sure you can quit at five and get home to do *that* job, the one you aren't paid for. You can't take on a top job and quit at five, at least not until you spread things around a little bit more, share responsibilities at home. Unless you have really good child care you can trust, where you work, for instance. Until these social needs are met, what is a woman to do? She's going to have to balance one thing against another. But I don't call that not taking on responsibility—it's just that some of women's responsibility is not taken on, not voluntarily. It's laid on them.

B.A.: During one of my probes a Frommian psychiatrist used this facetious example: She mentioned that she had a lot of women come in and say that they had problems. They would say, "I want to be free, and I want all this freedom now; I want to be equal to my husband—I don't want to be competitive with him, but I want to be co-equal." The response of this psychotherapist was very simple. She said, "Look, are you willing to share all of the responsibilities of your husband?" The answer usually was no. They didn't want to have to make the car payment and worry about the house payment and the insurance.

E.J.: Now we come right back to square one. If your expectation of income is sixty percent of your husband's—and that's the average wage differential between men and women—no wonder you don't want to share the car payments. If we had equal wages I would agree with that analyst. But we don't. So now we're coming around from the social to the economic and seeing how they become a vicious circle. Do you see? Now, in my case, as a freelance writer and lecturer I have made more than my husband does in a year—not often, but from time to time. Well, we've always put everything together, and we share it, and neither of us worries about it particularly. But if I was on a fixed salary, if I knew that no matter what I did I couldn't make more than fifty-seven percent of what he makes, even working flat out, what would I do? I would say, "Please, I'll pay my percentage share. Pro rata share. But for equal sharing, I want an equal share from society first."

B.A.: Fair enough. Changing the subject, what kind of psychological support do people need to develop? You have talked and written about the word *gradient.* It seems to be an outlook, an attitude that needs to be developed. Is this development dependent, though, on communication between men and women?

E.J.: It is dependent, I guess, on the social surroundings, on what's acceptable, or thought to be acceptable. There is a network of relationships, and we judge any relationship by the general ones around—the general ones we learned when we were young. Whatever happens to us we always test against what's in our heads already.

I don't know what I would say beyond that, but I think the support for change comes from finding that other people feel the same way. You find you've shared the same experiences with someone. You may very well have responded to them in the same way; and so you understand each other. This seems to me very true of women today. It's the ground for consciousness raising, sure, but I think it's true not only of women who think of themselves as being feminists. Women usually have shared quite a lot of experience.

I remember being on the Phil Donohue show in Chicago after my last book came out in the fall of 1974. Naturally all of television likes confrontations, so two busloads of Catholic women from Milwaukee were brought down to form the audience for the show. I'm sure the producers expected a confrontation.

We ended up sitting and talking about things working women were apt to run into, why they weren't paid equally, or didn't have equal chances for promotion. There were innumerable stories from these women about the treatment their daughters experienced in their work environment. As it turned out, we were on the same wavelength. Not everywhere, of course. I suppose if anybody had raised the matter of abortion, we might have disagreed—though I'm not at all sure that everybody there would have taken a hard position against the right of a woman to decide on an abortion if she felt she needed one. In general, I find there are a lot of areas of agreement among women.

B.A.: A lot of the real problems of women today seem to be contingent upon jobs, equal pay, and a lot of other socioeconomic questions. Is it reasonable to assume that women will have the time to realize their total potential? Or anyone for that matter?

E.J.: Yes, indeed—who does? I'd settle for simply the time to do both what I want to do and what I'm expected to do. Believe me, what you're expected to do usually gets skimped on because of *other* things you're expected to do. There is very little free-wheeling fantasy of the sort that says, "Oh, let me go out and be Isadora Duncan or someone, while I also hold a top-level job of meaningful work where I express myself." Women are torn by many, many demands on them and their time and energy, and few of these demands are narcissistic, believe me.

B.A.: Is it reasonable to assume that in a time of economic uncertainty women will have more difficulty than they do now in pursuing their goals?

E.J.: It's conceivable as long as the economic difficulties are small. On the other hand, if the economic difficulties become large, women will forge ahead because all of society will suffer, and old formulas will break down.

Robert Jay Lifton has an interesting study of women in China during the period of the Chinese revolution. Things went to hell in a hand basket, according to the old standards. Who held things together? The women held things together. Just got up there and did it. We have an awful lot of unused talent and energy among women. If things get tough enough that energy will be used.

No matter what the extent of gains for women, there will surely be costs for men if the bread-and-butter philosophy of the bulk of the women's movement is successful. If women continue to have success in the marketplace, men are going to feel the squeeze. And it will hurt. As Betty Friedan puts it, "Some men are going to have to be defeated or move over as women begin in larger numbers to compete for jobs or political offices that men now hold. But if we avoid female chauvinism . . . men may not find it any worse to be defeated by a woman than by a man."[2]

But there is the rub. Defeat! Competition! The very values that are so destructive to men. Some have seen this as a danger to women. Ashley Montagu told me, "The great mistake that many women make is to become like men. They think that equality means becoming like the enemy. I continually try to point out to women that when women claim equality with men, they are taking a step downward, if not backward. And this is, of course, a great error."

Of course, women must continue to seek liberation. And men must applaud and give full support to their effort. But if the cost is not to be too great, women must seek genuine liberation and not co-option into a pernicious system that will devour them just as it has always devoured us.

10
Men in the Wake of the Storm

THE WOMEN'S movement left many men confused and often scared. These were average men, the ones who have to struggle to keep everything together. Their jobs. Their families. Their house payments. Their car payments. Their heads. Ultimately, themselves. Some were resentful and angry about women's incursions into formerly male preserves. They were frustrated and disturbed as women rejected the roles and the values that had for so long defined woman's place in society. Many men felt they could no longer count on women to be what they were supposed to be—principally wives and mothers. Men felt they had a right to expect total and unquestioning care from women. The woman was expected to be a combination social director, social secretary, bookkeeper, housekeeper, child raiser, wife, and mistress. Already threatened from several sides, these men sensed in the women's movement an additional danger, one that seemed to be the greatest danger of all—the reversal of roles.

Many men, even those one would think most committed to political and social change, reacted with epithets when women sought a larger role. Cries of "She just needs a good screw" and "She's just a castrating female" echoed through the halls of leftist gatherings in the late 1960s. As Peter G. Filene notes, "When pushed, most male radicals revealed themselves to be usual men, defending sexual privileges against their female comrades as adamantly as the 'power elite' defended its economic and racial privileges against the New Left."[1] On the streets and in the offices things were no better. There, too, women had to endure the taunts of disgruntled men who charged that the woman who simply couldn't get a man was a "dyke," a dissatisfied neurotic, a castrating bitch. These men were angry and confused, unable to explain what was taking place, what was going on around them. So they reacted with name calling, much as a child might.

Other men were depressed by their confusion and dismay. They found it difficult to adjust to an "uppity" wife who questioned her role, to women who were saying to them for the first time, "I have ability, I have intelligence, and I'm going to do something with it!"

At their most paranoid, men feared that women didn't merely want to be equal; they wanted to dominate men. Males published books that described anti-utopias where men served in the harems of female sultans. Doomsayers like George Gilder wrote about "sexual suicide." Male prerogatives were declining, the male world was threatened. Nothing but disaster could result.

Gilder in fact charged that most of the social strains and disruptions of society in the United States could be traced to "the steady erosion of the key conditions of male socialization,"[2] a process exacerbated by the women's movement.

Gilder viewed this as a long-term trend, coincident with feminism in all its historical guises. He charged:

> From the hospital, where the baby is abruptly taken from the mother; to early childhood, where he may be consigned to public care; to the home, where the father is frequently absent or ineffectual; to the school, where the boy is managed by female teachers and excelled by girls; possibly to college, where once again his training is scarcely differentiated by sex; to a job that, particularly at vital entry positions, is often sexually indistinct and that may not even be better paid than comparable female employment—through all these stages of development the boy's innately amorphous and insecure sexuality may be further subverted and confused.

Now, in its most recent guise, the women's movement takes his job and his money and gives him in return what is for Gilder a dubious benefit, "the right to cry."[3]

Gilder has serious, if misguided, fears. Other men were only concerned about the competition from women. This was especially true among men who were most unsure of themselves or, in business, younger men who, according to Marc Feigen Fasteau, were "most concerned about proving their masculine worth. Younger men who haven't yet made it are more threatened by having female colleagues and competitors."[4]

Nevertheless, even in business there was no single response. Michael Korda has observed several responses among men. There are some men whose "residual guilt" at the knowledge they remain prejudiced against women has led them to give way before the female onslaught. According to Korda, these men "now find it impossible" to say they remain prejudiced, and they "feel guilty about it." There are still others who "are sufficiently doubtful about their own masculinity in one way or another as to be easily overwrought by a woman." Korda finds that there are also a great number of men—particularly in business and in the various news media—who are "quite honestly afraid of women." Finally, and perhaps most unexpected, he identifies some men, the most extreme male chauvinists, who get along fine with the new woman in business because they "couldn't give a shit. Once they have accepted the fact that women are going to be executives, fine: the woman is just another rival."

Because of these attitudes, women have made important gains in some areas. In publishing, Korda's field, all the copy editors were once women earning $150 a week, and all the editors were men, with salaries of $15,000 a year and up. Now, according to Korda, "in publishing the women have reached a point where they are close to equality with men, and in some fields they have been put ahead."

Women might have found men more congenial in recent years had it not been for the sluggish economy. Korda thinks that the failure of businesses to expand as expected had put women "somewhere between five and ten years behind where they ought to have been in terms of their progress to positions of responsibility and power. If it were a booming economy I think you would see enormous social changes—changes in attitudes between men and women. As it is, everything is fairly static."

Most commonly, though, men give up the semblance of advance while they retain the substance of power. Many men fight a rearguard action, and will do so as long as they can. Increasingly this becomes impossible as, for one thing, women are simply too smart to accept form without substance. Women want responsibility and, Korda says, "the truth is that women sometimes even take on too *much* responsibility."

As this suggests, men often don't understand women, and many make no real attempt to try. Too often they are satisfied trying to classify and categorize elements of the women's movement—simple responses from which nothing good can be gained. I asked Elizabeth Janeway about this, about the reasons why men should give up their attempts at classification.

E.J.: Well, the first thing to say to yourself is "Let's try to listen to women instead of making up our minds ahead of time." Men have their own preconceptions, their own "idea grid," so to speak, which they put down on top of the picture and draw lines along. Listen for a while. The patterns that women's lives and women's thoughts and women's emotions make are innate to their experience. Women are looking for connections, but they probably will not be exactly the connections men would expect to find.

B.A.: Does it seem to you that men are beginning to listen more? Has the situation changed?

E.J.: Quite a lot, yes. But it varies. I do know that men who have thought deeply about the women's movement and lived with change for a while understand what women are saying, and they seem to be so much happier—more hopeful and more clued in to life than the others.

B.A.: What in your estimation are some of the things men can do in terms of how they see themselves that will enable them, perhaps, to listen to women even better?

E.J.: I don't know if I can answer that. The answer to that seems to be a job for you. I do think that you should recognize that it might be helpful. You have to be motivated to want to do it. One thing, though: I went out to Missouri when I flew out for the Columbia conference and I met a man who is head of the Kansas City office of a large company. He told me they were having trouble with the women who worked there. They could get bright women to come in at the entry level, but the women kept quitting. Management was puzzled. They couldn't find out why. Well, how could I tell that man that he wasn't asking the right question? I did try to tell him, though.

I said it was because he didn't know how to ask. "But they all get married and go and have babies," he said. I replied, "Well, perhaps maternity leave would be a good idea." He didn't think so. Everything I suggested met with a negative response from him. I do think I finally persuaded him to write to the women who had quit within the last five years and say, "Since you are not here now, you really don't have to lie," or words to that effect. "Maybe you can tell us what would persuade you to come back, just blue-sky it along and see—think of what it is that might get you back here." It was hard work to make that man understand—not that he was asking the wrong questions, but that he wasn't asking any real questions at all.

He wasn't going to get an answer unless he came to grips with the fact that he really didn't want the answer. He thought he wanted the answer. He thought he wanted women working there. But he was in no way going to consider making any effort. He wasn't even going to see that changes were needed. For example, I said, "Was there any possibility of flex-time?" 'Oh, no. Not in this business!" he said. I'm not so sure. I'm not in his business. I don't know. But to *bang!* shut the door, shoot it down like that—it showed me where his head was.

And I do think the problem is in the male brain. We have to motivate men to want to take the trouble to think, to realize, perhaps, that they are asking the wrong questions. To admit that their premises are mistaken. Perhaps they would then find out what other premises might be if their ears opened up and they listened more. Because good will is not enough. Good will helps you spout panaceas like "Sure, we want to go on with affirmative action." But it's tokenism! It's asking questions but not really wanting to. Not seeing it as being useful to you, not seeing it as being productive, not being able to imagine that you might get something out of it. Really, that's the bottom line.

I can't tell you how strongly women believe that this change in male-female relationships is not only going to benefit women. I can't tell you how universal is the feeling that the women's revolution—if you want to call it that, or the end of the movement, if it ever ends—is going to refresh humanity. All of the things that we have, that we think are good, that we know are good for you, and for all of us—those things that have never been developed . . . simply to begin to bring them back or help establish a better way for people to live together . . . to recapture things that have been lost—all of this can come from the women's movement. And this is very, very important. It is the kind of consciousness raising that is awfully hard to go through. The men who have gone through it, who have done it, are so far ahead.

Actually the picture is not so bleak, although there still are disquieting signs that the old attitudes are firmly entrenched among teenagers. Among young adults, however, Anthony Pietropinto finds that "most men admire the new woman and are enthusiastic about the changes she has undergone. About two out of three men surveyed for *Beyond the Male Myth* expressed positive views and felt the modern woman had changed for the better." A less scientifically structured, mail-in survey in *Redbook* magazine confirmed this. Surprisingly, seven out of ten men report they have been relatively unaffected by the women's movement.

One unscientific observer, Art Buchwald, told me much the same thing.

B.A.: Art, what were your initial impressions of women's liberation when the whole furor started in the 1960s?

A.B.: It didn't bother me.

B.A.: It didn't? You didn't feel threatened by that at all?

A.B.: Hell, no!

B.A.: Why do you think so many men did feel threatened?

A.B.: I don't think they did that much, you know. I think that anytime you try to change people's habits, or change their thinking, you shake them up. And I think the feminist movement shook up the women more than it did the men.

B.A.: In what way?

A.B.: Well, everybody was role-playing. The man had a certain role, the woman had a certain role, and when you are a little kid, they tell you you're a boy or you're a girl, these are the roles you play as you grow up. Suddenly, someone tells you when you're grown up that this isn't the role you should be playing. It shook up the women in that they didn't know what role they should play.

B.A.: Don't you think that a lot of men felt that all their male prerogatives were going to be taken away?

A.B.: Well, I can only speak for myself . . . but I tend to see the humor in everything, so it is different for me. Nonetheless, I really don't think you can generalize that men felt and still feel threatened by women. They just didn't know where this thing was going—nobody knows where it is going—and there was so much going on during the women's liberation thing. The war was on. The kids were in the streets. The women's movement was part of other movements. I think that most white men worried far more about blacks than about women in the 1960s.

B.A.: I would agree with that. But did you see any humor in the women's liberation situation?

A.B.: No. Every time I write a piece—and it is usually pro-women's liberation—I get all these letters from women in the movement who claim that I'm making fun of them or I don't understand their movement. You know, the hard-liners in women's liberation have no humor either.

Tony Randall was another man who claimed to have been largely unaffected by the movement. He puts it this way: "This whole women's liberation movement, which has affected so many men so much, has never taken place in my world. Nothing has changed since I was a teenager, because I have always lived in a world of liberated women. From the time I got into show business it has been dominated by women. If it is not dominated by them now, it was then; and it will be again.

"The greatest stars were women, and they ruled the roost. Certainly no liberating action was required for the actresses of my time. I have always worked for women, women stars, women up there, women producers. When I was very young I started working for women. So this liberation took place long ago in the world of the theater. It has always been so—or at least so since I have been on earth."

Bruce Jenner has more of a firsthand view. He needed support while training for his chance at an Olympic gold medal, and he got it. His wife, Christie, fulfilled a traditional female role. But he did not expect it to continue, nor did he want it to. He puts it this way:

"I would feel terrible if somebody kept telling me I couldn't develop myself as a person, that I couldn't do what I wanted with my life, that I had to live totally for someone else. I would go bananas if someone told me to stay home and wash the dishes every day. A woman has a lot of things she wants to do. She is a human being, too. She has potential. She may not know exactly what it is she wants, just as many men don't always know. So she needs support and encouragement and opportunity.

"I try to encourage my wife to go out and do things. I think she has so many things going for her. She has so many things she could do, and do well, if she decided to pursue them."

"You don't need financial help. Does that bother her?" I asked.

"I don't think so. She works because she wants to get fulfillment out of it. She trys things she really enjoys. That is why she is on a committee that helps with rape cases. She is learning to counsel the victims. She is interested in real estate. Just now she is in the process of buying an old home. She plans to work with a carpenter, fix it up, and sell it. We just bought a summer home in Lake Tahoe, and she is working on that. She has other things going, too. Probably the biggest is the corporation we formed after the Olympic Games. She runs it, does all the work. She likes it, and it is a tough job. But she is good with tough jobs.

"People often expect that she does nothing but sit around and enjoy life. Sure, she doesn't have a formal job, but she works harder than anyone else I know. She runs the multimillion-dollar corporation. She runs the whole thing by herself. The corporation pays her for it. That plus her real estate. She has many jobs, not just one formal job."

Accepting new roles for women has meant that men like Bruce Jenner have had to rid themselves of many of our culture's myths. These are men who have fulfilled Ashley Montagu's prophecy of men who would "come to see their relationship to women as a partnership conferring mutual benefits as well as benefits upon all who come within the orbit of their influence."[5] These are men who do not fear that women will be turned into men. "On the contrary," Montagu says, "each of the sexes will for the first time function as completely as it has hitherto functioned incompletely, . . . to realize itself according to its own nature and not according to the nature that has been forced upon it."

These are the men who see great gains for themselves. Not in the traditional sense of a zero-sum game with a loser for every winner, but as part of a process that means liberation for all. These are men who see the expansion of the definition of female roles as leading to an expansion for men. They see that if women are freer, men will be freer, too. As Gael Greene told me, "If men can be silly and if men can be wrong, and if men can cry and be sentimental and frivolous, and all the things that women have always been able to be without even thinking about it, it is a great liberation." A liberation for both sexes.

11
Sex in the Twentieth Century

MAKE NO mistake about it. We are in the midst of a sexual revolution.

Some deny this. Bob Guccione, publisher of the slick men's magazine *Penthouse,* thinks the talk of a sexual revolution is overdone. He says: "One talks about the sexual revolution having taken place in recent years. I would like to say I have a very firm attitude, very firm beliefs about this. I don't think there ever was a sexual revolution. Many women are not doing anything today that they didn't do ten years ago, a hundred years ago, ten thousand years ago, a million years ago. We are doing exactly the same thing. Orgies have always existed; wife swapping has always existed. All of the things we think of as being chic sidelines to sex play, as being inventions of today or coming into fruitful practice today, are not new at all. What has happened is not a sexual revolution so much as a revolution in communications.

"This is something for which the media is directly responsible, because in recent years it has become chic to talk about what you do. Women are now prepared to talk about masturbation. They will talk with great zeal about how they masturbate, how often they masturbate, and what they get out of it. This was unheard of a few years ago. A few years ago, it was unthinkable that women should get together in an office and talk about some guy that they were screwing. It used to be guys getting together and saying, 'You know, I screwed so-and-so's secretary last night!' Now the roles seem to be reversed, but they aren't. Women always did that, but they did it much more discreetly. Men were never let in on it, so they didn't know that it was going on. Now the women talk. Women talk about their sexual relationships, their sexual encounters. People go to meetings and talk about these things quite openly.

"What has really happened is that we have come of age in

the sense that we are prepared to talk about the things that we only whispered about or hinted at in the past. Because of the revolution in communications, we now know where women's heads are."

In one sense Guccione is correct, though he may not know the real reason why he is correct. There is evidence that the amount of sexual activity has been growing throughout the twentieth century. Beginning first with the lower classes, those who were least affected by Victorian prudery. Sexual activity grew, particularly in the wake of World War I, when contraceptives, sex manuals, and a breakdown in middle-class morality led to increased sexual exploration among the young. From the 1920s on, one can chart the growth of premarital intercourse, as it rose at a steady pace.

Whatever the long-term trend, there is no question that from the late 1950s through the 1970s the liberalization of attitudes has expanded so much, the amount of premarital and extramarital sexual activity increased so dramatically, that these years do stand as a time of revolution in sexual attitudes and practices.[1] The statistics on nonmarital and premarital pregnancies—the latter shown when births occur less than nine months after marriage—rose precipitously at this time, ironically at the very moment when contraceptives and information should have made out-of-wedlock sexual activity less easy to spot.

Most of the increase in sexual activity has come among the young. As Morton Hunt shows in *Sexual Behavior in the Seventies,*[2] the young generation of American men, and, even more so, of American women, have adopted standards of sexual behavior different from those of their parents and grandparents. Today, over four-fifths, or 80 percent, of all married women had intercourse before they were married. What is crucial to remember, though, given the tolerance for premarital sex, is that in the majority of cases, the premarital experience was with the partner the women ultimately married. There is casual and promiscuous sex among the young but it is far less prevalent for them than it is among older single, divorced, or widowed adults.

American women have been especially affected by this surge of sexual activity. Women are now allowed to have their own sex lives. Men may want to marry virgins, yet they don't really expect females to remain chaste throughout their teenage years. Now, too, married women can be exposed in an extramarital affair, and it may not be an automatic cause for divorce. It certainly would have been so in the past. The male would have demanded some sort of retribution; he would have taken some sort of dramatic action. Not so now. Men have changed; women have changed. And most often, people will tell you that the change can be traced to the permissiveness of the 1960s. But this is, as I will suggest at length, far too simple an explanation. Signs of profound change in moral attitudes and practices were evident throughout the 1950s, and actually extended back to the destructive yet liberating period of World War II, an event that transformed life in this country to a degree that we have not yet begun to assess.

World War II marked the acceleration of changes in America's sexual habits. Lives in general, for both men and women, were altered to the extent that little of the prewar days seemed to survive the years of fighting. It opened new vistas to people who would otherwise have remained confined to their localities. People came into intimate contact with other societies whose moral practices were often different from their own. Although only a small percentage of the population actually participated in the fighting, for all Americans the war was the high point in their lives.

The war years gave many men the opportunity to live an almost bacchanalian existence underwritten by the necessities of the conflict. Old restrictions in many fields were openly disregarded. Religious strictures broke down among laymen. Clerics were not immune, either. One could kill others in the war and it would not be regarded as murder. People could watch while church prelates sprinkled holy water on bombers about to leave for Europe or the Pacific. Old definitions no longer had any meaning, especially since so many could be set aside so easily.

The war years were a dividing line between old ideas and new. For younger people the prewar years were defined by the Depression and by a far simpler pace of life. It was a time when traditional morality reigned in word if not in deed, when women's virginity at marriage was prized and monogamy accepted without question. The war caused the young to question everything their fathers and mothers had taught them, everything their neighborhood schools and churches and Kiwanis Clubs professed, everything the prewar community of the middle class represented as correct conduct. The war took three or four years out of young men's lives and separated them from everything they believed to be right and wrong. For those who survived into the postwar years, return to the simple ways of their parents was virtually impossible. How could they accept complacently the humdrum existence of the past after the exposure and experiences of the war years?

Also, the war gave women a freedom and independence that had been unknown, perhaps impossible to know before. Women were separated from their families and communities. They joined the women's armed services or war industries, or worked in offices or at innumerable other jobs that were suddenly opened to women because of the absence of men. Most women did not get as far away from their early experiences as did the men, but for the first time, they made as much money. And what is more, they spent it—often at night in the bars and clubs that flourished throughout the nation. For them, too, there was a new freedom from the old moralities. Many of the women lived away from home, in apartments of their own, helping pave the way to a new sexual freedom. In that expedient and tumultuous time of war, new and different behaviors were accepted.

Male and female moral attitudes were liberalized. Both had sexual affairs even if they were married. But the correspondence between wives at home and servicemen in Europe or the Pacific still abounded in the lies demanded by old morality. The husbands and wives expressed their fidelity to one another, a fidelity that neither observed in practice, but the façade had to be maintained. The war made it right. Only the "exigencies" of the war made it possible to justify the constant deviations from accepted moral conduct. Women, too, were looking for something different to emerge after the war. They, too, looked at things differently from their parents, even when they publicly professed the old moral codes.

Just how far they had come was reflected only a short time after the war by the studies of Alfred Kinsey. Kinsey's studies of human sexuality in America conducted in the 1940s showed that older sexual standards existed primarily in word and not in deed. The studies revealed that about half of all American women had premarital intercourse, a percentage growing with each generation. For males, the premarital sex figures ranged from a low of 68 percent for college men to 98 percent for those with only a grade-school education. If this was not disturbing enough, Kinsey sent shock waves through the country with his finding that 92 percent of American men and a wholly unexpected 62 percent of women masturbated to orgasm.

The report clearly indicated that traditional morality had broken down, but that it was still far from dead. The death knell for older values began to ring during the 1950s, a period we usually think of as quiescent.

The 1950s were a time when the nation once again returned to a kind of normalcy by electing Dwight D. Eisenhower to two terms as president. Aside from international affairs and the fears of domestic Communism, men were preoccupied with enjoying the good life, symbolized by a home in the suburbs, the ubiquitous station wagon and commuter train, a good, straight job, two kids, a dog, and a perpetually harried wife who somehow managed to provide a strong martini at the end of a tough day.

But that was not what the 1950s were really about. Actually, they were a decade of great fermentation. People were far from happy about their existence. Men were bored with their lives now that the great adventure of the war was over. Women, too, were disenchanted, and it was their disenchantment that produced the final break with traditional standards.

In one of the period's great coincidences, Kinsey's study of women was published in 1953 and at the same time a new magazine for men, *Playboy,* made its debut. *Playboy* revolutionized the magazine industry and made sex and a new moral code acceptable subjects for reading and conversation. In this, *Playboy* mirrored rather than provoked a change in attitudes. It answered a need felt by those who had experienced the war years and who longed for renewed excitement. *Playboy*'s suggestive pictures, titillating cartoons, and risqué stories answered part of the need. So, too, did the appearance during the decade of other harbingers of change. Lenny Bruce, with his black humor and profanity; the growth of nudist camps; the release of films like Russ Meyer's *The Immoral Mr. T;* and, on a more elevated level, the acceptance at law of a publisher's right to release serious literature with explicit sexual scenes.

At first, the liberalization of sexual attitudes did not alter the relationship that had existed between men and women. Each still had a prescribed role. Men were the aggressors, women the passive recipients. Women were still expected to adorn themselves to attract men, to invite sexual advances. Women remained sex objects, putting on their perfume, their makeup, their provocative clothing. In a way they were selling themselves, selling their sexuality, in the hope that by doing so they would attract a man who would, in time, propose marriage.

Sex, marriage, family—these remained a triad of traditional attitudes and desires despite changing attitudes toward sex. As Anthony Pietropinto puts it, beginning in their teens, women had fantasies that they would "meet their one ideal dream man, fall in love, and get married." Later, as adults, women continued to see sex in terms of love and a constant relationship. They could never be as impersonal about their sexual relations as men. Whereas men could buy sex from hookers on the street or the massage parlor, women virtually never purchased sex. Most found it impossible to engage in sexual relations with someone for whom they had no emotional feeling. Their sex lives, though freer than women's sex lives had ever been before, were still directed toward the same goals—marriage and family.

Moreover, liberalization of sexual attitudes created new difficulties for women. In 1974 Elizabeth Janeway noted that, before the sexual revolution, the male's traditional right of initiating sexual encounters "was balanced by a female right to refuse the man's request on general grounds of morality or propriety. Acceptance was seen as a personal sign of affection and favor, but refusal carried no stigma of personal rejection."[3] By the 1960s, women were finding themselves in an awkward position. Anthony Pietropinto reports that his female patients tell him that once they give up their virginity, once they go to bed with one guy, "they all expect it. They take you to dinner and you know you have to go to bed with them. Because if you don't, they will say to you, 'What's the matter with you? Why not? It's your body, enjoy it, have fun' and so forth." This advice not only applies to women individually but to women as a whole.

Elizabeth Janeway observes that the new, general assumption "that women enjoy sex as much as men, and that it is proper for them to do so, has been extended to the expectation that they will respond to a request for sexual relations by agreeing." Should the woman refuse to do what is now accepted as normal for her, for whatever reason she actually does so, the man is disparaged, his worth challenged; and a relationship that might have developed over time is endangered. The woman may want to terminate the relationship and her refusal might be an indication of that. On the other hand, ending the relationship might also be the furthest thing from her mind.

In short, Janeway notes, we have not yet got rid of the double standard. "Some women who still feel themselves to be secondary people whose role calls for them to please men accept sex as a duty in the same way their great-grandmothers did." Such "sexual liberation," which directs the response of women, whether it direct that they say no or yes, is in no way liberation for them. They are still seen primarily through men's eyes and not as autonomous creatures who can put their own choice of pleasure first.

The mid- to late 1970s have seen even greater changes in women's attitudes. American women have moved from their earlier acceptance of and fealty to the ideals of virginity, monogamy, and sexual fidelity to an attitude that accepted premarital sex as proper, always provided, however, that the woman had a strong feeling and commitment for the man. It's developed to the point, in Anthony Pietropinto's words, "where she had an obligation to enjoy her body, to have sexual relations, to seek out orgasm and not think she had to make a firm commitment to enjoy it." Women told each other that they did not have to be involved emotionally with a man, no more than men felt that they had to be involved emotionally with the woman they were screwing.

Advocates of women's liberation have been in the forefront of sexual liberation; none more than Germaine Greer, who is a powerful advocate of woman's search for sexual pleasure and fulfillment. Women like Greer tell other women to enjoy their body, have fun with it. And women seem to be heeding the message—at times with a vengeance. "Now," Pietropinto says, "it appears that a lot of women are going to bed with guys with the attitude, 'O.K., now please me!' or 'Let's see how good you are.' " Roles have changed. Now women are initiators of sexual relations. Now they often take charge.

Now it is all right for a woman to go to bed with a man—on the first date if she wants to. Women are now perceived as sexual creatures, too. They're expected to have strong sexual desires and responses. The woman no longer replies to a man's overture by saying, "What kind of girl do you think I am?" Now she asks, "What took you so long? I thought we would never get back to my apartment. Let's get going!" Or she lets the man know early on that she expects a good sexual performance from him.

Precisely what a woman means by a good sexual performance has confused many men—perhaps because they continue to project their own sexual preferences onto women. They assume that what they want, she must want, too. They are usually, but not always, wrong.

The male's own desire is primarily for penile-vaginal intercourse, to *screw.* But Albert Ellis noted in conversation with me that women are interested in noncoital sex for the most part. Men won't accept that fact. They wrongly think that women only want a big cock that can last long, but many of them really don't want this. "The male," Ellis says, "is satisfied when he gets a full erection, has intercourse and gets an explosive orgasm, so he wrongly thinks that the female is satisfied the same way. He makes innumerable errors in that respect. This doesn't mean that no women are satisfied by intercourse. There are some who want nothing else. But this is relatively rare."

Men could have learned this from Kinsey's study of female sexuality, which had a profound impact in the 1960s when debate raged over the precise nature of female orgasm. Freud and his followers, with customary dogmatism, insisted that the mature female's orgasms were "vaginal." The female had to experience intercourse before she would experience a mature vaginal orgasm. Freudians admitted that clitoral stimulation also produces orgasm but said that these were the orgasms of women who had not yet admitted their true femininity. Clitoral orgasms were, in psychiatrist Helen Deutsch's words, "rather like a good sneeze" in contrast to the complete gratification of the vaginal orgasm. It was Kinsey who pointed out that Freud and his followers had had their anatomy wrong. The vagina, Kinsey reminded readers, was virtually insensitive, lacking the nerve endings necessary for orgasm, while the clitoris was extremely sensitive to touch or even indirect pressure. And Kinsey reported for the first time that women were capable of repeated orgasms after only a short refractory period.

For most women, then, intercourse does not provide complete sexual satisfaction. Women have told men this. Whatever its flaws as a work of sociology, *The Hite Report,* by Shere Hite, does suggest a deep disquiet among women that men must take into consideration. Gael Greene commented on this. "If you read *The Hite Report,*" she told me, "you have to cry to think about all those women who have their best orgasms by themselves even though they would rather be with men."

There is among women an extraordinary anger at the way they have been used sexually. Gael Greene continued: "I think it is especially vivid in Barbara Howar's book *Making Ends Meet,* where the woman never has an orgasm; she has many affairs but only achieves orgasm at the end of a relationship with a lover who finally makes love to her orally. She thinks to herself, 'He knew all about this. He could have done it, but he never did!' And she is filled with rage about all of those times.

"And I think there is that rage in the antimale feeling that you hear expressed from some women in the movement. And I understand it. There is so much anger in all those years spent with so little sexual joy."

Now, with all that has been and is being written about sexual joy, women are hungrier for it and angrier to have missed out on it for so long. These are the women whom Shere Hite reports as feeling that men really don't care about women, that all men truly care about is their own gratification. These are the women who complain that men don't like foreplay, that they spend little time at it, that they want their women to be weak and passive, so the men can remain in control all the time. To be sure, Hite is wrong when she concludes from her unrepresentative sample that the self-centered singles discussed in her book are representative of all men. She nonetheless pinpoints a legitimate complaint of some women—how many nationwide is still impossible to tell.

Representative or not of men in general, *The Hite Report* is important as a document of how some, or perhaps many, women feel now that they understand and accept their own sexual selves. It is difficult not to believe the women who say they fake orgasm, who complain that men are not sensitive to their needs. Certainly there is a great communication gap between men and women. The man may think he is pleasing the woman, but the woman is afraid still to talk about it. So she fakes orgasm and then feels bitter and resentful.

Certainly the sexual revolution of the 1960s and 1970s has been liberating. "It is much better now," James Dickey says, "much freer." But there is another side to the sexual revolution. For one thing, the easy availability of sex has taken much of the mystery out of it—to our loss, Dickey thinks. "The way people live now takes the clandestine quality out of sex. It was the good part . . . it was right for me. I liked that. So did the women that I fooled around with. Now, the fact that sex is so easily come by has taken some of the adventure, of playing the great game, out of it. It is just as though you were surfeited with porterhouse steaks at every meal. You get tired of eating steak."

Tired of eating steak . . . tired of sex? Dickey recounts one incident of disillusionment at the new sexual freedom. "I was reading at Harvard once, and I stayed with a fellow whom I had known, who had once been a student of mine. He was living with a girl and not married to her. One day he went off to teach, and I was talking with his girlfriend. I said, 'Well, listen, how do you like the new life, the new freedom, you and Dick living together like this? Is it to your taste? Why don't you marry him?' And she said, 'We can't afford to get married.' 'Well, if you can afford to live together, you can afford to get married,' I said. 'Well, we just don't see it that way. We like it this way.' 'Well,' I said, 'are you completely satisfied with the arrangement?' She said, 'Yes, I am, but Dick is gone now, and I have the chance to talk to you and tell you some things I wouldn't tell him.' She said, 'I love Dick very much. I wouldn't be living with him if I didn't. But we just come home and take off our clothes and go to bed like old married people.' I said, 'Well, what's wrong with that? Isn't that the freedom that youth has always wanted, to do what they want to do in bed?' She said, 'Yes, but I just wish that we could sometimes just sit on the sofa and neck.' "

Dickey laughed loudly. "Now, that was a big thing in my day. Sitting around with someone necking. That was fun. But it is not fun when you can just go to bed any time you want to, any time of the day or night, and the other person doesn't object. So they don't like it as much as we used to."

Actor James Whitmore, deeply concerned about this question, sees the same thing happening. "There is a backlash already against sexual freedom," he told me. "In the colleges, many kids report that they have tried the permissiveness route. They've gone that way and they find out just what the problems are."

"Yes," I said. "You know I am a traditionalist, like you. I think sex is the ultimate manifestation of a love relationship. It has to be. But many have lost sight of that. Often people have sexual relations quickly so they can become familiar with somebody. They're afraid of the transience of society."

"Jesus Christ, yes!" Whitmore agreed. "They say, 'Oh, man, what is this?' More than that, it is confusing to them, this sense of loss, because they have, as we all do, this tremendous hunger to make contact with another person. Sure, sex is the closest physically that two human beings can get, other than being joined together at birth. But they find that sexual freedom is dross; it doesn't nourish. It doesn't nourish the human psyche. It doesn't fulfill the need for love. I think the backlash has started already."

What is clear is that there have been losses to women as well as gains as they understand themselves better. Women as well as men are responsible for the inability of people to sustain relationships today. Women are losing some of their sense of romance, their desire for mutual commitment. Anthony Pietropinto sees this as a disturbing evolution in our culture. "I get very distressed," he told me, "when over and over again, I hear statements, particularly from women, like 'You have got to be independent. You can't tie yourself down to any person. You can't ask someone else to meet your needs.' But is it really such a terrible thing to say, 'I need a person in my life whom I can rely on, whom I can trust, who is going to be there in the good times and the bad times, who isn't going to have one foot out of the relationship and one foot in'? There has always been this basic human need. But all of a sudden, this has become very bad. We are all expected to be little narcissistic islands unto ourselves. We mustn't get overinvolved."

Helen Gurley Brown sees the cost to women, too. "Women have lost something with the new sexuality." she said. "The thing that I think has been lost is a certain sexiness which came when men and women were very separate, when she was the pursued and he was the pursuer. Sex was a little more forbidden, a little more intriguing. It was a big deal to go to bed with somebody. Single girls did sleep with men when they weren't supposed to; they just didn't say much about it. They continued to be ladies. Women had sex lives, but they didn't talk about it. It was secret, sexy, naughty—and rather fabulous in one way because of that. But now everybody is supposed to sleep with everyone. You go to dinner and you go to bed. It is almost obligatory. So it's not as sexy."

The gains for women should not be disregarded. Now they can expect orgasms from oral sex or masturbation, and they can enjoy it. Those years have passed when a man could peak and climax and ejaculate but if the woman didn't have an orgasm, it was not very important. Women now expect orgasm, even multiple orgasms, more than they used to expect it. That is all to the good.

But orgasm for the woman is no more important than orgasm for the man. It is not the biggest achievement in life, no matter how pleasurable. All the orgasms in the world will not provide the emotional closeness human beings require. Women as well as men have a need to feel cherished and loved. Casual sex for women answers this need no more than it has for men. Women have simply accepted a male norm that has never worked for men. It is a loss for them just as it has always been a loss for us.

12 One Man's Odyssey Through the Sexual Revolution: A Conversation with Dan Greenburg

THE SEXUAL revolution affected American men in different ways. Not all were swept away. There were some whose need for sex was not strong. They were content with their sex lives as they were, satisfied with their wives and at times, perhaps, with a little extra on the side. Others, committed to monogamy, remained faithful to their partners. Still others felt the exhilaration of the new wind that was blowing. They took advantage of the new sexual liberation of women to satisfy their own long-repressed appetites.

One of the latter was Dan Greenburg, novelist and essayist, who has written extensively on sexual matters for *Playboy* and whose "memoir," *Scoring,* was a funny yet poignant examination of a young man on the make. Greenburg's sexual experiences in the 1970s constituted a sexual odyssey. He did it all. And his experience speaks to the elation and then the disillusion.

I asked him how it began, if he thought while he was married, during the first stirrings of sexual liberation, that he was missing out on a great deal, with all of these wonderful and willing women walking about.

D.G.: I thought at first it was all a conspiracy to get me. Especially when I first started researching my *Playboy* orgy article. I had never been involved in an orgy. I was terrified! I think I'd been married about six years by that time, and whoever I talked to, somewhere in the conversation, they'd say how drastically things had changed in sex in the last six years. I wondered why they all used that figure. It was as if the minute I took the marriage vows and said I do, a whistle was blown. Everybody said, "O.K., it's all right to fuck strangers, animals, orgies—anything goes! It's all right! Just forget guilt!" God passed a new law, you know? I really started getting incredibly bitter and frustrated. Everybody I knew was into it. All the stories that you would hear from your male friends just got outrageous. I mean, the stories in college were bad enough, but now it was really, you know—"Three girls came by and undressed me, and. . . ." I mean it was outrageous!

Anyway, about a year later I got separated from my wife and suddenly it was all possible. I didn't have to feel the guilt and I went crazy. I really started making love to three women a day—one in the morning, one in the afternoon, one in the evening. I walked around in a daze, bumping into doorways, falling down stairs, because making love was really all I was doing for the first couple of months. Just fucking my eyes out. Then there came a day when the girl of the night before, who I had just fucked in the morning, kind of straggled out the door at about eleven-thirty or eleven-forty and five minutes later, before I'd even had a chance to jump in the shower, my noontime date, a married women, showed up and proceeded to attack me. And I heard myself actually say, "You know what I feel? I feel used." I started laughing because I sounded so ludicrous. It was an exact echo of things that I had always heard *women* say. Then I actually heard myself saying, "How come we don't talk anymore? How come we just fuck?" I realized then that I had reached a certain point, the point of saturation. I didn't want to do that anymore!

So I decided to start getting a little bit more serious. But I did it the wrong way because I was unwilling to give up this incredible life of multiples. So I got serious with three women. Instead of doing it intelligently, what I did was carve my life into three equal parts and gave each of them a part of it. I felt controlled by each of them. It was as if I had three wives. I got them all the same number of presents for special occasions. I kept two of them totally in the dark about the others. The third was living with a guy. She wanted to know about the other two.

I experience all of the feelings that married men who have affairs must go through—looking at the watch, this one's coming in five minutes, so you get rid of the other one at the last possible minute, and so on. That pattern went on for about, I don't know, a year or so. Then I went into the next phase of going with one woman primarily while seeing a lot of others casually.

That phase ended around the summer of '77 and I have since then been faithful to one woman, which for me is an extraordinary accomplishment. I don't know what I think about it yet. I give myself a lot of credit, and yet I go through periods of incredible horniness.

B.A.: It is laudable. But it is so difficult, because temptation is rampant. Everywhere you look, every elevator you get into, every coffee shop that you stop in, it's there, dangling in front of your face.

During this period that you spoke of when you were seeing three women and parceling out equal proportions of yourself, did you feel fragmented?

D.G.: Yes, I felt that I was so-and-so's boyfriend and so-and-so's boyfriend and so-and-so's boyfriend— and almost felt that I had somewhat lost my own identity. In order, perhaps, to get over the guilt of cheating on all these other people, I saw myself as a put-upon "hubby," you know, the one who was just really trying to do the right thing. I felt enormously put upon to go here and do this, be available to do that—it was really like having three wives. Take it from me, it isn't such a terrific thing to do, despite the movies on the subject. Remember the Alec Guinness picture, *The Captain's Paradise,* the one where he had two wives? It ended in disaster.

B.A.: I'm reminded of the Warren Beatty film *Shampoo,* which is about that whole situation of multiple romances. The extraordinary thing was that the Beatty character seemed to be sincere! Of course, he wanted it all, like so many of us do, but he was sincere about it. When he said to a woman, "Baby, you're great, I love you, he meant it, even though fifteen minutes later, there would be someone else with him.

D.G.: Well, I honestly felt that I loved each of these three women, and I couldn't believe they could get jealous. I really thought that there was enough of me to go around. To some extent there was, except that there wasn't enough left for me. There wasn't enough left for me to do my work, and a lot of other things. But if all I needed to live for was to keep three women happy, I was almost able to do it. But at what expense? At what price?

Did I make them happy? I'm sure each of them, if you'd asked them, would have said they weren't in fact satisfied, that they weren't seeing enough of me. I think I was seeing two of them three nights a week and one of them two nights a week. Also many lunches. I was constantly with one or another of them.

Finally, the one who was living with another man was the

first to say "the hell with you." She was the one that felt most willing to give it up. The instant she said that, it was very clear that she was the only one that I cared about. I went insane. I wrote her long, soul-searching letters, got her gifts, and behaved in a fashion that, if it had been one of my friends, would have embarrassed me horribly. I would have said, "He's gone off the deep end. There's no hope for him!"

What finally happened is interesting. I was on the way to Haiti, with another of the young women. Just before departure, I hand-delivered a letter that took me two days to write. I was obsessed with this all through my Haiti trip. In Haiti, I got into all kinds of weird things, like taking part in voodoo ceremonies. When I got back from Haiti, I was still obsessed with trying to win the girl back. I even asked a witch to give me a magical spell that would get her back.

The witch said, "I will give you a spell, but you must understand that there have to be certain safeguards. For instance, you are not to use her name. You are not to make it too specific." I said, "Why?" She replied, "Because, then you *will* get her and perhaps you shouldn't."

So I took this spell and I tried it three nights in a row and nothing happened. I was very disappointed and decided to improvise a little. At that point, I felt I knew a little bit about the occult, so I started using the name of the young lady, against the witch's instructions, plus a candle to focus on, which is another good device. Also, I used an article of her clothing, an article of her jewelry and photograph. Now, they have done interesting studies on photographs—this sounds bizarre, out of context—but apparently a photographic likeness of somebody has some curious connection to them, and many occultists feel that it's almost as good as working with the person himself, should you want to cast a spell on him. That's why natives of Mexico and Africa are so camera-shy. It's because they are afraid that they will be vulnerable to your magic. Well, it turns out that they may not be so far off.

Anyway, as I told you, I started working with her photograph, plus an article of her clothing, and an article of her jewelry. About a day after I started working on the spell, she telephoned me. She said, "You know, I don't know why I'm calling you." It gave me an eerie feeling.

We had a two-hour discussion and I began to see what a fool she was. I began to see that I was right to have valued her least of all three. By the time the two-hour conversation was over, I was no longer mesmerized.

I called up the witch and I told her about it. I confessed to being a naughty person. I had done all the things she had told me not to do. I said, "Do you think this is a truly magical experience?" She said, "Well, what do *you* think?" She was almost like my psychiatrist. Anyway, after this incident, I broke up with the second girl and then the third. It seemed to be the end of a phase I was going through.

B.A.: Do you think that in the rush to arm ourselves with techniques of sexuality and a great deal of information that we are losing something in the process—perhaps spontaneity, sensitivity? It seems as if people are becoming obsessed with the means of sexuality as an end unto itself, rather than the true meaning of the act. Did you fall into that at all?

D.G.: You bet. In a certain way, I feel it is behind me, and I feel superior to that position. I have outgrown it. The instant that I became separated, I started dressing in a more provocative manner. I started hanging macho things in my bedroom, like a gunbelt and a fireman's helmet and pictures—all kinds of pictures of me in very macho pursuits.

I went down to the Pleasure Chest, only a half a block from my house, and got a lot of equipment. Long before I did the kinky sexual behavior article for *Playboy* on answering sex ads, long before that I went with a young woman to the Pleasure Chest and bought chains and handcuffs and we used them on each other. It was a lot more titillating in contemplation than in actual practice, but it led to a pattern. For months, every time that I went to bed with a woman more than once, I would say casually, "Say, listen, I have these chains. Would you like me to chain you up?" I don't think there was one woman during that period of time who said no. Not one! It was amazing because they didn't know me. They didn't know what I could have done to them. They just thought, 'Oh, well, that's amusing.' It was as if someone said, 'Listen, I have an interesting batch of grass here and would you like to smoke?' 'Oh, sure, why not? That sounds like fun.' I would say by and large—and we're talking about maybe a dozen women—I would say that all dozen mildly enjoyed being chained and spanked, or whatever I was doing in those days. They didn't seem to look upon this as very unusual behavior either.

I still have large iron screw eye chain retainers embedded

in the platform of my bed, both in the city and in the country. They haven't been used in a long time, but they're there, as a reminder of the old days.

Really, fucking—or sport-fucking, shall we say—has become one of the great indoor sports. We care now about how we're dressed for it and the equipment we use almost more than how we play the game. You could almost say there has been as great a proliferation of equipment stores for the sport of sex as there has for the sport of tennis.

B.A.: You mentioned that in the sixties people were into orgies, because it seemed in keeping with the whole collective energy of things, as they were evolving at that time. The innocence and the vulnerability. Now things have been kinked up quite a bit. People want to hold power over other people. They want to dominate them in some way. That perhaps has a lot to do with the whole current S and M movement. They want to tie people up and cause pain, yet spanking and pain-oriented eroticism have been around for thousands and thousands of years, but it's never been a sexual trend. Not only that, Madison Avenue has never used it to sell products.

D.G.: Well, the Establishment has always co-opted the revolution. In fact, the way that it's more often done is through commerce. My favorite example of that theory used to be a station I.D. on CBS-TV, "Channel 2, the People." I just thought it was hilarious. But, yes, it makes perfect sense that people would put S and M into ads.

Everything gets absorbed, you see. The further out we go to try to shock ourselves and our friends with weird new stuff—it all gets co-opted. Whatever drugs, whatever strange sex habits, all that gets assimilated. So we're seeing S&M and B&D [sadomasochism and bondage and domination] in ads—we're going to see golden showers in the media before very long too, I'd imagine. We're going to see bestiality. We're going to see all that, done very lightly and stylishly, using the most beautiful of animals and people together . . . the most gorgeous of golden showers—things of that sort.

I don't know what the next thing will be. Perhaps it will be stylish snuff sex. High-fashion ads, models killing each other and having sex with the corpse—very stylish, you know, in ads on TV. It probably isn't too far off.

B.A.: "Brutality chic" in the last couple of years is a perfect example of that. Very, very kinky images that are flashed; vehicles used by rock groups, et cetera, that become parts of the people's consciousness. When you see something looming above you on this larger-than-life billboard, it sticks, it really does.

D.G.: I think there's a hell of a lot more kinkiness going on in this country than anybody admits to. All you have to do is have a series of ads, the Bloomingdales lingerie catalogue of a year or so ago, something on that order. Things readily available to the public. Watch the fervor with which people pick it up, look it over voraciously, devour it, and then pull back and say, "Well, amusing, of course" or "Shocking" or whatever. It gives you an insight into the incredible amount of kinkiness that exists and will never be revealed. I certainly don't think there's more of it going on now than in the past. It's just better advertised. People are freer to talk about it.

In the last few years people have gone through an orgy of talking about themselves. I think psychiatry and the human potential movement have legitimized it. It's a great release, because I think people have always wanted to talk about themselves. They were dying to talk about themselves. And now they get a chance to. On reflection, you find that all those horrible secrets about yourself are in fact rather mundane, because everybody has the same secrets to reveal. Today, with a great sign of relief, everybody in the country is babbling about their sexual hangups, their kinkiness, and their latest trip to Plato's Retreat . . . or the affair that they've been having for some time with their Doberman Pinscher.

B.A.: The sexual experimentation at the retreat at Sandstone attracted much notoriety. What did you learn about yourself from your experiences there? Did you reach some kind of self-knowledge about who you are as a sexual person?

D.G.: Yes. That I considered a very good experience. I started out feeling almost the way I did when I began my article on orgies—terrified of not having a big enough cock, of not being able to be potent, of getting a disease, of not being as good as the other men, of being rejected, all the things that it's possible to be terrified of.

Fortunately, the first weekend I spent there consisted of a day-long seminar devoted to just getting used to our bodies, to each other's bodies. There were a lot of Esalen-type exercises, touching other people in a pool. Touching men as well as women, being touched, massaging, being massaged. It was a lovely, low-key introduction to a new world. Finally, on the second day, there came the party. Presumably anything you wanted to do was fine, as long as it didn't hurt another person. By that time I had passed into another frame of mind. I was certainly not divorced from my own considerations, but I was very proud of the way I "measured up" against the other men—how my body did, how my penis did, and so on.

I was very proud of the relative ease I felt being nude around a lot of other nude people. I thought less and less about the strangeness of it. On the first weekend or two at Sandstone, I only made love to one woman at a time, even though there were, say, a few different ones in an evening.

It wasn't until the second or third weekend that I got into groups. Even though I had participated in groups before, I never had indulged in threesomes with two other women—a longstanding goal! That turned out to be very nice, but not quite the big turn-on that I had expected.

After having been to Sandstone several times, I didn't feel the need to try and get threesomes or get groups together. I felt I had done it. I had come through the experience liking myself. I enjoyed the experience without getting a fixation on it. In a certain sense, I didn't feel I had to do it again. Rather, I was left with a feeling of warmth and sweetness about the people at Sandstone. I took great pleasure in simply sitting around having dinner or going into the Jacuzzi with them. There was nowhere near the obsession to score as before. That need didn't totally leave me, but I certainly felt that I had passed through to another frame of mind.

There's been a lot of mention in the media about Plato's Retreat. I have never been there, and it's all right with me if I never go because I feel that I've had that experience and I don't feel the need to do it again. I don't know whether I will or not. I feel that's all in my past and that I'm ready for . . . what? I don't know. Maybe the seriousness of my current relationship and hoping that will endure. I feel good about it, so it must be a good thing.

B.A.: You deal with a very interesting facet of human relations in your last article, your final trip to Sandstone. You deal with the whole theme of jealousy and possessiveness, how you related to that with a woman you met there.

D.G.: Yes. I met a woman leaving Sandstone the time before last. I corresponded with her. Then we got together for a very steamy weekend, but she was married and brought her husband with her to Sandstone. I was extremely nervous about making love to her anywhere near where he was. I found myself getting a big crush on her. The very first time that she was with a man other than me or her husband, I felt betrayed. I felt that Bill's wife was cheating on me, an extraordinary thing to feel. Even when I was able to view it in its most ludicrous terms, it didn't help much. I must say that particular experience was very strange. I spent the whole day with her and him, and it ended in both of us making love to her but not to each other. It was a very weird experience.

Sandstone, as you may know, was located in a very beautiful and very weird place on top of a mountain. The day of that incident was particularly strange and eerie. They were playing weird German electronic music. It really felt as if I was in another world—a feeling heightened by the fact that I felt I was breaking the last taboo. In a sense with her I was fucking Mommy with Daddy. Needless to say, it was very odd . . . probably the single strangest experience I've ever had. I believe it shocked me in some very deep way. Yet I think it's alright now. I think that it's also in my past. It's also something that I don't ever have to do again. I'm glad I did it. I think it was an experience that caused more growth in important areas, probably because it was such a shocking and taboo-shattering experience.

B.A.: The husband's attitude, though, seemed to be typical of a lot of men who have been able to rationalize the infidelity of the people they care about—a man who felt that by allowing his wife to make love with other men, he would strengthen and enhance his relationship with her.

D.G.: In fact, it didn't. In fact, the postscript to that story, which will never be published, unless you publish it, is that shortly after our experience, Diane and Bill broke up. She fell in love with another man, moved in with him, and has been faithful to him ever since. She has totally given up the swinging life, the Sandstone life, all that. Of course, that totally surprised me, and yet when you look back on it, it makes perfect sense. Because those who lead one extreme form of life at some point always, or most always, change a hundred and eighty degrees.

B.A.: Is it reasonable to assume that if any man cares about another woman, there is a degree of possessiveness that's almost intrinsic to that caring?

D.G.: I think so. I think it's certainly part of very important moral codes that we're brought up with. Maybe it's even deeper than that. Maybe it is really animal.

It is interesting to look at animal behavior patterns and see the possessiveness that certain species display for their mates. Not all species, but certain species. The terrible jealousy fights.

I don't really believe, or quite know what to do with, men who tell me in a Sandstone situation that they truly aren't jealous. Maybe they're telling the truth. Perhaps many of them believe that themselves. I tend, on the other hand, to think that in some cases, the men are bisexual and enjoy the idea of making love to their woman with another man, and/or it's a way to put distance between a great intimacy that might develop between them and their mate. Perhaps it's a way to get back to an Oedipal situation. It's almost like saying, "See, Dad, I don't really want to take Mom away from you—let's have her together."

I certainly think that most, if not all swingers, are very concerned, while swinging, about not getting too intimate with their mates. Certainly a big part of it is trophy hunting—simply fucking as many other people as they can. However, I'm sure that they would be horrified at the suggestion that one of the prime purposes of their swinging was to make sure they didn't get too close to their mates! Many of them, probably most, would tell you that it was a way of getting even closer. I'm sure many of them believe it. By letting other men sleep with their wives, they then feel freer to come closer to their mates than they would otherwise.

B.A.: What do you see as the future trend on sexual attitudes and practices?

D.G.: I think that the pendulum is swinging back the other way. We're becoming more puritanical, even though there are places like Plato's Retreat now. They may not go on very long. I, for one, will be sorry to see it all end.

I think we're going back to the very rigid and stultifying puritanism that existed before all this happened. That's going to be too bad. I think it's almost inevitable. Just as people are starting to wear suits more now. They get tired of one thing, and then they go to the other. Then it will swing back. But it will take a while, perhaps a generation. I just hope when it does swing back, if it does, that *all* the things won't swing back and be the way they were before. I hope we don't surrender all the growth that we've achieved in the last ten or fifteen years, that we don't surrender all the healthy developments, all the honesty, all the freedom, all the permissiveness, all the experimentalism, the lack of condemnation about practices that we're afraid of. I hope there will be some residue left when it swings back, as it now is beginning to.

Some of the obscenity codes being enacted in various places across the country are an indication of that trend at a legal level. At a personal level maybe it's getting slightly harder to get laid. Maybe women who were up for sex on the first date before, or on first encounters, are now waiting for the second or third. I don't know, but that's my feeling. It's certainly not anything like it was ten or fifteen years ago, but who knows? It could swing even farther back.

B.A.: I think what people are coming to understand now is that sex, as an experience, is better for a lot of people when there is some kind of emotional commitment.

D.G.: Yes. And that's very healthy. I think it would be a shame, though, if we prevented people from exploring all the kinds of superficial sex available, because the minute we prevent them, I think it'll become an obsession and a fixation again. If you permit people to do everything that it occurs to them to do, everything that's not harmful to themselves or others, that is, then they'll find their own level of health.

An oft-cited example of permissiveness centers around an elementary school experiment where little kids were given complete freedom about what they could eat at lunchtime, even if it were just cookies, cake, and ice cream. By God, for the first week they went crazy with cookies, cake, and ice cream—they overdosed. But eventually they started eating other foods, healthier foods. They got the cookies, cake, and ice cream down to a level that perhaps even their parents would have been comfortable with.

The same phenomenon, I think, applies to grown people and sex. Take my own case. My own sexual behavior following my separation was a lot like stuffing myself with cookies, cake, and ice cream. Eventually, I calmed down. Nobody put a gun to my head and forced me to get more serious about one woman and to give up others. I have done it of my own free choice. And I suspect that most people would behave in a similar manner.

B.A.: I do, too.

13
Hors de Combat: The Walking Wounded

ALL REVOLUTIONS have their victims. The sexual revolution is no exception. The surprise is that all the most pathetic victims seem to be men.

In general, men have reacted rather badly to the female initiative in sexual matters. Before, sex was a male's prerogative —it was his option. If he felt like it, she did it! If he said, "Now, honey," she sighed and said all right. There was no consideration for the timing of a woman's moods or needs. Sex was all up to the male.

Now, however, roles are a bit reversed, for a man is often required or expected to make love when his partner wants to. It may be at a time when he is not really up to it. The woman may announce at breakfast, or any other time of the day or night, that she feels like making love. If the man has had too much to drink, is not in the mood, has something else he would rather do, then it's just too bad for him and the image of masculinity he wants to project and protect.

It was all so convenient for him when he didn't have to make a move except when he felt like it. Now he feels intimidated. He is on the defensive. He can no longer choose the moments for sexual encounter. He is no longer in control. He is in the very position no man ever wants to be in—at the mercy of someone else. And because that someone else is a woman, his manhood is threatened.

Men are uncertain. Of course, some have reacted well to changing attitudes and behavior among women. Many men, especially those who are less rigid, have become sensitized to women's needs. These men have paid attention to media discussions of women, their expectations and desires. Many men now understand how women achieve orgasm. They realize the importance of oral sex, lengthier and more imaginative foreplay. They have at least a working knowledge of the female anatomy.

They know where the clitoris is, what it is like, and how it responds. They are willing to discuss mutual needs with women, admit ignorance and failings. They try to establish a relationship based on more than their own sexual or ego gratification.

Many men, as well as women, are beginning to realize that sexual relations should not be limited simply to coitus and ejaculation—especially for those whose relationship develops into something more intimate and open. Just touching each other becomes an extremely pleasurable and erotic experience. Touching is an important part of a deeply emotional, intimate partnership, one in which there is a large measure of mutual love. Perhaps touching will never substitute for a good orgasm, but if there is really a love relationship, the whole body becomes an erogenous zone. There is pleasure in just holding hands. Touching even the nongenital areas of the body can be an electric experience, sometimes more pleasurable than genitality. The more openness there is in a relationship, the more relaxed it becomes. The more we in the West explore nongenital contact, the more we will emulate and enjoy the sexual experiences advocated in the classics of some Eastern cultures, where couples are taught to spend hours touching each other, holding off orgasm.

Many who are able to achieve true fulfillment in sexual relations recognize that good sex is a continuing process. They know that a satisfying relationship has to be built gradually. It doesn't happen immediately. You cannot operate on the assumption that the first time you go to bed with a person it is going to be perfect, that it has to be perfect. The partners must take time to learn about each other's bodies. They must talk to each other, communicate, learn, what the other likes. That is the only way forward to a complete rapport.

On the whole, men have had a difficult time of it, trying to preserve the power of the traditional masculine roles of our culture—as prime breadwinners, leaders, fathers at home and in society—while threatened by yet a new challenge, the demands of the liberated woman's sexual life style. To cope with this, some have given up the pose of superstud or man-on-the-make, though we still see this role being played, even among the most intelligent and highly educated. Now, Anthony Pietropinto reports, "we also see role reversal. We see for the first time things like men going out on dates and saying to a woman, 'I want you to understand right off I don't go to bed on my first date.' I've got college boys who tell me, 'These women want to go to bed with me, and I tell them I can't do it unless I have a strong emotional feeling.' I know it sounds ludicrous, but it is happening. Some men are trying to restore the balance. This is something we have not seen before."

For far too many men, however, the task of reorienting themselves sexually to the new attitudes and practices of women has proved too much. To get a better insight into this recent phenomenon, I talked to experts who were more conversant with the subject.

I asked Dr. Albert Ellis what type of man he finds has trouble reorienting himself sexually. He replied: "Well, first, the stupid man, the uneducated man, the unsophisticated man. Second, the disturbed man who rigidly holds on to his hypothesis and won't consider that he might be wrong. Of course, this second type may be sophisticated, too. In fact, I have a man right now in therapy who is a college graduate, very sophisticated, does very well in business; but his wife is one of those women who insists on intercourse largely because she thinks that if he doesn't get it up and keep it up to satisfy her, he doesn't love her. (You see, women may want intercourse for other than sexual reasons.) This man has difficulty accepting the fact that if he doesn't get or sustain an erection, it is not the end of the world."

I asked Anthony Pietropinto what he thought were some of the sexual characteristics of the sort of man who can't deal with a sexually aggressive woman. He replied: "I think these are probably men who are very uneasy with their own bodies and who are uneasy dealing with women in general. We saw some men, for example, who said things like 'Women scare me,' or some who said, 'I can't talk to any woman except my wife. She is O.K., but other women make me nervous.' And I think the man who doesn't want a sexually aggressive woman is the one who feels that he basically wants to take the lead, because if the woman makes demands on him he may not be able to perform for her. In other words, he just doesn't trust his own body, his own sexuality.

"At times, and especially in the early phases of a relationship, men may realistically equate this with experience. To me, this is another way of feeling their own inadequacy. They say, 'I can perhaps be an adequate lover, but if she has known a lot of different men, then she is bound to have found somebody who is far superior to me.' They have this kind of feeling."

"Almost a fear of grading," I suggested.

"Yes."

A fear of grading. Something new? Perhaps not entirely. Helen Gurley Brown told me that women have always graded men. Pietropinto says he knew a woman who actually kept score cards on them—for pleasure. The important thing, though, was that women never let the men know about it. Brown says women just never made a big deal out of it. "They just knew whether they were happy sexually with somebody, and if they were, they stayed with him. And sometimes they stayed even if they weren't all that happy with a man sexually."

Now the situation is far different. Women still grade, but they often do so with a vengeance. The recent furor at the Massachusetts Institute of Technology illustrates the point. There, young women on the campus newspaper staff decided they were going to perform an experiment, to let the men know what it feels like to become a sex object. What they did was publish a list of all the well-known lovers on campus, some thirty-six in all, the ones who "got around" a lot. The reporters interviewed the women who had slept with "the big lovers on campus," took a poll, and published it. The women rated the men rather explicitly on a scale that ranged from no stars ("Turkeys") to four stars ("Close your eyes—waves crash, mountains erupt, and flowers bloom").

Predictably there was outrage. After a barrage of obscene and threatening phone calls, protests from parents and alumni, plus probable pressure from the school's administration, the newspaper ran an apology. Anthony Pietropinto was distressed by this, too, for he sees this as particularly threatening to the male sexual ego. "What they are grading them on is not how they looked, but on how good or bad they were in bed. This is *really* a terrible thing. Sure, men used to rate girls on looks, which was cruel. But rating someone on his ability as a lover is bad. It is attacking a man right at his core."

This suggests that sexual performance, even if only the illusion of satisfactory sexual performance, is one measure of the male's sense of his own manhood. He has to feel that he is able to please a woman in bed. Ideally, the male should try to attune his own sexuality to the needs of the woman. Unfortunately, perhaps inevitably, men remain just as genital as they always were. I delved into this question further with Pietropinto, who agreed: "Yes, men are genital, insofar as their sexuality is always going to center on their penises to some extent. And I think they are going to be even more preoccupied with orgasm than women are, although it is interesting to note that Morton Hunt has found that there are more and more men who are not having orgasms during intercourse, even though they are able to penetrate and maintain an erection—something that was an *extreme* rarity in Kinsey's time.

"But sure, they are going to be more genital. The only thing about it is that they now seem more willing to vary their sexual experience. They know they can bring their penises into play in a lot of different ways—orally, tactilely, and so forth.

"Now, some women like Shere Hite seem to want to get rid of the penis somehow. I'm not sure I understand completely what she is advocating when she says, 'Well, why does intercourse have to culminate in orgasm for a man?' Because you don't arouse him and leave him hanging, that is why! Hite complains about men who do this to women, and yet it is supposed to be all right to do it to a man. It isn't right for either."

Even if men are going to remain genitally centered, it is true that male sexuality is becoming more eclectic. At the same time, however, it seems to be becoming more automatic, more mechanistic. Men, even those attuned to women, have a fixed repertoire. They know exactly what they need to do to please a woman. They have read articles by women; they have read the sex manuals. The end result is that there is danger that a certain spontaneity is being taken out of sexual relations.

Sex should be fun. It is fun and it is healthy. Ideally, perhaps, sex should be spontaneous, inventive, funny, and a little bit wild and playful. In adjusting to the new woman, and the new sexuality, men are often a little too serious about it. They can be remarkably businesslike about sex and approach a sexual engagement as if it were a board meeting. They often act as though an efficiency expert were going to rate them. Technique becomes all.

Pietropinto sees this as one of the problems with men. "But, you know," he says, "we always get attacked whenever we say men do this or women do this. Somebody will say, 'How can you talk for all men or all women?' Well, you can't. Not for everyone. But because men are to some extent conditioned, goal-directed, achievement-oriented, performance-oriented, they do tend on the whole to get stuck in ruts. They prefer to go with a tried and sure method of anything.

"You are absolutely right in your remarks about the danger of mechanization," he continued. "I think if a guy suddenly finds out, 'Well, the best sex seems to be when I linger a little bit, and we have a little bit of cunnilingus, and then do this,' and the woman doesn't modify this, then that will become his routine. And pretty soon she will start getting bored with it, and he will say, 'What happened? It worked great last February. Why isn't it working now?' Men will do that, because so much of it is important to them, that is, about things going right, not making too many waves. It depends on the man.

"Of course, a lot of people are interested in experimenting. They like to try a lot of new things. But I think this is going to depend on the partner. If, for example, a man has a wife or a girlfriend who really enjoys experimenting, and he feels she likes it as much as he does, fine. They will experiment. On the other hand, if every time he wants to try something new he gets into a little fear scene—you know, 'God, will she think I'm kinky if I try this?' or 'How is she going to feel about this?' Then he is not going to experiment, even though he may want to.

"So even this sort of thing—experimenting, trying to keep the romance lively, and so forth—that may again be a way of reassuring him that he is doing what the woman wants, that everything is going to go well in the relationship."

Albert Ellis sees things a bit differently. I asked him if at the same time that some men seem to be bringing their sexuality more into harmony with women's and developing a greater sensitivity and sense of eclecticism about sexuality, there is also a mechanization of men's sexuality. In other words, is the man being trapped by a whole other system of guidelines, roles, and expectations?

He replied that this was true of everything that takes a degree of skill. "Let's take the art of cooking—and most chefs, don't forget, have been males rather than females. If you are a very good cook, you have creative urges, and you mix things a little differently. But you always have to take care of the temperature of the oven and lots of other mechanical things. Sex has to be somewhat mechanical to be enjoyable and creative. Unless you do certain things, you are not going to get the greatest joy out of it. So the more you know to some degree about cooking or sex, the more mechanical you had also better be.

"You know, there are a lot of mixed-up people. I just wrote an article for *Psychiatric Opinion* answering some well-known psychiatrists who insist this very thing, that sex is becoming mechanized and alienating—who won't face the fact that a certain mechanization is inevitable. It is also a part of the human condition. The reason you become more mechanical in, let us say, driving a car or inventing other kinds of cars which have no shift, or something like that, is because you are human and you want to act more efficiently. It isn't antihuman to be mechanical. It is human to use mechanistic processes in the service of enjoyment and creativity. You can't simply denigrate the mechanical in, of, and by itself."

"When you use the word *efficiency,*" I said, "that brings up another question I have, which deals with sex in our American culture. It seems that in America, sex, like much else, falls prey to certain cultural manifestations of our national identity. For instance, we like to be efficient. We like to control things. We like to compete with each other. We like to compare things. Do you find this true in the realm of sex?"

"Yes, but it is not a cultural phenomenon," Ellis replied. "You are wrong in thinking of it as cultural. It is a human condition to compare yourself with others. Now this has advantages —you learn how to do things a bit better. It is also a human condition not merely to rate your own traits, deeds, acts, and performances, but to rate your worth, your being, your essence, your psyche. Now this is foolish, since self-rating is a form of overgeneralizing that often leads to dismal results.

"But this is a biological phenomenon. There are no humans I know of who do not do this. So don't think we do it only because of our American culture. Our culture may be one of the most competitive—we really don't know if that is true. But even assuming it is, the competition is not the bad part. The bad part is the *self*-rating, or globally rating oneself as a person because one has some good or bad traits. We all rate our traits to see whether we play tennis better, screw better, or love better than other people. But when we rate ourselves for having certain traits, this is deadly. But again, there are no humans I know of who don't do this.

"Practically all humans are out of their goddam minds in this respect. They *all* engage in continual self-rating and they do it because they think crookedly, because they are human. It has little to do with culture. In rating themselves for their sex performances, men become casualties, or victims, if you will, of the sexual revolution and apparently the new assertiveness of women."

I said, "This is getting very close to a fundamental issue, the notion that American men are consumed with this desire to measure themselves against some standard or against some other person in order to define themselves. They compare the amount of money they have, how much power they can exercise, their athletic ability, their sex life. A very few succeed in various realms and become the ideal which others seek to emulate. However, the great majority of men, the marginal men who do not have any kind of great success in any of these areas, usually spend a lot of their lives trying to compensate for not measuring up to the ideal."

Ellis quickly interjected, "Or they withdraw from the competition. But again, that is a human trait. And it exists in business, sports, all kinds of areas. The person who thinks he has to do well, *has* to perform up to a certain standard—and, as a male, he would be the vast majority of any culture—and then actually doesn't do that well, he will compensate or withdraw.

"For all of us, or at least most of us, are average by definition. We won't do *that* well in most areas. Only a few really perform greatly at anything. Some males will focus on one or two fields that they do well in and accept themselves for that reason. But others will put themselves down for their poor traits; and they will be marginal men who hate themselves because they are not superb, not up to some ideal standard."

Today many men are simply withdrawing from the sexual arena. They are unwilling to risk encounters with women. Some worry about competition with other men, the invidious comparisons that might be made between their performance and some ideal performance, or even whether some other man is better-looking, richer, more successful. Some, too, fear women, in some cases because they have at some time in their lives suffered psychosexual damage or ridicule for poor performance.

I asked Ellis what in his view were the usual causes of sexual timidity, of ambivalence or sexual avoidance among men.

"It is almost always fear of failure," he replied. "The man fears he will fail and that would mean he was a failure as a person. He feels he must be perfect and not have any significant failings." According to Ellis, men tell him: " 'If I get rejected it means something about *me* rather than about the taste of the rejector,' but the latter is really the truth." These marginal men can't tolerate even the possibility of failure, so they withdraw, just as other people don't try for certain professions or sports because they fear they will do too poorly at them.

"They are afraid to put themselves on the line," Ellis said. "Because they are not just putting their traits on the line and saying, 'Well, shit, I'm not good at tennis,' or 'I'm not good at screwing.' No, they tell themselves, 'I am a *rotten person* if I am not good at tennis or screwing.' Again, it is their self-rating by which they downgrade themselves in many areas. And sexual performance is one of the chief areas where men rate *themselves,* their entire being."

Some men retreat into fantasy and masturbation. They experience several masturbatory ejaculations a day. There are theorists who feel that masturbation itself is the villain, a practice that encourages a man to retreat from the real sexual world. I asked Albert Ellis, "Do you think that in some cases masturbation drives a man into withdrawal, or does it merely reinforce an individual's tendency to withdraw?" Ellis argued that the latter is true.

"It is just like crime movies," he said. "Crime movies may encourage *some* people who are very disturbed and are therefore apt to be criminals. These few do things they see in the movies. But the same films don't encourage most of us to go out with a gun or a bomb! If you are disturbed to begin with and then you masturbate, you *may* use masturbation to withdraw from heterosexual or even homosexual activity. That is quite possible. But if you are *not* disturbed to begin with, then you will masturbate and *not* withdraw. In fact, because you will find interpersonal relations better than masturbation, you will probably favor them more. It depends on your basic tendency."

I remained curious about men who seem to be increasingly afraid to risk encounters with women, so I asked Anthony Pietropinto if he lent credence to the notion that a lot of men who are sexually timid have, at some point in their lives, suffered psychosexual damage or perhaps ridicule at the hands of a woman. "Yes," he replied, "I think that tends to be true. And it need not be ridicule. It might be some kind of strong feeling or taboo against sexual expression, or just guilt about it. The problem might stem from an overtly seductive mother, forcing the man to repress his sexuality. But remember, obviously if a man has a severe problem relating sexually, it has to stem from some other place."

Many men with sexual problems have suffered a deep emotional wound from a woman somewhere along the line. It might have been a man's mother, his first lover, or some erotic experience that has wounded him. Often, the man develops a built-in defense against further wounds. Never again will he relinquish control and power. Never again will he leave himself exposed and vulnerable to a woman who might abuse him, hurt him, humiliate him, leave him. He cannot allow himself to be caught between his human need for intimacy and his fear of suffering again. If the psychologically scared man does not withdraw, if he does seek another sexual relationship, it will be with someone whom he perceives as absolutely safe and unthreatening, someone, perhaps, who has no power, no money, little education. But even in these cases a man may still experience a conflict between the head and the penis. And that is a battle from which the male's sexuality rarely emerges unscathed.

14
Sexual Dysfunction

WITHDRAWAL MIGHT be a good tactical maneuver for the man who is unsure of himself. In war, armies often withdraw only to regroup, add reinforcements, size up the opposition. Then they sally forth again. So, too, with men. Even the person who withdraws and masturbates can learn something important about himself. In masturbating, Dr. Ellis says, the individual "learns to focus, learns to fantasize. He learns what sensations to focus on, what kind of stimulation he requires to get aroused and come to orgasm. So all down the line, both ideationally and physically, he gains knowledge about himself which he can then take into the arena of interpersonal sex."

For many men, however, withdrawal is not voluntary. In fact, there is an inability to perform, even in situations where a man desires, or thinks he desires, intercourse. Sexual dysfunctions, as they are called, have been with us for a long time. In recent years there has been talk of "the new impotence," a feeling that sexual dysfunctions are on the rise. There is no way of knowing for sure. There are no reliable statistics on which to base a sound judgment. So I asked Dr. Ellis: "I realize that when you try to talk statistically about this you are in for a lot of trouble, but is there a greater incidence of sexual dysfunction, or are men just more open about doing something about it?"

He replied: "There was that *Esquire* article several years ago, 'The New Impotence,' arguing that there was a greater incidence of dysfunction. Well, it is probably the opposite. There is probably less male impotence, in proportion to the total population of males, than there was years ago, because men are gaining more experience. The more experience you get, the better you tend to function. When you get used to doing an unfamiliar thing, you do it more competently. In absolute numbers, sure, there is greater dysfunction because, in the first place, the population has increased—everybody always forgets that little thing—and second, more people are having sex. If fifty million were copulating twenty years ago, and a hundred million are doing it today, there will be more cases of sexual dysfunction. Psychiatrists, psychologists, and urologists will see more men with problems. But that does not mean the proportion is higher. The proportion is probably lower. I really haven't seen any evidence whatsoever that a greater percentage of men are impotent today than, say, twenty years ago, and I personally find that it is a smaller percentage."

There are two primary sexual dysfunctions among men, impotence (or erectile dysfunction) and premature or fast ejaculation. Of the two there is, according to sex therapist and author Helen Singer Kaplan, "probably no other medical condition which is as potentially frustrating, humiliating, and devastating as impotence."[1] In our culture, masculinity is directly related to virility, to the ability to get and sustain a hard erection. Not to do so is to be less than a man. The male's self-esteem is deeply involved in this aspect of his sexuality, and failure can lead to severe depression.

As defined by experts, impotence is divided into two types. First is primary impotence, the most severe, which is a dysfunction among men who have never been potent with a sex partner, even though they may well have complete erections either spontaneously or during masturbation. Men who have secondary impotence have functioned capably for some time before the onset of their erectile problem. Primary impotence is by far the more difficult to treat, because it is the product of serious, deep-seated psychiatric disorders or some physical disability that is not easily corrected.

For men with secondary impotence, erection fails at some point in a sexual relationship, usually at the point that a man becomes overanxious. The precise moment of impotence varies with each individual. As Helen Singer Kaplan notes in her book *The New Sex Therapy,* "there are wide variations in the pattern of impotence." Some men, she continues,

> cannot achieve an erection during foreplay. Others attain an erection easily, but lose their erection and become flaccid subsequently at specific points in the sexual response cycle, e.g., at the moment before entry, or upon insertion, or during intercourse. Other men are impotent during intercourse, but can maintain an erection during manual manipulation or oral sex. Some can have an erection while clothed, but become flaccid as

> soon as their penis is exposed to view. Some men become excited and have erections during foreplay when they know that intercourse is not possible, but lose their potency when they are involved in situations where intercourse is not only feasible but is expected. Some men can erect only if the woman dominates the sexual situation, while others become impotent if their partner tries to assume control. Some men are capable of partial erections but cannot achieve firm erections. . . . Others suffer from purely situational impotence and experience erectile difficulties only under specific circumstances.[2]

Whatever the circumstances, whatever the situation, it is thought that over half the male population has at some time experienced impotence.

Anthony Pietropinto attributes the incidence of erectile dysfunction to a fear of rejection by the woman. "In the past," he says, "if a guy was in bed with a woman, either he had to feel that she cared for him—which he obviously knew because she would not have gone to bed with him unless he meant something to her—or he really didn't care—she was a prostitute, he was paying her, or she was a bar girl, and he bought her a couple of drinks, so it was O.K. He never had to ask himself, 'Does she really care about me? Does she want me in this way?'

"Now it seems that a lot of women are going to bed with guys and the attitude is 'O.K., now please me' or 'Let's see how good you are.' This is very threatening to a man. She hasn't gone to bed with him because she necessarily likes him. She may be there just to try him out—something he never had to worry about before. So, you see, this is a problem.

"I had a woman in therapy who would routinely go to bed with a guy on the first date and then refuse to do it thereafter. She didn't know why he felt so terrible about that. After all, hadn't she gone to bed with him on the first date? What more did the guy want? I pointed out how terribly hostile this was, that what she was saying to the guy was, 'Boy, you were so bad I'm not going to go back to bed with you again.' Now, obviously this was what was going on within her.

"I don't think it's right to say that a man is going to be turned off or intimidated because a woman has a well-paying job or because she has a college education. That isn't the point. What he wants to know is—within the context of this encounter—'Are you interested in me? Do you want to please me as much as I want to please you? And if things don't go too well, is it O.K.?' "

Still, there has been a tendency among some writers to lay the blame for men's impotence on the women's movement and the demands for performance by aggressive, liberated women. In her novel *Blue Skies, No Candy,* Gael Greene describes a women's consciousness-raising group. Her protagonist, Kate Alexander, attends and thinks to herself about the women there and the movement generally. "They're like mutating insects, women feeding on the poison they condemn, absorbing sexism and hate into the bloodstream. I worry they will immobilize the drones that adore them and become a tribe of queen bees with no males left strong enough to survive contacts with their cunts." Strong words, which Greene qualified somewhat in our conversation.

She said, "I think it is true that a small fraction of the movement is using the same kind of sexism they condemn and that anger and sexism are very threatening to men. There *are* men today who don't know what to do and feel overwhelmed, feel that they are constantly asked to perform, sexually and otherwise. And these men are immobilized. I couldn't guess how many, though."

"Is that what all this premature ejaculation and situational impotence are all about?" I asked. "Do you think it is like a psychosexual catch 22, that men are getting lost at this point, that it has become a problem for them?"

"Well, I think some men feel they are being asked or required to perform rather than feel they are doing what they love to do or what they have always wanted to do. I think that it has to do with a little boy's fearing that love will be withdrawn if he does not perform for Mama. 'You eat your dinner or I am not going to love you.' Women, on the other hand, have received loving, cuddling, kissing from their fathers, who coo, 'Aren't you adorable.' They do not get commands for performance from their fathers. Father-daughter relationships can create their own special problem. The point I'm making is that girls are not asked to perform for Daddy. And when a man equates his sexual communication or sexual expression with that kind of performance, it is the end."

This remains an "alleged phenomenon," according to Dr. Helen Singer Kaplan's writings. But she warns us that any "demands for sexual performance can have deleterious effects on the male sexual response."[3] The same applies to women, and Kaplan reminds us that "through the ages women have experienced the destructive effects of 'sex on demand' to a far greater extent than men." She cautions that "commands or demands" from either side will impair a sexual relationship. *But neither Kaplan nor the majority of sex therapists finds any correlation between the sexual liberation of women and the incidence of male impotence.*

I also asked Dr. Albert Ellis if he found the blame placed on the new liberated woman to be true or false.

"Largely bullshit," he replied. "It is probably just the opposite. Many men now are able to go to bed with women because the woman has been more assertive. She goes out actively looking for men. Sometimes, after reading books like my *Intelligent Women's Guide to Dating and Mating,* she picks them up. She is more overt and assertive about sex. She has a better attitude. And when she gets into bed, the really sexually liberated woman doesn't demand intercourse or anything like that. And many men know this. If anything, sexual liberation in women has helped make millions of males less inhibited. Men now know that even if their cock doesn't get big and hard they can still satisfy, even better satisfy, a woman with their mouths or their fingers.

"Now some will still feel that they are below average sexually. They may feel they are not sexy enough, that women demand that they be supersexy, and they are not. In view of the fact that women are more available today—and not only for hand-holding or petting but for full sexual relations—a few men will make themselves more disturbed than they used to. But the few are not necessarily typical of the vast majority."

"And is it a negligible few?" I asked.

"Well, it is a few million, probably, so we can't say negligible. But it is a small proportion compared with the bigger proportion who are screwing liberated women more often and getting less inhibited."

In fact, therapists report that while some men are turned off by the demands for performance and satisfaction, the greater majority of men with erectile failures have partners who are too gentle or too rigid. They are turned off by women who just lie there very passively, who don't touch the man's penis. There is no communication of sexual needs and desires. These are women who expect penetration only, not clitoral stimulation or more varied things. The man gets anxious. He is in charge, but he is alone. Being alone, having full responsibility, is a source of anxiety for these men. Thus, it seems to be a myth, not borne out by men entering therapy, that the new, aggressive woman is causing impotence.

Anthony Pietropinto provides an illustration. "A guy called in on a radio show I was on and said, 'I'm so glad you were talking about it, because just tonight I tried to have sex with a girl who didn't seem that interested. I found I was unable to keep my erection, and even though she was willing to go through with it, I couldn't. This is the first time it has happened. What's wrong with me?' 'Nothing is wrong with you,' I replied. 'It is quite common. It happens all the time.' "

Therapists also find that one of the greatest sexual turn-offs for men is anger at their partner, especially anger that festers over a long period of time. Of course, as mentioned earlier, there are some men who are quite capable of having sexual relations with their wives, even though they have terrible marriages and really can't stand their spouses. Yet they manage to do it anyway. Most deeply angry men—and women, too—will find it difficult, if not impossible, to be sexually desirous of the other. They may not express it verbally. But if the anger is there, deep inside, it can show up in bed.

Also showing up in bed is the second of the male's dysfunctions, premature or "fast" ejaculation, as Albert Ellis prefers to call it. In fact, premature ejaculation is considered to be the most common of all male sexual problems. Albert Ellis is one therapist who disagrees. He admits that most of the men who come for sex therapy do suffer from fast ejaculation, but he claims that he had a greater proportion of premature ejaculators "years ago." "Why?" I asked.

He replied: "Again, the reason is the same as I gave for dysfunction in general. First, the population is greater, so even if there is an absolute increase there is not necessarily a proportionate increase. Second, there has been an explosion in the publication of sex books that deal with the problem and with ways to overcome it, including books that show men they don't have to use their sacred penis to satisfy the female. Also, just the fact that people are having more sexual experiences has a tendency to decrease the amount of premature ejaculation. The more sex you have, the slower you will tend to come. If you have sex only a few times a month you will come much faster. Consequently, the sophistication and greater experience of American men are both leading to proportionately less fast ejaculation."

One problem for men is that there is a lack of agreement as to what constitutes premature ejaculation. Different authorities demand that there be a definite, though varying, amount of time from reaching the plateau of excitement to ejaculation before they will label a condition one of premature ejaculation. One textbook mentions thirty seconds. At New York University they specify a minute and a half. At Cornell it was two minutes. At UCLA it is eighty seconds. Others specify a certain number of thrusts after entry. Masters and Johnson even said that if the man ejaculates in half the time it takes his partner to reach orgasm, his ejaculation is premature.[4]

None of these definitions is sufficient. As Helen Singer Kaplan puts it in her writings, "Prematurity cannot be defined in quantitative terms because the essential pathology in this condition is not really related to time. Rather the crucial aspect of prematurity is the absence of voluntary control over the ejaculatory reflex, regardless of whether this occurs after two thrusts or five, whether it occurs before the female reaches orgasm or not."[5] Premature ejaculation occurs when it is beyond the male's capacity to control his intense level of sexual excitement at the plateau stage.

To Kaplan this is a problem of voluntary control. As she defines it most simply, "Prematurity is a condition wherein a man is unable to exert voluntary control over his ejaculatory reflex, with the result that once he is sexually aroused, he reaches orgasm very quickly." It is essentially the inability of the male to have voluntary control over his ejaculatory response.

Most people can attain voluntary control over some of the body's reflexes. Other reflexes are simply beyond the ability of the nervous system to exert voluntary control. You can swallow, for example, if someone tells you to swallow. But, unless you are an advanced practitioner of yoga, you cannot exert voluntary control over heartbeat. If someone tells the ordinary person to accelerate his heart rate five beats per minute, he could not do it. It is beyond the ordinary person's control.

Under ordinary circumstances, both men and women have the capability to voluntarily control their orgasmic response. However, there are a certain number of men who are unable to control their ejaculation. When they reach a high level of sexual excitement, they will ejaculate involuntarily. That is premature ejaculation.

Premature ejaculation may or may not interfere with lovemaking. It all depends on the attitudes of the man and his partner. Generally, however, it does lessen the quality of sexual relations, because the man who knows he ejaculates quickly tends to be afraid, nervous, anxious. He is unwilling to be too fancy in foreplay because he is worried that he will become too excited, that he will come and that will be the end of it. So it is an inhibitory factor to some degree.

Both premature ejaculation and erectile dysfunction (impotence) demand therapy, especially if they recur. And it turns out that many men eagerly seek help. They know they can do something to have their sexuality restored, enhanced, improved. In many cases these are the very men who most relate their sexual problem to their sense of masculinity. Self-esteem is a highly motivating force.

A man might neglect a penis that refuses to function in any circumstance. This is a visible problem, a visible dysfunction, and when it becomes apparent, men have always run for help. They go to urologists, internists, take hormones. They do not hesitate to try everything to regain their "masculinity."

Men who are reluctant to seek help are those with hidden problems that they are unwilling to face. These usually have to do with the man's desire and sexual appetite, his inability to get aroused except with certain women. For this, a man seldom seeks help. This seems to hit at the core of his being, in the area where he is most vulnerable—his masculinity. These men are aroused by certain women but not by others, even those they deeply admire. For example, they can get aroused with prostitutes, someone they can look down upon—a very young woman, a powerless woman who makes the man feel superior. This is the kind of problem men hide. Even if he does enter therapy at the insistence of his wife or lover, he is still reluctant to admit the problem, simply because his identity is too closely tied to virility and sexuality.

Once a man comes to grips with the problem, treatment of secondary impotence, either persistent or occasional, is likely to be successful. It appears to be far more difficult to cure primary impotence, a phenomenon more likely to be associated with serious underlying psychiatric disturbance or endocrine disorders.

For secondary impotence, the therapist's goal is to diminish the anxiety that impairs the male's erection before or during intercourse. His confidence has to be restored, so the therapist's initial goal is to facilitate one erection and one successful coital experience. The therapist assumes that success at an early stage will make easier the subsequent treatment of more deep-seated anxieties. If the man with secondary impotence has a cooperative lover or wife, he may be completely relieved of his impotence within two months after beginning therapy. Those with more serious sources of anxiety require longer therapy, but these men are, in virtually all cases, improved to the point that they experience only infrequent erectile dysfunctions.

Premature ejaculation is one of the easiest conditions to cure. Basically, voluntary control has not been learned because men find it difficult to focus attention on the sexual sensations prior to orgasm. If men don't pay attention, they cannot control their rising excitement. Being aware of sensations, for example, is the way the little boy learns control over his urinary reflex. He first learns what a full bladder feels like. Then he learns to hold it back. He learns control. Similarly, men who become so anxious during the high excitement phase of lovemaking have not focused their attention on the sensations, with the result that they have no control. It is a learning disability, pure and simple, but one that can be overcome. In contrast to the treatment for impotence, the therapist does not have to get to the origin of anxiety. Therapy bypasses the anxiety. The man is taught to focus his attention on the sensations, the high excitement sensations prior to orgasm. As he does so he learns control. About 90 percent of men can be taught voluntary control within a dozen therapeutic sessions, over just a few months.

Pay attention to his sensations—that is what the American male must do. But he often finds that impossible. Most American men find it too difficult to be sensitive, open, and intimate with another person, so they find it difficult to be open with themselves. All too often men are overanxious about their relations with women because they are overanxious about their own feelings. They deal with this anxiety by becoming supermacho, hostile, and aggressive; or they become intimidated by women and may, in the end, be unable to engage in sexual relations at all.

It would seem, then, that it is neither the sexual revolution nor the new, liberated, sexually aggressive woman who is the male's worst enemy. Instead, the male has once again fallen victim to the masculine role he must play at all costs. It is his need to compete at the sexual game, just as he competes at other games, be they business or sports. He rates himself at sex, just as he rates himself in all matters. He has a tendency to equate inability to live up to an idealized standard of performance with failure, which he feels minimizes his entire worth. He defends himself by blaming women and their drive for liberation. But he deludes himself. As men we will continue to delude ourselves until we can say, with Pogo, "We have met the enemy, and it is us."

15
Out of the Closets: Homosexuality and Bisexuality

JAMES DICKEY recalls the feelings of many people who grew up in the 1930s and 1940s: "Homosexuality was as bizarre as seeing a gorilla walk down Fifth Avenue dressed up in a tuxedo. I knew that there was such a thing, but I didn't know any homosexuals. Or at least I didn't know they were homosexuals. There were some fellows that were kind of sissies, but I would never have dreamed in my wildest imagination that they were doing something with another man. People would have killed themselves in my early years before they would have had such a thing imputed to them."

That was America a generation and three wars ago. "Now," Dickey says, "it is different—and, I think, much better. I don't think people should be persecuted for their sexual habits, for their sexual nature. A person's sexual nature is just as much a part of him as the color of his eyes. He does not do what he does by choice, he does it because he must. And there should not be laws against that sort of thing. I believe in people doing what they need to do. Or want to do."

If, as Dickey's remarks suggest, more Americans now accept homosexual behavior in others, it is also true that powerful sentiment against homosexuality still exists. Stringent laws remain on the books in many communities. With each session of a state legislature, as with each election, there is pressure to pass even more oppressive laws against homosexuals. Part of this compulsion can be explained by studying the beliefs of fundamentalist religious groups. But that is not the whole story. For present among men is a deep objection to homosexuality, particularly the male variety. This phobia cannot be explained away simply in terms of religious beliefs. It is also the product of the male's fragile psyche.

I asked Albert Ellis what he saw as the psychological basis of homophobia. He answered: "Well, first of all, I must say that there are probably less homophobic males than there used to be—proportionately, that is. There may be a greater number of homophobic males because the population has gone up. Also, more men may express homophobic sentiments because they see more homosexuality, and they react against what they see. But the proportion is most likely lower, because almost all males were homophobic years ago.

"When I was a youngster, if a man put his arm around my shoulder I would feel uncomfortable about it. Today, that is not so. We have many more males who have had experiences touching each other in encounter groups.

"But as for the psychological basis for homophobia, the reasons are usually the fear men have that they, too, might become homosexual. They fear this because they have had some homosexual desire at some time and are afraid it will grow and become paramount.

"This fear goes directly to their sense of masculinity. They fear that if they had homosexual relations they would be unmasculine—they would be feminine in our culture. We still mistakenly tend to see it that way. Consequently, men are terribly afraid that they will be contaminated, that they will do it. Men are disturbed about other men, because all men—you, me—relate what they do to what we might do ourselves, just as when you cry at a funeral you are probably not crying for the dear departed but because you are reminded that you might die, too."

The pressures of the male role certainly do cause great anxiety. Men who do not measure up to the masculine standard live in fear that they may in fact be homosexual. They experience the fears, the doubts, the anxieties. Yet they don't engage in the homosexual experience. They are pseudo-homosexuals. I asked Anthony Pietropinto to define the term "pseudo-homosexuality" as it is used in his book.

"First of all," he answered, "let me say at the outset that I did not invent the term. Others have used it before. Pseudo-homosexuality is a term that is used to describe men who present to their therapists worries about being homosexual. Generally they are men who have not acted upon them, or if they have acted out their fears, they have done it in a rather ambivalent fashion. They are truly afraid of being homosexual. They are preoccupied with it. They sometimes have homosexual fantasies, maybe even homosexual dreams—they see themselves as being unable to please women and feel generally inadequate, feel unmasculine, may even feel very threatened in places like men's rooms, locker rooms, and so forth—may find themselves peeking at other men's genitals. This is different from true homosexuality, because given the opportunity, these guys would not really become aroused or want to enter into a homosexual relationship. It's more that they're constantly worried about it, because they have some of these feelings about it. It seems to stem—let's not go into what causes homosexuality—not so much from an ambivalence about the female, but rather a sense of competition with men and a feeling that somehow they have not lived up to what in their mind is the prototype of masculinity. They see themselves as generally being inadequate and weak in areas that really go beyond the sexual. This is what we define as pseudo-homosexuality."

If the roots of pseudo-homosexuality are easily traced, the causes of real homosexuality are not. At some time or other everything from genetic endowment, hormonal deficiency, childhood trauma, and a myriad of psychological problems have been cited as the true source of homosexual development. In truth, no one knows for sure. For example, even in the most recent study, *Homosexuality in Perspective,* William Masters and Virginia Johnson have to conclude that "in view of the current lack of secure information in this field, we must maintain an intellectually open stance, acknowledging that in at least some instances—though clearly not in most cases—hormonal predispositions may interact with social and environmental factors to lead toward a homosexual orientation," a statement which says everything and nothing at the same time.

It is also possible that for some men homosexuality is an outlet which enables males to escape from the pressures of modern life and the anxieties caused by the women's movement. One therapist, who requested anonymity, said she found more of her male patients experiencing disorientation at this particular time, that more males were wondering if they were not homosexual, or questioning whether they should turn to homosexual relationships. Men expressed anguish at the pressures they feel from many directions, especially from outside the traditional male world: pressures in the home, pressures to perform, to be different kinds of men. A lot of them seem to be becoming more selfish, and asking if they would not be better off with exclusively homosexual relations.

Certainly, several of those with whom I spoke related instances in which an apparently heterosexual man suddenly, late in life, began to talk about going to bed with another man. These men were husbands and fathers, apparently not the kind of men one would expect to hear this from. Unfortunately, what they did not tell me was whether any of these men had acted on their expressed desire.

If it is true that some men are turning to homosexual relationships, then it may mean that gayness is a means of coping with their lack of desire for a male-female relationship. Bob Guccione agreed. "It seems to me almost a natural way of coping. I think that a man who goes from genuinely straight to gay is a man who would feel that he has lost some terrible internal battle with himself, would feel that he had let himself down. Now, I used the phrase 'genuinely straight to gay.' I don't know that it really happens like that. I think there are guys who are bisexual, but more inclined to be gay, who could be put off by the changing attitudes of women today and feel, 'Well, this is really not for me. It's really not my scene. I'm really not happy with women anyway!' They may change or become more oriented toward gayness, possibly for that reason."

I spoke about this phenomenon with several people. Early on, I said to Helen Gurley Brown, "It seems that more men are turning to homosexuality than they have in the past. I don't know at this time whether one can describe this as a response to the women's movement. Certainly, as the female begins to manifest herself in various ways, the male becomes more and more introverted. Do you think that what is happening today has a direct effect on male sexuality? Are men turning inward and turning toward their own sex for gratification as a means of escaping responsibility? Sex without obligations?"

She replied: "Burt, we have never had really accurate statistics about the incidence of homosexuality in our country."

"No, we haven't," I admitted. "Perhaps it is just more visible now than it once was."

H.G.B.: That's definitely a possibility. Who knows how many closet homosexuals there were back when being open was incredibly risky? Remember, we've become a lot more accepting of homosexuality during the last decade, and a gay man doesn't have to be as afraid as he once did that he'll lose his job, or be run out of town if he's honest about his sexual preference. Perhaps there only *seem* to be more homosexuals because they're not hiding anymore. Still, there may actually be a greater number of gays today, and I'd say that this might be related to the current low birth rate. As a nation, we've had to admit that we don't *need* a lot of babies—that there are already enough people to get all the work done—so men are not pressured to father children anymore. They're free to be themselves and find whatever sexual identity suits them best. I think in times of lessening procreation, there has *always* been an increase in homosexuality.

B.A.: Maybe that's also the reason men aren't marrying. We know there are fewer marriages and more divorces today."

H.G.B.: That's right. But the decreasing population isn't the only factor that's causing these trends. You mentioned that men may be shying away from heterosexuality because women are becoming more sexually demanding—and I certainly think that's true. I have no doubt that some men turn to homosexuality because they just cannot face the pressure. (In fact, my feeling is that a fear of not being able to live up to the expectations of the opposite sex is the origin of almost all homosexuality.) In spite of my conjectures, however, I'm not sure anyone could *prove* that there are significantly more homosexuals today than in the past. But let's assume there are—well, that's rather sad for women. Heterosexual men are important to us, whether we're interested in making babies or not. And, of course, by being more demanding and responsive in bed than we used to be, we don't mean to drive men *away!* We want men to desire us even if—indeed *because*—we're more in touch with our own sexuality than women have been in the past.

Although, as Brown pointed out, we don't have accurate statistics, Dr. Albert Ellis does think homosexuality has "increased significantly" over the last ten years. "For two reasons," he says. "First, gay liberation has allowed homosexuals to come out of the closet. They are now more open, especially in the big cities, but even in other places, than they used to be. The desire for homosexuality may not have increased, of course—we really do not know. We only know that homosexual activity has increased. Second, the revolution in sexual values and practices has led a great many more straight men to engage in homosexuality occasionally as part of threesomes, orgies, parties, and other unusual situations. More men today have experimented with and performed homosexual acts once in a while.

"In the past many males would have some homosexual behavior when young, masturbating in the company of other boys, for example. But you wouldn't find much of it after the age of fifteen or sixteen. Today more males start after that age and engage in some amount of homosexual activity. In both respects, then, homosexuality and bisexuality have increased overtly. But again, I must caution that nobody knows whether they have increased in the sense of desire. To some degree the homosexual desire may actually be less, because of the phenomenon I have mentioned before, that we are seeing much more open heterosexuality. One of the reasons in the old days for homosexuality was that heterosexual relationships were not easily available or were considered sinful. A lot of Catholic males, for example, who in the past actually would be horrified at sullying a female, had homoerotic urges. There would be a lot less of that today."

Anthony Pietropinto, on the other hand, is not so sure that homosexuality is increasing in any sense. At least that is what the sample for his book *Beyond the Male Myth* indicates. Most important, though, Pietropinto does not see any move to homosexuality that can be linked to the pressures of the women's movement and the inability of men to deal with it. He says, "I see homosexuality as an avenue that is not really one of free choice where men can have relations exclusively with men or with women and choose one or the other. To me there is an underlying inadequacy among men who have difficulty relating to females or competing with other men. The inadequacies drive more men into withdrawal, into celibacy, not into contacts with their own sex. Men may wind up having fewer and fewer sexual contacts. The women's movement may ultimately result in fewer marriages—although as things stand, people are getting married as much; they are just getting divorced more. Certainly it will lead people into more trial relationships. You will see a rise in men and women living together. But I do not think it is going to cause homosexuality."

Pietropinto also disagrees with the notion that homosexuality should be seen as some sort of haven from pressures. He says: "My own feeling is that homosexuals have their own share of, if not more, difficulties and adjustments. Many people argue that if you could turn gay it would be so easy, because men are so loving and men are so good, and men really care about one another, and so forth. But it doesn't work that way. Homosexuals experience the same difficulties in establishing relationships, defining their own concepts of masculinity. Homosexuality would raise as many problems as it solved for most men."

Sex therapists would agree with Pietropinto's conclusions. They find, for example, that homosexuals seek help for the same psychosexual reasons as heterosexuals. A lot of gays who enter therapy feel the same types of anxiety as heterosexuals. Performance anxieties affect people with delicate reflexes, and therapists find that the homosexual is just as likely to have performance anxiety and lose his erection or ejaculate prematurely as the heterosexual.

In general, the sources of anxiety are the same for homosexuals and heterosexuals. In this, as in most areas, as Ashley Montagu has observed recently, homosexuals are as essentially normal as anyone.[1]

Another fascinating phenomenon among homosexuals, confirmed by the Kinsey Institute's first volume on homosexuality in the United States, is that female homosexuals are better adjusted than male homosexuals. Witness the greater instability of male homosexual relationships, as testified to by the Kinsey report, wherein it was demonstrated that the male was far less constant. The female homosexual typically has only a small number of liaisons in her life, while the male's affairs number in the hundreds. This stems in part from the fact that a woman adjusts more readily to her nature, whereas a man does not. Why is this so?

Bob Guccione provides a clue. Men, he says, "feel that a homosexual encounter drains or acts against their masculinity, that it is antithetical to the image of masculinity which they wish to protect at all costs. Women just don't have these kinds of homosexual hangups. They do not feel that it in any way detracts from their femininity. I think, in fact, that it contributes to their femininity. It adds to it. You see young girls going to school holding hands, you see girls kissing and embracing when they meet. You never see men doing these things in our culture."

Gael Greene agrees that homosexual play is easier for women. She says, "I find that there are some women who are able to make love with another woman in a totally free way without thinking of it as a homosexual experience. Some women are more adventurous about sex and find it easy to try a homosexual relationship most likely in a scene with a man or another couple. It is not threatening as it is to most men."

I asked Greene, "As women become much more overt and

open about their sexual needs, do you find them turning increasingly to homosexual relationships as well as bisexual relationships? Are they now trying homosexual relationships whereas before they wouldn't consider them?"

"Well, I don't find that to be true in the women with whom I am a confidante. I don't find that they are turning to women as a possible source of love or sex. Most of my friends are extremely old-fashioned heterosexuals. They are romantics, waiting for the right man and a real relationship and involvement."

Nevertheless, there is a large population of gay women, and the women's movement, or at least one part of the women's movement, has endeavored to make female homosexuality more open, more accepted. Of course, there has never been as strong a taboo about female homosexuality as there has been about male homosexuality. This is in part due to the ability of women to conceal it. Women over the centuries have had sexual friendships with other women, and few people suspected them of being lovers. Women found it natural to stroke or make love with another woman. It seemed an extension of what they did as babies and as youngsters, especially if they attended a girls' boarding school in England, on the continent, or even in this country.

Natural or not, desirable or not, male and female homosexuals find themselves in the same bind as male and female heterosexuals. Their relationships often parody the old-style possessive marriages that many heterosexuals are attacking. Instead of a relationship of equals, homosexual relationships often have one dominant and one submissive partner. And possessiveness and jealousy between gay couples can be as frightening and destructive as it is for heterosexuals.

Whatever the problems, and whatever the numbers, it does seem clear that homosexual relationships now provide a real alternative for men and women. This suggests that the United States is moving away from the old stereotypes, possibly toward a more bisexual society at the least. Men and women are freer to indulge their personal proclivities without fear that they are engaging in something that will do irreparable harm to their psyches.

I asked Dan Greenburg if he, too, felt we might be moving toward a bisexual culture, or if he thought America was intrinsically too homophobic to "really get into the possibilities of bisexuality."

He replied: "I think that homosexuality will not be snickered at quite as much as it was in the past. But I don't think the average person is going to be very much at home with it.

"My experience in places like Sandstone, in orgies, in post mortem discussions, has indicated an ambivalent feeling about homosexuality. By and large people don't think that two women together is a very big deal. Perhaps enough to raise an eyebrow, but men seem to find it a turn-on. I know I do. And women seem to find that 'Oh, yes. Well, of course, it makes sense.' Not so with males and other males. At most, many men say their attitude is 'Well, that is all right among consenting adults, but I don't think I want to get into it.' Now, that is my personal attitude. I think it is all right if men make love to men. I just don't think I would want to do it.

"That is probably the prevailing attitude among liberated males who have had some experience. Probably the blue-collar guys who have not been exposed to a lot of different sexual experiences find even this liberated attitude revolting. That, I think, probably grows out of their feeling of being personally threatened, wondering about their own well-repressed instincts toward homosexuality.

"I'm sure everybody has homosexual instincts, and I think probably the more repressed groups of individuals really fear it to an incredible degree. If they actually went through analysis or were exposed to anything approaching homosexuality, they would find little danger of suddenly giving up their construction work for interior design, hairdressing, or any of the other gay stereotypes."

Alvin Toffler agrees that we are moving toward a different society, but, as usual, he put things in a larger perspective. He had mentioned in *Future Shock* that society seemed to be becoming more and more lenient and willing to accept homosexuality, so I asked him if he still felt the same way. He answered: "My feeling about the society generally, not just about sexual relationships, is that we are moving from a mass society to a much more diversified society with a multiplicity of social groupings, ethnic groupings, life-style groupings, value groupings, sexual groupings, political groupings—call them what you will. Instead of a uniform industrial mass, we are becoming a highly differentiated, market-segmented, psychologically segmented, religion-segmented, sexually segmented society.

"These trends suggest to me that no one political attitude, no one economic policy, no one sexual program is going to prevail. There will be a multiplicity of life styles which include homosexual life styles, and down the line there will be lots of conflict as these groups come up against each other."

"And as a militancy develops within the group?" I asked.

"Yes. Militant groups pass through a phase during which they hate those who do not share their beliefs or practices. They have to 'hate whitey,' 'hate men,' or 'hate straights,' until they become sufficiently secure and have confidence in themselves. Once they come to the other side, they can have better relationships with the rest of the world.

"To me," he continued, "there is a perfect analogy in the psychological development of a black friend of mine. He was a real tough kid who was very militant—not a juvenile delinquent but a political street fighter, a radical of the 1960s. He drew the line at weapons, but nothing short of that. He went through a black consciousness-raising period during which he hated whites. Then he came out the other side. Now he can relate easily to other races, to the rest of the world—but as a *peer,* never again as a subordinate.

"And I think that is what will ultimately happen with many other groups as well. It has happened with many feminists. As they have developed support systems for themselves and strengthened their own egos and come to value their own heritage, they, too, moved away from the 'hate men' attitudes.

"On the one side we see some gays going overboard in their detestation of outside society. And that may be necessary for them, until they have a stronger sense of their own competence. Conversely, it is going to be terribly hard for the Anita Bryants and John Briggses of the world to come to terms with diversity. But they ultimately will have to come to terms with a lot of other things—not just homosexuality—that will make them uncomfortable. All of us are going to have to come to terms with a diverse, fast-changing society. The toleration of diversity is going to have to be a primary value.

"We are never going to move back to the pre-1970s condition of homosexuals or blacks or any other group in society. We are not going to have an Anita Bryant or John Briggs world, although we will—and *should*—have pockets or subcultures in which their values prevail. The same will be true for gays. Both groups are likely to come to terms with each other eventually, or each will move off to a different part of the turf and ignore the other. One way or another, they will coexist."

In time they may want to coexist, particularly if they become receptive to the lessons they can learn from homosexuals. The new work of Masters and Johnson, for instance, speaks directly to many of the problems of heterosexuals, to the lack of communication between men and women, to the persistence of male dominance in bed, to the male's sense that his sexual expertise should remain unquestioned. From homosexuals, and especially from homosexual women, straight males can learn, as one reviewer of the book observed, "that nothing succeeds so much as treating sexual partners with consideration, understanding, and unhurried gentleness." If they can learn that, all men will gain. Until then, all people should ponder and accept Ashley Montagu's wise words from an article in *Psychology Today:*

> Homosexual men and women are best understood when they are seen as whole human beings, not just in terms of what they do sexually. And that, surely, is the important point about any class of human beings that are in any way distinguishable from others. By virtue of the fact that a person is a human being, whatever his or her biological or behavioral traits (so long as they are in no way damaging to others), the person has a full right to his or her growth and development as a human being. What he or she does about sex, whether to remain celibate, heterosexual, homosexual, bisexual, should always remain a matter of individual right.[2]

16 The Gospel According to Gore

NO ONE is better placed or better qualified to discuss America's sexual mores than Gore Vidal. No one is better able to bring into sharper focus many of the issues raised in this book. In sixteen novels, countless essays, and numerous plays, Vidal has touched on every aspect of human sexuality from classical times (where "the range of vice revealed was considerably beyond the imagination of even the most depraved schoolboy") through the shocking though, perhaps, prescient vision of *Myra Breckinridge* and *Myron,* to the apocalypse of his latest novel, *Kalki*.

I asked Gore if he thinks Americans are now preoccupied with sex.

G.V.: Well, *Time* magazine had a poll on what people are up to and what they think sexually, and they turn out to be more liberal in some ways than you might at first think . . . and in some ways less. One thing which would not have been true twenty years ago is that a majority says that the government has no right, state or federal, to legislate the sex lives of people. Now that is something new. I would say that twenty or thirty years ago they would have wanted the law to punish everybody —adulterers, illicit fornicators, antisocial masturbators, and so on. On the other hand, what people think is morally right and what is morally wrong have not changed all that much.

On the dark side, the Kinsey Institute out in Bloomington, Indiana, recently published a report. Apparently, researchers were astonished to find that in heart of the country some thirty to forty percent of the people, not all of them twice- or even once-born Christians, regard all sexuality as wrong except for procreation within marriage to make babies. They also feel very strongly that their views should be forced on others. These people are natural fascists. At election time, they are the ones who respond with votes and money when demagogues push such hot buttons as "Get the fags," Get the niggers," "Get the media"—which means "Get the Jews."

B.A.: And that is what you refer to in one of your essays in the *New York Times Book Review?*

G.V.: The *New York Review of Books.* We do not write for the *New York Times.* They are the enemy.

B.A.: You refer to it as the "heterosexual dictatorship"?

G.V.: Yes. For example, Alfred Kazin—one of the dictatorship's minor Gauleiters, attacked me in *Esquire*[1] for trying to undermine the sexual Reich. Yet it is perfect lunacy to think that one way of performing the sexual act is the right way when in nature there is extraordinary diversity. Certainly, at any given moment, one-sixth of the American population's primary sexual instinct is for their own sex. Now, are we to say that since this statistic makes the score one to five that the five are "right" and the one is "wrong"? Or to go back to the old Kinsey findings: Since nearly forty percent of the male population has had some homosexual experience, are they—or were they—bisexual? Or were they just experimenting? Or were they so drunk that night that they still don't remember what happened?—an old joke when I was in the army. The dictatorship is so confident that heterosexuality is the preferred, the only "right" sort of sex, that anyone who does not go in for this marvelous practice, so natural, no normal, so blessed by God and Freud, should be imprisoned or psychoanalyzed or have civil rights denied him in such odd places as Dade County, Florida, and New York City. Yet, if heterosexuality is so natural and so wonderful and so obviously right, then why do so many millions prefer their own sex? And why make such terrible laws to force them to conform? The Gauleiters like to depict me as a wicked person who hates heterosexuality—which I don't. What I detest is the heterosexual *dictatorship.* The emphasis is on the noun, not the adjective.

B.A.: Do you see homophobia in the country as more or less a product of a particular mentality that stems from . . .

G.V.: Well, it stems from the law of Moses. Currently it is particularly strong among right-wing Jews. This would be understandable, if not admirable, were they rabbis. But those solemn folk who might have been rabbis in the last century are now psychiatrists, literary critics, journalists; and they enjoy laying down the law of Moses as if it were scientific truth and not Bronze Age superstition. They are great bigots.

Needless to say, our Christian fundamentalists are just as bad. But no one expects an Anita Bryant to be intelligent. On the other hand, we do like to think that our intellectuals are without prejudice—so it's dismaying when they go in for fag-baiting, for putting down women, for playing into the hands of our home-grown fascists.

In the last two years, right-wingers have been raising enormous amounts of money to elect such paladins as Helms and Hatch. To get the money, they must push those buttons that make people react viscerally. Nixon was a master of this sort of thing. Ask him what he is going to do about inflation and he'd say, without blinking an eye, 'Marijuana is a halfway house to something worse.' *You* were talking about inflation. *He* shifts to marijuana. He knows that that will excite the crowd. It also helps him avoid a real issue—like inflation. Lately, intellectuals, who should know better, are employing the same technique.

There was a piece in *Harper's* last year that made the point that the U.S. was losing its love of war because the fags had taken over the culture—the way that they took over England in the thirties and appeased Hitler because the English fags did not want beautiful boys killed. Needless to say, the author is a professional Zionist with no knowledge of history. The American ruling class has always liked wars. As a nation, we are seldom at peace. As for the notion that fags don't like war—well, putting to one side the homosexual capers of Alexander the Great, Caesar, Frederick of Prussia—the army, like professional athletics, has always been a haven for those who take pleasure in the sexual act with their own gender. The ultimate in masculinity, or so this society thinks, is sport and war, two activities traditionally dominated by those with an enthusiasm for their own sex.

B.A.: Is homosexuality more prevalent nowadays—or just more open?

G.V.: Obviously, the subject is more discussed now than it was thirty years ago. But the terms of the discussion are totally cockeyed—to make no pun. There is no such thing as a homosexual, no such thing as a heterosexual. Everyone has homosexual and heterosexual desires and impulses and responses. The balance in each person varies—from those who are most enthusiastic about the opposite sex to those whose sexual enthusiasm is aroused primarily by their own sex. But trust a nitwit society like this one to think that there are only two categories—fag and straight—and if you're the first, you want to be a woman, and if you're the second, you're a pretty damned wonderful guy or gal. Very few so-called fags are feminine in their ways and very few heteros can be regarded as wonderful. Ultimately, everyone is a mixture. Most men whose principal enthusiasm is for boys are married and they are seldom found out—until a scandal breaks like the one in Boise, Idaho, that gave rise to a fascinating book, *The Boys of Boise.* The entire male leadership of the town was busted for sex with consenting adolescent males. The banker, the baker, the publisher, the lawyer—all of them fathers, even grandfathers, were boy-enthusiasts! Oh, the shame! The horror! Look not upon thy father's nakedness!

Yet what they did was perfectly natural and no one would have thought it strange in a civilized society like Athens. Unfortunately, the United States seems farther away than ever from achieving a civilization.

B.A.: Though Anita Bryant represents a distinct part of this country in terms of attitude, mentality, philosophy, what she said was picked up and carried all over, and the sheer stupidity of what she has said has been ridiculed all over the land at the same time. Isn't someone like that ultimately good, because she sets up a point of reference for people who are beginning to think about this subject a little more?

G.V.: I don't know. Look at the recent vote in Dade County, in the City Council of New York. On the other hand, the Californians rejected Proposition Six, a license to hunt witches, and that was encouraging. But those millions of signatures that the local demagogue got in order to put Proposition Six on the ballot do cause alarm. Those who press hot buttons will eventually start a fire.

B.A.: To get back to one point that you mentioned, the question of man and war as affirmation of masculinity . . . what was Dr. Johnson's phrase? "All men think less of themselves for not having been soldiers?"

G.V.: Having spent three years as a soldier in the second war, I neither thought more or less of myself for the experience. It was pretty dull. Dr. Johnson is parroting macho nonsense. I suggest you read a book by Marvin Harris, *Cannibals and Kings.* He looks at human history with an eagle's eye. He demonstrates how *people become whatever their circumstances require.* The Aztecs lacked domestic animals. They needed protein. They became cannibals. To justify what they had done, they institutionalized cannibalism and made it an integral part of their religion.

People become whatever a situation requires. A boy goes to prison. He's an enthusiast for heterosexual relations. Denied those relations in prison, he turns to homosexual relations. Then when he gets out of prison, he goes back to women. What does this mean? It means that he adjusted himself to a situation which he may have enjoyed or not enjoyed and, when it was over, he returned to his principal interest.

B.A.: But aren't sexual roles inherent? Programmed?

G.V.: Not really, beyond physiology. Certainly it is nonsense to say there is an absolute ideal of what male behavior or female behavior ought to be. How he and she behave depends entirely upon conditioning and environment. With one proviso: Strong sexual drives can be frustrated or diverted but they don't go away. They are imprinted for good at the beginning, and the society that tries to thwart them will grow sick and die. As for aggression and war . . . well, if a given society didn't believe in war, then no man would want to be a soldier. He would regard war as an aberration. Dr. Johnson's quotation simply reflects the masculine ethic of his time, place, class.

B.A.: Well, Lyndon Johnson thought that he was ultra-masculine.

G.V.: Oh, yes. The character of Buck Loner in *Myra Breckinridge* was based on Lyndon Johnson.

B.A.: That's interesting. In *Myra Breckinridge,* I remember one particular passage where Myra and Rusty and Mary Ann are sitting together in a restaurant, and Myra is giving advice to Rusty about how there are other ways to swing in the world. But later on you mentioned something very interesting that I wanted to get to with you. You talk about, what it boils down to is that once people can manage to develop this kind of eclecticism sexually, that will free the human spirit in some way to go in all sorts of directions that we restrict it now. Can you elaborate on that?

G.V.: Well, that's Myra. That is not me. I mean Myra Breckinridge is not my voice any more than you can say that Gulliver's adventures represented Jonathan Swift's view of the common man—in an uncommon situation. Myra does seem to be proposing some kind of pan-sexuality, which I don't entirelv understand.

My own view of sexuality is benign. Consenting sexual relations are a good thing, regardless of number, gender, or positions assumed. Incontinent baby-making is a bad thing in an overcrowded world. The muddle the Judaeo-Christian nightmare has made of our sexual attitudes is something not to be believed. Yet people do.

B.A.: Changing the subject somewhat, in the postscript to *The City and the Pillar* you talk about how one man will normally reject sexual advances because he is afraid of losing his autonomy, of feeling used by another person, of feeling like a sex object.

G.V.: Did I write that? I've often thought it but I don't remember writing it.

B.A.: It seems to ring true, especially from the standpoint of male sexuality, which has always been one of poker and pokee . . . fucker, fuckee.

G.V.: It is part of the whole crisis now—the boy-girl with the girl wanting to be on top, which, in symbolic terms, is important to many women who want to do the fucking.

B.A.: Now that women are feeling their sexual oats, they want their time on top.

G.V.: The most interesting aspect of sex is power. In fact, it is the only interesting thing about a subject that is . . . simply *is,* and obvious. But for a man to play sexual games in order to gain power over women—economic as well as physical—that is a great and never-ending theme.

B.A.: Now that men are learning how it feels to be a sex object, what do you think of this new phenomenon of male nudes in magazines?

G.V.: I asked one of the editors of *Playgirl* if he knew how many readers—or viewers—were men and how many were women. He thought a third were fags; the rest were women. I was not convinced. I thought they were all fags. Then one day, walking along the Ringstrasse in Vienna, I saw two stout Austrian women in their thirties rush up to a vendor to get the latest *Playgirl.* As I watched, they tore off the cellophane wrapper, riffled the pages, mouths ajar. They were like two men looking at the gynecological studies in *Hustler.*

B.A.: But isn't male sexuality more compartmentalized than female? It's more concerned with the object per se as a turn-on, tits and ass, that kind of thing. Whereas female sexuality is more of a totality in sex, where the woman is interested, of course, in having sex and orgasms, yet she's more interested in intimacy, in warmth, in touching, afterglow, all of these things.

G.V.: Oh, yes. Holding. But how much of that is conditioning? Other societies haven't featured holding. Look at those

Amazons who used to throw boys onto the ground and mount them—a common *male* sex fantasy, by the way. But all in all, people will try to behave as society wants them to.

B.A.: Then is society's attitude unnatural?

G.V.: I'm sure that a million or so years ago the DNA (a.k.a. God) worked out the logistics of human survival. Thus far, *she* lays the egg. *He* forages for food while she's nursing. Then *They* bring up baby. This still holds—to a point. But things change. Today an economically independent working woman can bring up a child by herself. That's new. That could be the end—for many people—of the family known as nuclear. Certainly, the family is not a biological unit. It's an economic one.

B.A.: The unfortunate thing about this whole situation now is that we are all right now experiencing in this country a state of *sexual overload*.

G.V.: Well, that applies to the ten percent who read magazines like *Cosmopolitan*. The ninety percent go on as before, with two exceptions. One, the fact that the world is seriously overpopulated has got through to every American, and he's figured out that there is no need to marry if one isn't going to have children. Second, the "independence" of women is making for freer, less tribal arrangements. As a result, every relationship is bound to be a bit strained. We have Judaeo-Christianity to thank for much of the mess. Happily, our dismal culture is disintegrating rapidly.

B.A.: Personally, I think that change is going to come when people begin to realize that we've all been turned into a bunch of arteriosclerotic and sexually dysfunctioning shells of human beings. Do you think change is possible for all of us, or only within ten percent of us, the people who read? I don't know. I think, perhaps, I am just a bit more optimistic.

G.V.: Who can predict the future? I can't. But change is the nature of life. So is stupidity. Whatever comes next, we'll adapt —unless the race is extinguished, always a possibility. There is nothing written in the stars that says we have to continue. We have been here a very short time, and we have fucked up beautifully. But then that's the fun of being human, isn't it? Unlike the ants, we're temporary. But the ants don't have as good a time as we do, and so who cares if they're still trudging about in single file long after we're gone, as they were doing before we came down from the trees?

17

Now and Beyond: A Conversation with Alvin Toffler

ALVIN TOFFLER is one of the most astute critics of contemporary society. His best-selling book *Future Shock* reached millions with the message that the acceleration of change in the twentieth century has proven too much for individuals as well as social and cultural systems—that these have a finite capacity for adapting to rapid transformations.

Toffler sees the sex-role crisis as one aspect of this larger problem. He recognizes that men are disoriented and unsure of what it means to be a man today, what women expect of them, and what they should expect of themselves. He believes that the male crisis, however, is indicative of a more general role crisis in our society. But if Gore Vidal is pessimistic about the future, Toffler is optimistic about what he sees beyond. We talked about this.

A.T.: Every society has an internal role structure, an invisible architecture of roles. And that invisible architecture of roles is usually very, very rigid and solid. But if you look now, you see not just the blurring of the line between males and females, but a blurring of the line between doctors and nurses, between consumers and producers.

What I see is essentially a honeycomb of role configurations in the society. This is a cop, this is a lawyer, this is a doctor, this is a nurse, this is a man, and this is a woman—all the definitions are now blurring, and as a result we see conflict and confusion all around us. When that happens inside the society, good-bye Congress, good-bye President, good-bye economic structure, good-bye the rest, because the role structure is part of the basic glue that holds the system together.

So, to me, the masculine crisis is part of a larger picture of role crises. And that, in turn, is part of the breakdown of industrial civilization and the emergence of a new civilization in its place.

B.A.: "What do you see as the source of the blurring of sex roles?"

A.T.: "What's interesting about the blurring of male-female roles is that it actually has very deep sources in the economy and the technology. When we moved from an agricultural to an industrial society, we fundamentally changed the consciousness of both men and women. For example, we now assume that men are more "objective" and women are "subjective." There probably is a small grain, not a big grain, but a small grain of truth to this common view. But if so, it isn't a biological condition. Rather, it reflects the changed nature of work in industrial society.

Before the industrial revolution, the entire family—men and women—worked together as an economic unit. They worked in an essentially decentralized economy, a local, self-sufficient economy—and, therefore, a noninterdependent system. If one peasant didn't show up to cut the hay that day, it didn't prevent the next one from doing so. They were not tightly interdependent. The same was true for household work. If a woman didn't take proper care of her child, it didn't prevent the woman in the next household from doing her job.

In factory life, by contrast, most work *is* interdependent. If a worker doesn't show up, he or she disrupts all the workers downstream in the production process. That's a very big difference, and it has psychological consequences for both men and women.

As men moved into the factories and women stayed or were forced to stay home, there was a sharp divergence in the nature of the work done by the sexes. And this affected their psyches.

Men, by and large, became totally involved in highly *interdependent* work in which everything they did had effects at a distance. They were part of large organizational systems and they were taught to think of their relationship to the larger, distant, impersonal world. Women, by and large, remained home and continued to work under decentralized and basically noninterdependent circumstances. They focused on the close-in world of family and personal relationships.

I think this difference between high interdependency work and low interdependency work came to correlate with objectivity and subjectivity. The high interdependency of "men's work" bred an awareness of relationships with the outside world; the low interdependency of "women's work" emphasized subjective, private experience.

Today I see the rise of unisex fashions and the blurring of sexual roles as related to new changes in work. As more women move into the high interdependency sector, you can expect them to assume so-called masculine characteristics—that is, to become somewhat more objective and less subjective. By contrast, as more men stay at home and do less interdependent work, as they care for kids and take care of homes, their consciousness softens, becomes more private and subjective.

Moreover, the work itself is beginning to change. Millions of people are "doing their own thing"—they are working at home, they are working at odd hours, they are doing work which is less repetitive and more creative. We're moving from the factory production of goods into the manufacture of symbolic goods.

So while some women are moving in toward the center and becoming somewhat "masculinized" and "objectivized" by the process, a lot of men are moving in the other direction.

B.A.: That's a very interesting perspective, but if you extrapolate that out, what you're really saying is that we're going to reestablish the small familial relationship.

A.T.: Well, I'm not an Aristotelian. I don't believe in either/or. Therefore, we won't go back to a purely subjective, noninterdependent system for both men and women, but rather toward some synthesis or fusion of the two forms of consciousness—which is much healthier, it seems to me, and yields a more balanced view of reality.

B.A.: Will it have ramifications culturally? And emotionally?

A.T.: Oh, yes.

B.A.: Sexually?

A.T.: Yes. I think there already are.

B.A.: To what do you attribute a lot of this "feel-goodism," in the seventies—est, and a lot of these mystical purists, and the new spiritualism?

A.T.: Well, to me these are evidences of the breakdown of a three-hundred-year-old epistemology, which came essentially with the industrial revolution. The industrial revolution was not only a matter of machines. It was also Descartes and his idea that the universe is composed of discrete particles. In physics you got the unsplittable particle, the atom. In sociology you got the ultimate, inalienable individual. In economics you got the corporation as the ultimate, atomic unit of the economy. In journalism you got the idea of the event, unconnected with any other event—therefore we tend to report who-what-why-and-when, but seldom the meaning of these events.

Throughout the industrial world we operated on the basis of a common set of fundamental ideas. These included a common conception of time—seeing time as linear. A common conception of space, logic, and causality. This industrial culture, which I call "indust-reality," is present in all industrial societies, capitalist or communist. It's the culture most of us were raised in. It has given us a very powerful handle on certain kinds of problems—on physics, mechanics, engineering, space shots, technology, and so on. But as the industrial age ends and a new civilization makes its appearance, we are now reevaluating it.

We are finding that it is increasingly inadequate to solve some of the social, political, cultural, and psychological problems we face. Thus we see a tremendous disillusionment with industrial-era ideas and an enormous attack on the epistemology of industrialism. That explains the rise of cults and the interest in Eastern mysticism. All of these quasi-religious movements are essentially critiques of the industrial epistemology. Ninety-five percent of them are quackery and nonsense, no doubt. They are not an adequate substitute for indust-reality. But they *do* call attention to the weakness or limitations of the existing epistemology—the industrial mentality.

They get a lot of people seriously searching, thinking about alternatives. But we also see a lot of desperate searching for an answer, any answer, a supersimplistic explanation of everything. Plenty of religiocultural quacks and salesmen are beginning to offer just that.

When we add the breakdown of our epistemology to the breakdown of the old social institutions like the nuclear family, and you turn up the transience level, you get a lot of lost and lonely people, candidates for future shock.

In fact, we are suffering from a plague of loneliness as people try to cope. It affects men as well as women, although men may have a harder time admitting or expressing it.

B.A.: Do you see transience as part of the way our culture, our society, has developed?

A.T.: The society is shot through with temporariness, and it clearly affects man-woman relationships. You see it in sequential polygamy in marriage—marriage, divorce, remarriage, divorce, remarriage, and so on. You see it in the frequency of affairs. You see it in the search for instant intimacy—particularly in young people.

In a more stable society, where relationships were more long-lasting, you first built a relationship with someone, then you hopped into the sack. Sex was the culmination of the relationship. For the generation that has grown up since the 1960s, the reverse is true–you hop into the sack because, deep down in the recesses of your brain, you realize that if you don't achieve intimacy with somebody quickly, you may never do so. He or she may very well be out of your life—transferred to California or hitchhiking to Vermont—before you have had the chance to establish an intimate relationship.

A lot of kids surveyed about sexual behavior say, "Sex is a way to get to know somebody better." What they are really saying is that sex is a way to *accelerate* the relationship. I think this is a direct psychological reflection of the acceleration of technological change, the acceleration of social and political and other changes in this society.

What we have, then, is a crisis for the individual, for personality, and for the family system as well. With so many people now knowing who they are, what they are, or what to do—and feeling awful about it—there is an enormous market for psychological and religious hucksters.

Toffler does not think there will be any easy solution to this problem, "short of political, social and technological changes that create the matrix for a more stable culture."

I asked him: "You have talked about the liberating possibilities of the new revolution for men. You say that it will liberate them from many of the barbarisms that grew out of the restrictive, relatively choiceless family patterns of the past and the present. That it will offer to each a degree of freedom hitherto unknown. But that it will also exact a steep price. Can you expound on that a little more?"

A.T.: If you're in charge of yourself, having a wider range of choice is great, because then you can put together a set of experiences, or a life style, or a set of relationships that really fit your own individual needs. If you are out of control of yourself, if you are not deeply aware of your own values, then all of those choices merely make life more difficult for you. They confuse or paralyze instead of liberating.

For example, during the past century or two, since the industrial revolution, the nuclear family was the standard model for society. We grew up more or less assuming that we would all be a part of the nuclear family system. But we are now seeing the breakdown of the nuclear family. It's not going to disappear, but it is no longer going to be the *central* model, or the *standard* model, to which everybody has to adhere.

With respect to family, as well as everything else, there are going to be more choices—single parenthood, childless marriage, homosexual marriage, expanded households, two-paycheck or three-paycheck families, et cetera.

Rather than our coming down hard on all the people who are trying out alternatives to the nuclear family—often at great personal cost—we ought to recognize that they are performing a social service for us. They are, in fact, acting as a social laboratory. From their painful experiments we will discover which family forms fit the matrix of the future society. Nobody now knows which family forms will survive and dovetail with the new forms of work, the new nature of technology, the new economy, the new political order, the new cultural system.

So I think it is valuable for us to have a lot of people experimenting with different familial forms. And we really ought to subsidize them, rather than punish them—which is what we basically do.

B.A.: This whole splintering of all the social structures and the regrouping over the next century—I would like to be there looking back, because it is an interesting phenomenon. I have been trying to figure out where it is all going. We do seem to be moving into lots of little groups and lots of little satellite groups that are all banging against each other.

A.T.: Temporary clusters of minorities.

B.A.: A psychological minority, a sociological minority . . .

A.T.: But not just in the United States. This is happening in every industrial society.

B.A.: I find also a homogeneity in problems—in any industrial civilization.

A.T.: That's because we're experiencing the general crisis of industrial society. Industrial civilization, not just in one country but across the planet, is in its death agony. This doesn't mean we are going to slide back to some pretechnological condition.

Unless we incinerate ourselves, we're not going back to the cave. Rather, we're going ahead to some new stage of society with highly sophisticated technology—but also with very different social, cultural, and political institutions.

B.A.: Over the last two, three, four years, we've seen a total disenchantment with our political system as it exists today.

A.T.: Today's political systems are obsolete. So the question is, how do we design new ones? And how do we make it legitimate for people to start thinking about alternative political institutions in societies in which even to talk about an alternative is dangerous?

B.A.: Blasphemous.

A.T.: Yes.

B.A.: You can't do that sort of thing. Perhaps a younger generation will be more willing to consider that. I like to think so, although I'm not sure.

A.T.: I'm not even so sure that it's generational. I've been saying for five years that it's time for us to reexamine the Constitution, the entire structure, the framework of our government. I've said that to audiences all over the country. I've had elderly John Birchers and young long-haired radicals both come up afterwards and say, "Yes, you know, you're right. It doesn't work." Mainstream audiences, too, recognize that the present structure doesn't work—and this is as true of the Communist structure in Moscow, or the semi-Socialist structure in Sweden as it is in Germany, Japan, France and the United States. The institutional structure we have was created by social and political inventors—people like us. It wasn't God-given.

B.A.: Now we've got to redesign it—go back to the drawing board. What about the possibility for change?

A.T.: Tremendous.

B.A.: Fundamental?

A.T.: Yes, fundamental change. But the questions are what kind of change—and guided by whom?

What kind of change? In the past, as we have seen, the male role has led to confusion among men and subservience among women. It has worked to the benefit of neither. Fundamental change will come about only when men begin to reevaluate themselves, their lives, their roles in society. Some have already begun. And it is to them and to the goal they seek that we now turn.

18
Men's Liberation: A Talk with Warren Farrell

THERE IS a new generation of men, particularly young men, who take women's emancipation and liberation for granted, as a fact of life. In many cases these are men in their twenties and early thirties who were in college during the height of the women's movement, men who may well have started as traditional chauvinists but who discovered either that they agreed with the new ideas of the women's movement or that they would not get far with liberated women if they did not accept, really accept, their program.

These men look at life differently. They see male-female relationships as a process of sharing. They value fatherhood in different ways, thinking of it as more than throwing a football on a Saturday morning. They expect to be complete parents, to deal with their children on an emotional level. They don't leave the housework and the cooking to their wives. They participate. And they are proud of it.

They accept the need of many women to have some interest or job outside the home. Few want to be totally responsible for a woman, and they don't feel that their only desirability as men rests on their ability to provide. They feel instead that their desirability rests on being good companions, lovers, and friends. They might even accept that a woman might be the provider for a brief period or all the time—that she may be in a position to make more money. They are comfortable with the new arrangement. It doesn't threaten their masculinity.

The women's movement has opened the eyes of these men. It has shown them that liberation for women can mean liberation for men, too. For several years men have been meeting together across the nation, talking about masculinity, about what it means to be a man in America today. Doing this they have to be open with each other. The barriers that men usually put up have to be down.

The movement for men's liberation, like that for women, has many voices, serves many constituencies. At the fringes are those with special concerns, often with radical political and social programs that would require the overthrow of institutions as we know them. At the center, however, are moderates who address issues of concern to the mass of men, the issues raised in this book. Perhaps no one is better known for his work on behalf of men than Dr. Warren Farrell, a moderate, who spends nearly all of his time speaking and appearing in all parts of the country. His book *The Liberated Man* sold 225,000 copies in hardcover and paperback. He has appeared coast to coast on television with the message that men, too, can be free.

We spoke in New York, and I asked him about the functions, the advantages, and perhaps the limitations he sees in the movement for male liberation and in the drive for consciousness raising among men.

B.A.: Warren, I sensed in your book, and in the whole nature of what you and others have done in the last five years, that you have created a foundation on which further gains are possible. That is the beginning of the process; that gets the juices flowing. Just the beginning. Getting men to start asking serious questions about their lives and their values; to look at themselves honestly; to think about how they really feel about things. Do you think that men's liberation has the potential for this further expansion, the potential of being a mass movement?

W.F.: In the formal movement sense, the very nature of the men's movement will always limit its ability to reach the masses *as a movement*. For example, if seven men sit around in a men's group learning how to listen, we're unlikely to see the front page of a newspaper with headlines saying "Seven Men Learned How to Listen." The women's movement has more concrete goals. A woman becoming a senator can make headlines. The men's movement, therefore, has limited inherent visibility through which to communicate with the masses.

Despite the limitation, the movement has expanded from a few men's awareness groups in 1969 to about three thousand in 1979. From no men's courses in 1969 to hundreds in 1979. From one men's center in 1969 to forty-two in 1979.

The men's movement will probably have its greatest impact on the personal level—in its communication to men of a new "permission system," a new set of options for men, that will reach down to the mass of the male population. This will allow those who find themselves dissatisfied with the usual male role and the usual male values to explore new alternatives. They will find other options open to them. Perhaps that is the most a movement can hope for. A new series of options. New alternatives. In a sense this is well under way.

B.A.: Do you consider yourself to be a revolutionary?

W.F.: I consider myself radical—in the Latin sense of the word, meaning "root." I try to address the root of a problem. But I have trouble with the word *revolutionary,* for a couple of reasons. One is that it suggests to the average person a type of violence, with overthrow and total replacement. And it also suggests disregard of the present values. I see myself as an "evolutionary" revolutionary—in the sense that I want fundamental change, but with care.

I have a lot of patience. I have the patience to devote full time to weeding out the worst, to reeducate, but also to try to preserve some of the best things. For example, I don't want men to lose their desire to be athletic. I don't want men to lose their ability to make decisions. But I also don't want men to be compulsive about their athletics and their decision-making ability. I want men to be able to cry and express feelings, but I don't want men to use their feelings as a way of manipulating other people. I would like change to be faster, but I realize these things take time.

Where I am most revolutionary, in the standard sense, is when I consider the ways that advertising and commercials, in order to sell, attempt to associate a product with a standard like a Marlboro Man. It creates such insecurities because everyone sees the gap between himself and the ideal. It creates role-strivers and a basic anxiety level. And yet there is so much more money and psychology and carefully planned effort to put into that, so that they overwhelm my power to do very much about it.

B.A.: Is there any way that the mass media can be made to work for men's liberation, in the same way that the media aided supporters of cultural revolution in the 1960s? That would be one way of countering the pressures of the economic system.

W.F.: Well, most people in men's liberation would say no. They don't want to truck with the media. But I guess I am one of the few who say yes. My whole approach is to struggle for alliances, to search for aid. Alliances and aid are necessary for success. But to give a concrete answer to that question, I've done things like men's beauty contests in order to manipulate myself into millions of homes. By appearing on TV shows like "The Mike Douglas Show," with some fifteen million viewers a day, I am communicating men's liberation as a concept to as many people as I could if I spent five full lifetimes speaking to two hundred persons an evening, seven evenings a week! That's a literal computation. We can use the media if we understand the difference between *compromising* and *introducing*. Many people who never read *The Liberated Man* give themselves permission to have a lot of feelings they're half suppressing as soon as they're articulated. That's the value of introduction. Compromising is changing the essential truth of something. We must used the media for the former without giving into the latter.

B.A.: You will certainly reach far more people than the fringe magazines.

W.F.: We have to use the media's desire to report on change, and the economic system's need for change, its need to open up new forms of dress, handbags, colors, all the things that keep sales high. And it pays off. People can now do things, wear things, they "couldn't" only a few years ago. These are, of course, only symbols of some minor changes. But more significantly they are permissions to deviate (until they become a new form of conformity). There are more important things, though. . . . We might call them "men's issues." Like developing flexible jobs such as two-for-one jobs so people do not have to choose between working full time or not working at all. Or men's birth control. Or developing new forms of sports that integrate cooperation with competition. Or calling attention to the way companies like Johnny Walker's Black Label manipulate men as success objects. Or obtaining paternity leaves.

B.A.: What is it, normally, that makes a man join a men's consciousness-raising group? Is it something that happens in his life, something obvious?

W.F.: No, it is a lot of different things. It may start with a wife or woman friend getting involved in a woman's group and starting to change. She then suggests or demands that the man start to change, too. If he doesn't, well, too bad for him. That's one impetus. Increasingly, and we have only begun to see this in the last few years, the source is internal. It comes from men beginning to say, "I want to do something different with my life —regardless of whether the woman I am involved with or the man that I'm involved with also wants that. If necessary, I will find someone who does want that." For some men it is forty, forty-five years in a corporate system, or a government system, or an academic system. It is having worried constantly about publishing, having worried about pleasing the next level up in the hierarchy, and worrying, "Have I really spent my life most creatively? Where are all my values? What have I gotten out of it? I've lost my wife in the process, I've lost my children in the process (that is, I really don't know who they are). I don't even know who I am. I've lost the creative parts of me that used to be there, used to be so vital. Something is wrong, but I don't know what it is.

In some ways the underlying impetus for all these men can be seen as either dissatisfaction or "failure." I put quotes around failure because it's actually our first success. For example, I failed my doctoral orals first time around. My adviser said, "You'd benefit from a year looking inside yourself." I did just that—with immense pain. It was my first major failure and my first major success. When I redid my orals and my dissertation, I had a different internal value system, was less nervous, less dependent on the expectations of others. I, like a number of men, merely heard of consciousness-raising groups. I first joined just to "check things out." When I evaluated it, it seemed to be the first time in my life I was developing deep male friendships. I didn't feel as odd questioning old values. I was setting aside a time to look inside myself, distinguishing between rough edges I wanted to eliminate and those I wanted to keep.

That is probably a good range of reasons for men to join. I'm sure there are many other reasons, too, probably some we couldn't guess if we sat here all night.

B.A.: What do you see as the primary cause of male confusion in the 1970s? Do men seem disoriented about what it means to be a man in this world? And if they are, is it just a product of this particular time?

W.F.: I think it's cultural. This culture has taught people to accept a set of rules as a way of defining ourselves. So when a new *option* is introduced, people fear they must further redefine themselves or resist the option. If the option becomes very popular, they adopt it because their underlying value system is to not appear different or "weird." This type of mentality can't easily accept the concept of real alternatives. They are "societal approval seekers"—looking outside themselves to find the right rule rather than inside themselves to find what feels right.

B.A.: Fine. But that is abstract. What, on a more concrete level, are the goals, the purposes of the men's liberation movement as they apply to work and achievement, in terms of the accepted male role in society?

W.F.: First, I mentioned before the concrete "men's issues" of flexible jobs, men's birth control, new forms of sports, and so on. To expand on men's relationship to work, I see the men's liberation movement as asking men to distinguish between becoming a success and becoming a success object. The moment a man is afraid to look outside his area of specialization to see if anything else might be more fulfilling and at least ask himself how he can rearrange his life to do what is most fulfilling, he is becoming a success object. Obviously, rearranging a life is a complex operation. And that's one of the functions of men's support groups—to do that without depriving ourselves of five thousand dollars of therapy money in the process!

B.A.: That certainly squares with much that I have found so far in my research. Would you elaborate a bit more?

W.F.: Sure. Let me redirect it somewhat. One of the goals of the men's movement is to have men consider that if they share the child-care and housework while their partners—female or male—share the responsibility for producing income, it frees us to start taking some chances with our work, protesting when we want to, getting involved in new areas when we want to, working in one area until we feel we are no longer growing, and then trying something new. Ironically, the Marlboro Man image of being adventuresome and creative is exactly opposite of what the average man is now—a bureaucrat seeking the approval of the person above him at work to get to the next highest step on the ladder to support a family. He's in a straightjacket. *We're proposing an option to free men's "internal Marlboro Man" so we don't have to spend our lives smoking the image.*

B.A.: This would apply for the woman, too, wouldn't it?

W.F.: Of course. Whenever the income producing is shared, *either person* can afford to take risks te (my word for "he or she") couldn't afford to take when te was responsible for the whole burden—when the risk fails, it doesn't mean putting the family in the poorhouse. The couple has to consider whether the tradeoff is worth it. Do they want income for two weeks' vacation or less income doing something they enjoy year round? Often the choice does not have to be made, since when one enjoys something, it often leads to better income-producing capability as well.

B.A.: How reasonable or realistic is it to expect a man to accept making less money in this culture? In other words, even if he knows his job is hurting him physically, even if it is making him miserable, it is reasonable to expect a man to make less money at any particular time—a typical man who derives a great deal of his identity, of his self-image, from how much money he makes and what he does, as so many of us do? For so many men, work is ninety-five percent of their identity. And that is why so many men, when they retire, go to pieces.

W.F.: They lose their identity, sure. And it is difficult for many men to accept these ideas. But there could be nothing less reasonable or realistic than putting all one's identity into one basket. And then giving an institution control over that basket of identity. And then accepting the idea that you will trade the identity in for a permanent vacation called retirement. What we call realism is killing us. Men's liberation is the creation of new forms of realism.

B.A.: Don't you think there would be a male backlash against these ideas? In fact, don't you think there is a backlash already?

W.F.: To some extent. Anytime you have people taking the offensive, you have someone taking the defensive. I think the men's movement is now taking some of the criticism and heat that used to be directed at the women's movement. This was inevitable, especially as I think the women's movement has declined in its intensity and visibility recently. As a result, the attacks on it have declined, too.

But I think we are seeing another phenomenon. When Nixon was president there was a political justification for a conservative social ideology. Now there is a political justification under Carter for a slightly more liberal social ideology, a slow progressivism with a careful rhetoric that appeals much more to the mass mind, the more conservative mind, than the liberal mind.

Of course, one of the values of the Carter type of liberalism is that it has a minimal potential for backlash. At the same time, it is not oriented toward a fundamental questioning of certain dimensions of our value system.

B.A.: So, in other words, you think that the men advocating men's liberation are now taking the attacks that were once directed against women?

W.F.: To some extent.

B.A.: Let me change the subject a bit. Do you think men have become lazier?

W.F.: Yes, some men have. As the women's movement's intensity has declined, the pressure on men to change has declined, and men who responded only through the pressure of women have become lazier, yes.

I think in relationships men need the type of mentorship from women that women need from men in finances and business. It means learning new personality traits. Women need to learn how to invest, how to look to the future, how to make decisions, how to have sexual relations with more confidence. And there are certain positive, helpful characteristics about relationships that men don't know very much about—like learning how to be sensitive, learning how to listen, learning how to increase their capacity for intimacy. In addition to "The Managerial Woman" we need "The Listening Man."

B.A.: What about helping himself sexually?

W.F.: I feel the most important thing a man can do about that for himself is to start focusing in on his nongenital sexuality—sucking, loving, touching, focusing, playing, cuddling, doing a whole series of other things—all the time making sure that he connects with lovers who understand that these nongenital activities are acceptable and beautiful parts of sex.

B.A.: Do you find many of the men with whom you talk affected by situational impotence? And what do you recommend for them?

W.F.: Some of them. And I find that many of them are nervous and self-conscious. And, ironically, when they learn to stop being so genital, to stop worrying about an erection, they find their penis getting hard anyway.

I recommend we apply to ourselves what I call the "acid test" of a sexually secure man. The first state is seeing if, the moment my penis gets hard, I feel compelled to stick it into something. Or can I let it get soft again without worrying about it? The second stage is not worrying about whether it gets hard again. Once I do that with a woman, I find I take the pressure off myself to perform. Impotence becomes not being able to relate sensually, emotionally, with fun and laughter. The moment we define impotence as a soft penis we are oppressing men. We are saying, "Your power, your sexual power, is wrapped up in the hardness or softness of your penis." Sexual potency is wrapped up in a whole range of sensual, sexual, and emotional interactions. Look at the number of women turning to other women sexually. It's not for hard penises.

B.A.: Changing the subject a bit, does it take much time for men to open up in your consciousness-raising sessions? Do they surprise themselves with how rapidly they are able to open up, how honest they can be about their feelings?

W.F.: I think they usually find it is much more difficult than they expected. They often feel required to defend themselves. They often find it impossible to be personal with another man on any but the most abstract level.

B.A.: How do you help? Perhaps you could talk about the presentation you do on campuses, for example. What type of material do you present, what do you wish to convey? What are some of the typical responses?

W.F.: I start with an intellectual overview, followed by an audience exchange of experiences and ideas. I don't want to be the only problem solver, the one with all the answers. My objective is to let people know at the outset that they have valuable things to contribute to each other. So I facilitate that process. That is the first step in getting away from stereotypes. They expect me to lead, and I have to lead to a degree. But they must take over leadership with me. Then we are all participants.

From there Farrell subtly directs men and at times women into a series of exercises—a men's beauty contest, role-reversed dates, sensuality feelings—that enable each to empathize with the other. It enables each to understand the dominant and passive roles culture directs men and women to play. Men find out what it is like to be passive sex objects. Women discover what it feels like to be strivers for success, to compete with other "successful" and dominant women for a date with a passive "boy." Both men and women find themselves exaggerating their new roles, parodying the roles of each other. After a time, each can see the gap that exists between the role they play and experience, what they actually are, and what they hope to be. Wearing someone else's shoes becomes a liberating experience, the first small step toward ultimate emancipation for all.

19
Toward the New Male

WHAT DOES emancipation mean for men?

To some who have thought long and hard, it means that men and women will adopt traits normally associated with the other sex. Women will continue to assume many of the traits and behaviors traditionally considered masculine. They will narrow the gap in education and their attitudes toward careers acceptable for women. They will close the gap in salaries and levels of attainment in all fields. And they will come to terms with the new understanding of their sexuality.

On the other side, men will develop their feminine nature, that part of the personality which is usually hidden behind a tough, masculine exterior. At its most elementary level, feminization of males will produce men more in touch with the full range of emotions and feelings common to all human beings. They will become more intimate in their relationships, more eager to form close bonds with women and other men, without the debilitating fears of losing their independence and of appearing homosexual. They will be willing to be dependent in all relationships, including their sexual relationships, where once they had to be dominant.

Within their families they will find a primary outlet for a new role as they make the transition from breadwinner to full partner. They will become willing to share earnings for the support of the family and they will participate fully in the tasks traditionally done by the wife. They will do these things without suffering pangs of anxiety that their identity as males is in any way threatened. They will see that their identity as humans is in fact augmented.

They will also bring a more mature attitude to their relationships. Increasingly, the male's essentially adolescent sexuality, his belief in male dominance, and his adherence to the values of traditional masculinity have made it difficult for him to work seriously at making a relationship endure.

If he enters a relationship with more than sex on his mind, if he chooses to live with someone whom he loves, admires, respects, and with whom he shares interests, he will seek to find solutions to the problems that inevitably plague any relationship. He will not take the easy way out and look elsewhere, dismiss fidelity as childish and passé, or walk out completely. He will try to attune his work with his home life. He will, in Tolstoy's words, seek to live "magnificently in this world." He will know "how to work, and how to love, to work for the person he loves, and to love his work." He will have a unity of existence and purpose.

In achieving this goal, men can learn much from women, something they have been loath to do in the past. "Women," Ashley Montagu has written, "are so much closer to the fundamental problems of life than men, are more sensitive to the needs of human beings than men. It is women who know better than anyone else that man cannot live by bread alone and that human beings are something more than slaves of the idea that men exist to earn a living and beat the other fellow to the mark."[1] Men will have to realize and accept that humanity is interdependent, that men need women as much as, if not more than, women need men to satisfy their needs for domicile and children. They will have to admit, as Montagu puts it, that "the sexes need each other because they are precariously dependent upon each other for their functioning as healthy human beings."[2] They will have to admit that "self-sufficiency usually winds up as insufficiency, which is the usual fate of the self-sufficient male."[3] Woman has always been "the firm rod" upon which man could lean for support in time of need. He must do so again.

Already some of the male's values have changed. There is a much greater involvement among men in taking care of their children. That is now not only acceptable, it has become a kind of status. Men are proud of the time they spend with their children. Some of them even feel they can be better parents than women, and if a marriage breaks up, we witness more and more men contesting for custody of the children. All of this is part of a changing notion of what it means to be masculine. Now parenthood is a trait that men can accept without feeling their manhood is threatened every time they change a diaper or hug their children.

Women have noticed the changes and view them favorably. I asked Helen Gurley Brown if she saw men opening up more.

"Oh, yes," she replied. "They don't all necessarily want to do so, but they are forced to deal with reality. The reality is that women are changing, and we are the only other sex that men have. To get along with us, men pretty much have to accept us and our changes. These changes among women redefine the values for both. Also, I think women's attitudes toward what they want in a man are undergoing a similar transformation. Women no longer demand that a man be steely, tough, and invincible. They are more willing to accept that he may be out of a job, or he may be sick sometimes. He doesn't have to be the strong, stalwart, unassailable male that he used to be. That was a terrible thing to have to live up to—never to be soft, never to be sad, never to cry, never to hurt, never to do anything that would mark you as a sissy.

"Women accept that men are human and not invincible, that they are quite vincible at times. In that sense, what is happening is very good. I see no loss of sexuality. People still have the hots for each other. Just the mode of getting together has changed."

So, too, evidently, is the old equation of power and success with sexiness changing. Gael Greene, herself a very sexy lady, maintains that "the idea that power and success are very sexy and that a woman wants this in a man is just so old-fashioned."

"But it exists," I said.

G.G.: Yes, it exists. It exists just as there are probably twenty-five-year-old men today who want women like their mothers. But there are also women who are not at all interested in power, who really have the new head and believe in it.

B.A.: And accept the responsibility of it?

G.G.: Yes, women who will accept responsibility, or at least an equal responsibility. Or who are interested in a very simple life, an artistic life or a rural life. You know, I got a phone call from somebody doing a magazine article who argued the old idea that power is sexy, that rich is sexy. She started asking me questions and I said, "Well I understand that phenomenon," but then I realized that I don't find power or wealth to be sexy. And in the middle of the conversation, I said that what was really sexy in a man was the man doing something well. The man doing what he does well. It doesn't matter what it is he does. He could be a great chef, or a dancer, or a carpenter. Physically at ease. That is sexy.

She kept trying to change my words. She wanted me to say that I found power sexy, but I just said, "I'm realizing you are talking to somebody who does not find power sexy. I would be very comfortable with a man who is less successful than I am, perhaps even less intelligent, somebody that I could take care of in some way who would take care of me the same way the rest of the time."

I'm not concerned with what New York thinks. I can't say that all the women I know would necessarily agree with me. But there are women who just don't have to have men more successful than they are.

B.A.: I think it is wonderful that you know enough about yourself and have enough confidence in yourself to be that way.

G.G.: Perhaps it's the time. Perhaps it's being a grown-up woman. I'm sure I didn't think that at twenty. It is something I have come to realize. Ideally, two healthy people, or reasonably healthy neurotics, should achieve a kind of balance where they can support each other and take care of each other and be adults and children together. That is what I am hoping for.

As Gael Greene's remarks suggest, women can make important contributions to men's ability to understand themselves. Ashley Montagu agrees. He says, "We are going to move into an era where the new woman is absolutely indispensable for this. She will bring the arguments for humanity up into the consciousness of men where it has never existed before. It will develop on the basis not of women's rights but of human rights —the notion that women as human beings have all the rights that any human being should enjoy. They are going to have in addition, a special contribution to make. That is the humanization of humanity, part of which consists of the males they will marry. Men must be aware of this and be ready to participate not as parasites or by living symbiotically with women but as we see many younger married couples doing now. They share: The father shares in the birth of children; he holds the baby and participates in its care to the fullest extent possible. Of course this is wonderful, because the bonding that takes place there between the mother and her husband is strong and enormously important. All too often this does not occur and a great opportunity is wasted."

Men, according to Montagu, have "lost all sense of understanding of the meaning of humanity." They depreciate humanity and denigrate the humanistic qualities in women. "Men despise 'femininity' in other men." But these very feminine qualities that men so dislike are "really human qualities," Montagu says; "common human qualities that men should have as well as women, that boys and girls should share."

Montagu thinks that men have to reach a point where they can begin to see life in its full meaning, to see that "androgyny, a combination of those traits that we think feminine and those traits we think masculine are the traits that we should all aim for in the development of a human being. It should be open-mindedness and adventuresomeness, spiritualness and imaginativeness, and explorativeness rather than aggression. We should all have the quality of gentleness. Imagine calling a man gentle! And yet if you speak to most women, they will tell you that the one quality they miss beyond all others in most men is gentleness. They tend to liken male behavior to that of gorillas, and in doing so, they slander the poor gorillas, who are very gentle creatures.

"We are just beginning to talk seriously about these ideas. But they are not new. They have been around for centuries. When I was eighteen, I wrote a manuscript on androgyny. I sent it to a publisher and he sent it back immediately. He thought the whole idea was ridiculous. We have come a long way since then."

Albert Ellis also sees us moving toward a more androgynous society in which men will recognize their femininity or feminine side more, while women develop the more masculine side of their personalities. He says, "The tendency now is for us not to define one particular set of traits as masculine, such as assertion and decisiveness, and another set of opposing traits as feminine, such as niceness and warmth. Human beings all have a good degree of masculinity and femininity and we seem more and more willing to give into our complete natures.

"The old test of masculinity and femininity which designated any male who liked the arts and ballet as effeminate or homosexual is changing. There is more freedom for males to do the so-called feminine things and for females to do the so-called masculine things. It hasn't changed completely, but it has to a great degree. Androgyny is a much more acceptable and accepted ideal than it was ten or twenty years ago. It probably will increase, because among other things, it is the human condition. We are naturally both masculine and feminine and practically nobody is one hundred percent 'male' or zero percent 'female.' So I think we are becoming more liberal, individuated, in that respect."

Will that have bisexual ramifications? "Probably," Ellis says. "But you see, the mere fact that a male is now allowed to be 'feminine' and a female accepted as 'masculine' does not mean that either will be homosexual. They may or may not be."

Will that have bisexual ramifications? "Probably," Ellis says. "But you see, the mere fact that a male is now allowed to be 'feminine' and a female accepted as 'masculine' does not mean that either will be homosexual. They may or may not be."

Others see development of a more bisexual society resulting. Warren Farrell says: "I believe most people go through three or four sexual stages in this society. First, we are all born sexual, although with a different hormonal orientation than after puberty. That is, we're potentially open to sexual contact of any type—hetero, homo, or bi. Second, we learn to inhibit and repress our sexuality. Parents and friends refrain from the genital touching that is part of natural desire. Third, we learn to redirect it into a compulsive heterosexuality. Men mix the compulsiveness with conquest and women mix it with a continuation of the repressive stage. And fourth, some of us learn to regain a portion of our natural sexuality again. It's like recovering from a disease."

I asked Farrell to explain "compulsive heterosexuality." "Well, let me give an example," he said. "I often conduct an experiment with three men and three women touching a person sitting in the center of the circle. The person in the center can never guess more than half the time whether te [Farrell's word for 'she or he'] is being touched by a woman or a man. The person in the center almost always enjoys being touched by everyone when tes [his or her] eyes are closed. Yet when we open our eyes, we almost reflexively withdraw from same-sex touching. We socialize ourselves to use our eyes—supposedly given to us to increase our sensual receptivity—to cut off our sensual receptivity to fifty percent of the human population. That's what I call training for compulsive heterosexuality. It's compulsive in that it cannot float freely, but imprisons our senses with roles. We open our eyes to discover is it a male, a female? Is the person too old? Too young? Too fat! Too thin? We don't simply ask, 'Does it feel good?' That's compulsive heterosexuality."

One objection to androgyny is that it suggests a kind of conformity for all people, a conformity that could be as stifling as other forms of behavior. Two psychologists, Frank Wesley and Claire Wesley, who are sympathetic to the concept of an androgynous society, put it this way:

"The teaching of androgyny would require discrimination learning because an individual would have to learn at which moments or in which situations to be aggressive and at which to be submissive, or when to be daring and when to be cautious, etc. . . . If the situations in which it is better to act feminine and those in which it is better to act masculine are not clearly differentiated, a middle-of-the-road personality may develop. Instead of fighting in certain instances and running away in others, an individual may simply stand still in all instances."[4]

They continue: "Individual androgyny would require that both females and males be aggressive in the same situations; otherwise, sex-role behavior may again precipitate. This would necessitate a more-or-less definite reaction pattern for all individuals, and in the final analysis, they would not be freer in their actions than they are in the present sex-stereotyped society." The kind of regimentation necessary to sexualize behavior, to ensure androgynous behavior in men and women, might, the Wesleys caution, "eventually create individuals who are all alike —doing Huxley's Brave New World one better!"

Of course, the advocates of androgyny are not crypto-totalitarians. Their goals are humane, and their methods never hint at coercion. Warren Farrell puts it this way: "Androgyny is the encouragement of every human being to be as individual as a snowflake. It is not unisex. It is multi-individuality. It encourages a constant search for our true selves. Not a competition for the artificial standards of a stereotype which creates stultification if achieved and insecurity if not achieved. Androgyny is hardly stultifying. It's a challenge to the self. The only thing stultifying about androgyny is the word. As a word, well . . . as a word, it's just not . . . sexy."

The most enlightened solution is to accept that humans will exhibit the full range of human behaviors. One can advocate expansion of consciousness, a widening of personality to include for the men the feminine side of their being, while accepting the probability that there will be women who continue to exhibit behaviors that we now label as purely feminine and men who will adhere to the masculine ideal. Within the social group, there will also be individuals who combine to differing degrees the qualities of both. As the Wesleys put it, "The group rather than the individual would be androgynous."

This implies a great degree of toleration for the full range of behaviors possible to both men and women. For men, it will mean abandoning, if not for oneself at least for others, the notion that one has to adhere to the stereotype of manhood. It will mean accepting that some men will be "effeminate," some homosexual, some androgynous, and some the same tough, steely-eyed individuals they have always been.

There is no reason for undue optimism that there will be toleration. The barriers to further change among men remain strong, and will not easily fall. Many men who want to change find the sledding tough, as they face the ribbing of unsympathetic male colleagues and superiors. At times, there is overt pressure and there are threats. Elizabeth Janeway gives the following example. "I won't give you the name of the university," she says, "but it is one of the most prestigious in the country. A young male graduate student was completing his doctorate in math and he had a very good job offer. He went to his department chairman, who was active in placement for the department's students and he asked, 'How would it be, would it be possible, I wonder, if I could put this off for a year? My wife is finishing law school. She has one more year to go. And I have a chance to do some postdoctoral work that would be of interest to me. Would they hold the appointment for a year?' And he was told by the department chairman that if he did not take the job, and if he persisted with such a frivolous reason for not taking it, he would never be recommended by the department or the university again. Isn't that a terrible story?"

Indeed it is!

There are psychological barriers, too. Throughout their lives men live a life marked by a "masculine-feminine polarity." Virtually all men have an identity formed by images of masculinity learned as they grew up at home, at school, and in their neighborhoods. At every turn, the ideas of manhood and masculinity are reinforced. Deviations from the norm are brought to the attention of all. A man may want to break free of stereotypical male values, but he is hard pressed to conform.

Joseph Levinson puts it this way in his book *The Seasons of a Man's Life:* "No matter how much a young man wants to grow beyond the traditionally narrow view of masculinity, the idea of manliness is still of great importance to him. He strives to take his place in the world as a male adult. In doing so, he must feel some anxiety about the feminine and must control or repress it to some degree. He must give greater priority to the masculine as he understands it. He can make room for the feminine, but he cannot fully integrate the two."[5]

For the male who desires to integrate his masculine and feminine sides, the battle rages and ebbs until midlife when he is finally able to reconcile the two sides of his nature. Levinson described the process. "The difficulty in integrating the masculine and feminine in early adulthood has many sources. It stems partly from cultural traditions, partly from personal immaturity. A young man in his twenties is just barely out of adolescence; he is not developmentally ready to resolve all his pre-adult conflicts and achieve a highly integrated personality. He has to 'go with what he's got,' which means building a first adult life structure that reflects and sustains his inner conflicts. The difficulty in integration stems also from the magnitude of his evolving life tasks. In the twenties and thirties, his energies are devoted to forming an occupation and a family. Ordinarily, he must meet heavy financial demands, pursue his goals, and face the stresses of day-to-day living. There are also biological reasons for the usual predominance of the masculine over the feminine among men in early adulthood."[6]

As he ages, the male is able to meliorate and integrate the opposing parts of his being. But most men arrive at the end of their thirties with about the same "balance" of masculine and feminine traits that they had when they reached adulthood.

But even if individual men could conquer the barriers of personality, they may be defeated by forces over which they have no control. For to a great extent, the future values of men as well as women will depend on economics. If we could guarantee a long period of prosperity, we might have more reason for optimism. Since we cannot, it is difficult not to feel ambivalent about the shape of things to come.

If relative affluence continues, we will see a tremendous increase in male sensitivity, a softening of the compulsions that drive men to self-destruction. But if we face economic hardship, prolonged recession or inflation—or both—one of the first things to go will be the changes we have witnessed over the past several years. We shall witness another hardening of sexual roles as more and more men feel threatened with loss of livelihood, status, manhood. Men will not have the free time necessary to expand their softer side—they will be ulcer-bound and scared. They will have no chance to indulge. If there is an economic crunch, the situation can only worsen.

This is not doomsaying. It has happened before. In other periods of recession and depression, we have retrenched. We are lucky if we can preserve even some of the social changes that have occurred. The women's movement is a prime example. It has retrogressed before. We know the movement is not just a recent phenomenon. In the 1920s there were sexual freedom movements. People lived together, refused to get married. But these movements and many other feminist initiatives were undone by the Depression. It took thirty years to bring the women's movement to a head again. The same things were discovered as though they had never been discovered in the first place. During the late 1960s and early 1970s we had a honeymoon with the women's movement. Now we are in a period of backlash against women's books, women's plays, women's political rights, everything.

So it may be with the men's movement. For many people want to go back to the way it was before. The comfortable way. The time when all persons, men and women, knew their place.

References

Chapter Two

1. Leonard Kriegel, "Hemingway's Rites of Manhood," *Partisan Review* XLIV (1977): 430.
2. Harvey Kaye, *Male Survival: Masculinity Without Myth* (New York: Grosset & Dunlap, 1974), p. 3.
3. Gore Vidal, *Myra Breckinridge* (Boston: Little, Brown and Company, 1968), p. 66.
4. Dan Wakefield, *Going All the Way* (New York: Delacorte Press, 1970), p. 195.
5. Robert Brannon and Deborah David, eds., *The Forty-Nine Percent Majority: The Male Sex Role* (Reading, MA: Addison-Wesley, 1976), p. 12ff.

Chapter Three

1. Margaret Mead, *Sex and Temperament in Three Primitive Societies* (New York: William Morrow, 1935), p. 190.
2. Carole Offir and Carol Tavris, *The Longest War: Sex Differences in Perspective* (New York: Harcourt Brace Jovanovich, 1977), p. 127.
3. Offir and Tavris, *The Longest War,* p. 172.
4. Offir and Tavris, *The Longest War,* p. 172.
5. Offir and Tavris, *The Longest War,* p. 172.
6. Warren Farrell, *The Liberated Man: Beyond Masculinity—Freeing Men and Their Relationships with Women* (New York: Random House, 1974), p. 33.
7. Harvey Kaye, *Male Survival,* p. 34.
8. Philip Slater, *Footholds: Understanding the Shifting Sexual and Family Tensions in Our Culture* (Boston: Beacon Press, 1977), p. 21.
9. Ruth Hartley, "Sex Role Pressures and the Socialization of the Male Child," in *Men and Masculinity,* eds. Joseph H. Pleck and Jack Sawyer (Englewood Cliffs, NJ: Prentice-Hall, 1974), pp. 10–11.

10. Jack O. Balswick and James L. Collier, "Why Husbands Can't Say 'I Love You'," in *The Forty-Nine Percent Majority,* eds. Brannon and David, p. 59.
11. Hartley, "Sex Role Pressures," p. 9.
12. Offir and Tavris, *The Longest War,* pp. 174–175.
13. Offir and Tavris, *The Longest War,* pp. 177–180.
14. Offir and Tavris, *The Longest War,* pp. 180–181.
15. Kaye, *Male Survival,* p. 3.
16. Herb Goldberg, *The Hazards of Being Male: Surviving the Myth of Masculine Privilege* (New York: Nash Publishing, 1976), p. 183.
17. Goldberg, *The Hazards of Being Male,* p. 59.
18. Brannon and David, eds., *The Forty-Nine Percent Majority,* p. 36.
19. Goldberg, *The Hazards of Being Male,* p. 123.

Chapter Four

1. Nancy Gager Clinch, *The Kennedy Neurosis* (New York: Grosset & Dunlap, 1973), p. 266.
2. Marc Feigen Fasteau, *The Male Machine* (New York: McGraw-Hill Book Company, 1975), p. 106.
3. Michael Novak, *The Joy of Sports: End Zones, Bases, Baskets, Balls and the Consecration of the American Spirit* (New York: Basic Books, 1976), pp. 209–212.
4. Jack Nichols, *Men's Liberation: A New Definition of Masculinity* (New York: Penguin, 1975), p. 101.
5. James A. Michener, *Sports in America* (New York: Random House, 1976), p. 15.
6. John Gagnon, "Physical Strength, Once of Significance," in *The Forty-Nine Percent Majority,* eds. Brannon and David, p. 173.
7. Fasteau, *The Male Machine,* p. 105.
8. Michener, *Sports in America,* p. 524.
9. Konrad Lorenz, *On Aggression,* trans. Marjorie K. Wilson (New York: Harcourt Brace Jovanovich, 1966), p. 178.
10. Anthony Storr, *Human Aggression* (New York, Atheneum, 1966), pp. 117–118.
11. George F. Gilder, *Sexual Suicide* (New York: Quadrangle/The New York Times Co., 1973), p. 220.

Chapter Five

1. Fasteau, *The Male Machine,* p. 115.
2. Joseph Heller, *Something Happened* (New York: Knopf, 1974), p. 30.

3. Fasteau, *The Male Machine,* p. 116.
4. Nichols, *Men's Liberation,* p. 67.
5. Margaret Mead, *Male and Female* (New York: William Morrow, 1948), pp. 311–312.
6. Kaye, *Male Survival,* pp. 50–51.
7. Myron Brenton, *The American Male* (New York: Coward-McCann, 1966), p. 199.
8. Nichols, *Men's Liberation,* p. 134.
9. Michael Maccoby, *The Gamesman: The New Corporate Leaders* (New York: Simon and Schuster, 1976), chapter 4.
10. Michael Korda, *Power* (New York: Random House, 1975), pp. 12–14.
11. Korda, *Power,* p. 9.
12. Fernando Bartolomi, "Executives as Human Beings," in *Men and Masculinity,* eds. Pleck and Sawyer, p. 101.

Chapter Six

1. John Lippert, "Sexuality as Consumption," in *For Men Against Sexism,* ed. Jon Snodgrass (Albion, CA: Times Change Press, 1977), p. 208.
2. Avodah K. Offit, *The Sexual Self* (New York: Ballantine Books, 1978), p. 39.
3. John Gagnon and William Simon, "Psychosexual Development," in *The Sexual Scene,* eds. John Gagnon and William Simon (Chicago: Aldine Publishing Co., 1970), pp. 31–34.
4. David J. Fox and Anne Steinmann, *The Male Dilemma: How to Survive the Sexual Revolution* (New York: Jacob Aronson, 1974), p. 80.
5. Rollo May, *Love and Will* (New York: Dell, 1974), p. 89.

Chapter Seven

1. Kaye, *Male Survival,* p. 55.

Chapter Eight

1. Daniel Levinson, *The Seasons of a Man's Life* (New York: Alfred A. Knopf, 1978), pp. 25–26, pp. 191–200.

Chapter Nine

1. Peter G. Filene, *Him/Her/Self: Sex Roles in Modern America* (New York: Harcourt Brace Jovanovich, 1975), p. 226.

2. Betty Friedan, *It Changed My Life: Writings on the Women's Movement* (New York: Random House, 1976), pp. 319–320.

Chapter Ten

1. Filene, *Him/Her/Self,* p. 224.
2. Gilder, *Sexual Suicide,* p. 109.
3. Gilder, *Sexual Suicide,* p. 109.
4. Fasteau, *The Male Machine,* p. 54.
5. Ashley Montagu, *The Natural Superiority of Women* (new revised edition, New York: Collier Books, 1974), p. 230.

Chapter Eleven

1. Edward Shorter, *The Making of the Modern Family* (New York: Basic Books, 1975), p. 84.
2. Morton Hunt, *Sexual Behavior in the Seventies* (New York: Playboy Press, 1974), pp. 142–155.
3. Elizabeth Janeway, *Between Myth and Morning: Women Awakening* (New York: William Morrow, 1974), pp. 81–82.

Chapter Fourteen

1. Helen Singer Kaplan, *The New Sex Therapy* (New York: Quadrangle/The New York Times Co., 1974), p. 257.
2. Kaplan, *The New Sex Therapy,* p. 256.
3. Kaplan, *The New Sex Therapy,* p. 262.
4. William H. Masters and Virginia Johnson, *Human Sexual Inadequacy* (Boston: Little, Brown and Company, 1970), p. 92. See also Kaplan, *The New Sex Therapy,* p. 290.
5. Kaplan, *The New Sex Therapy,* p. 290.

Chapter Fifteen

1. Ashley Montagu, "A Kinsey Report on Homosexualities," *Psychology Today* XII (August 1978): 66.
2. Montagu, "A Kinsey Report on Homosexualities," p. 66.

Chapter Sixteen

1. Alfred Kazin, "Gay Genius and the Gay Lot," *Esquire* LXXXVIII (December 1977): 33–36.

Chapter Nineteen

1. Montagu, *The Natural Superiority of Women,* p. 123.
2. Montagu, *The Natural Superiority of Women,* p. 113.
3. Montagu, *The Natural Superiority of Women,* p. 112.
4. Claire Wesley and Frank Wesley, *Sex-Role Psychology* (New York: Human Sciences Press, 1977), pp. 187–188.
5. Levinson, *The Seasons of a Man's Life,* p. 235.
6. Levinson, *The Seasons of a Man's Life,* pp. 235–236.